SIXTH EDITION

HEALTH POLICY
and POLITICS
A Nurse's Guide

JERI A. MILSTEAD, PhD, RN, NEA-BC, FAAN
NANCY M. SHORT, DrPH, MBA, BSN, RN, FAAN

JONES & BARTLETT
LEARNING

World Headquarters
Jones & Bartlett Learning
5 Wall Street
Burlington, MA 01803
978-443-5000
info@jblearning.com
www.jblearning.com

Jones & Bartlett Learning books and products are available through most bookstores and online booksellers. To contact Jones & Bartlett Learning directly, call 800-832-0034, fax 978-443-8000, or visit our website, www.jblearning.com.

Substantial discounts on bulk quantities of Jones & Bartlett Learning publications are available to corporations, professional associations, and other qualified organizations. For details and specific discount information, contact the special sales department at Jones & Bartlett Learning via the above contact information or send an email to specialsales@jblearning.com.

12698-3

Production Credits

VP, Product Management: David D. Cella
Director, Product Management: Amanda Martin
Product Manager: Rebecca Stephenson
Product Assistant: Christina Freitas
Production Manager: Carolyn Rogers Pershouse
Production Assistant: Brooke Haley
Senior Marketing Manager: Jennifer Scherzay
Product Fulfillment Manager: Wendy Kilborn
Composition: S4Carlisle Publishing Services

Cover Design: Kristin E. Parker
Director of Rights & Media: Joanna Gallant
Rights & Media Specialist: Wes DeShano
Media Development Editor: Troy Liston
Cover Image (Title Page, Chapter Opener):
   © Visions of America/Joe Sohm/Photodisc/Getty;
   © csreed/E+/Getty
Printing and Binding: Edwards Brothers Malloy
Cover Printing: Edwards Brothers Malloy

Library of Congress Cataloging-in-Publication Data

Names: Milstead, Jeri A., editor. | Short, Nancy Munn, editor.
Title: Health policy and politics : a nurse's guide / [edited by] Jeri A. Milstead, Nancy Munn Short.
Other titles: Health policy and politics (Milstead)
Description: Sixth edition. | Burlington, MA : Jones & Bartlett Learning, [2019] | Includes bibliographical references and index.
Identifiers: LCCN 2017029269 | ISBN 9781284126372 (casebound)
Subjects: | MESH: Legislation, Nursing | Health Policy | Politics | Nurse's Role | United States
Classification: LCC RT86.5 | NLM WY 33 AA1 | DDC 362.17/30973--dc23
LC record available at https://lccn.loc.gov/2017029269

6048

Printed in the United States of America
21 20 19 18 17   10 9 8 7 6 5 4 3 2 1

Contents

Chapter 11 The Impact of Globalization: Nurses Influencing Global Health Policy 193

Dorothy Lewis Powell, Jeri A. Milstead

Chapter 12 An Insider's Guide to Engaging in Policy Activities 215

Nancy M. Short, Jeri A. Milstead

Preface

This is a contributed text for healthcare professionals who are interested in expanding the depth of their knowledge about public policy and in becoming more sophisticated in their involvement in the political and policy processes. The scope of the content covers the whole process of making public policy within the broad categories of agenda setting; government response; and program/policy design, implementation, and evaluation. The primary focus is at the federal and state levels, although the reader can adapt concepts to the global or local level.

▶ Why a Sixth Edition?

The *Sixth Edition* began with succession planning, when Dr. Nancy Short became co-editor and took on the serious job of planning for this and future editions. Dr. Short's expertise and credentials demonstrate her comprehensive viewpoint, and she is dedicated to the continuation of this broad-based text on the whole policy process. As founding editor/author, I could not have turned over this text to just anyone. Nancy is an astute editor, has asked relevant and incisive questions, and has been encouraging to me personally. It has been a real pleasure for me to work with her and get to know her deep intellect and caring personality.

The *Sixth Edition* also introduces new authors with fresh perspectives, all of whom have a significant experiential basis for their expertise. We welcome Dr. Leslie Sharpe, Dr. Toni Hebda, Ms. Catherine Liao, Dr. Anne Derouin, and Dr. Dorothy Powell. We also delight in those who have continued to contribute to this text over the years: Dr. Elizabeth Furlong, Ms. Jan Lanier, Dr. Jaqueline Loversidge, Dr. J. D. Polk, and Dr. Patrick DeLeon. They build on the work of Ardith Sudduth and Dr. Patricia Smart, who retired, and of Dr. Marlene Wilken, Dr. Kimberly Galt, Troy Spicer, and Elizabeth Barnhill. We pledge to continue to challenge our readers to understand the serious business of making public policy and demonstrate their commitment to a democratic republic through their advocacy and involvement. We welcome your comments—let us know how this text has influenced your practice.

▶ Target Audience

This text is intended for several audiences:
- Doctoral and master's-level students in nursing can use this text for in-depth study of the full policy process. Works of scholars in each segment provide a solid foundation for examining each component. This text goes beyond the

narrow elementary explanation of legislation, however: It bridges the gap by supporting understanding of a broader policy process in which multiple opportunities for involvement exist.

■ Nurses who work in professional practice in clinical, education, administrative, research, or consultative settings can use this text as a guide for understanding the full range of the policy components that they did not learn in graduate school or may have forgotten. Components are brought to life through nursing research, real-life cases, and theory. This text will help the nurse who is searching for knowledge of how leaders of today influence public policy toward better health care for the future. Nurses in leadership positions clearly articulate nursing's societal mission. Nurses, as the largest group of healthcare workers in the United States, realize that the way to make a permanent impact on the delivery of health care is to be a part of the decision making that occurs at every step of the healthcare policy process.

■ Faculty in graduate programs and other current nurse leaders can use this text as a reference for their own policy activity. Faculty and other leaders should be mentors both for their students and for other nurses throughout the profession. Because the whole policy process is so broad, these leaders can track their own experiences through the policy process by referring to the components described in this text.

■ A wide variety of healthcare professionals who are interested in the area of healthcare policy will find this text useful in directing their thoughts and actions toward the complex issues of both healthcare policy and public policy. Physicians, pharmacists, psychologists, dentists, occupational and physical therapists, physician's assistants, and others will discover parallels with their own practices as they examine case studies and other research. Nurses cannot change huge systems alone. Members of the healthcare team can use this text as a vehicle to educate themselves so that, together, everyone in the healthcare profession can influence policymakers.

■ Those professionals who do not provide health care directly but who are involved in areas of the environment that produce actual and potential threats to personal and community health and safety will find this text a valuable resource regarding how a problem becomes known, who decides what to do about it, and which type of governmental response might result. Environmental scientists, public health officials, sociologists, political scientists, anthropologists, and other professionals involved with health problems in the public interest will benefit from the ideas generated in this text.

■ Interest groups can use this text as a tool to consider opportunities to become involved in public policymaking. Interest groups can be extremely helpful in changing systems because their members' passion for their causes energizes them to act. Interest groups can become partners in the political activity of nurses by knowing how and when to use their influence to assist advanced practice registered nurses (APRNs) at various junctures in the policy process.

▶ Using This Text

Each chapter in the text is freestanding; that is, chapters do not rely, or necessarily build, on one another. The sequence of the chapters is presented in a linear fashion, but readers will note immediately that the policy process is not linear. For example, readers of the policy implementation chapter will find reference to scholars and concepts featured in the agenda-setting and policy design chapters. Such is the nature of the public process of making decisions. The material covered is a small portion of the existing research, arguments, and considered thought about policymaking and the broader political, economic, and social concepts and issues. Therefore, readers should use this text as a starting point for their own scholarly inquiry.

This text can be used to initiate discussions about issues of policy and nurses' opportunities and responsibilities throughout the process. The case studies presented here should raise questions about what should have happened or why something else did or did not happen. In this way, the text can serve as a guide through what some perceive as a maze of activity with no direction but is actually a rational, albeit chaotic, system. The case studies and discussion points are ideal for planning a class or addressing an audience. Many ideas and concepts are presented, and we hope they serve to stimulate readers' own creative thoughts about how to engage others. Gone are the days of "the sage on stage"—the teacher who had all the answers and lectured to students who had no questions. Good teachers always have learned from students, and vice versa. Today's teachers are interactive, technically savvy, curious and questioning, and capable of helping learners integrate large amounts of data and information. This text can serve as a guide and a beginning.

Acknowledgments

We continue to thank the staff of Jones & Bartlett Learning for their encouragement and guidance when we were writing the *Sixth Edition*. Their confidence in all the contributors has been consistent and unwavering. Christina Freitas, Product Assistant for Nursing, and Rebecca Stephenson, Product Manager for Nursing, have kept the authors on track in meeting deadlines and provided astute editorial assistance.

We also thank the readers of this text for their interest in the policy and political processes. For those of you who have integrated these components and concepts into your nursing careers, we applaud you. You will continue to contribute to the profession and to the broader society. For those readers who are struggling with how to incorporate one more piece of anything into your role as professional nurse, remember that you are advancing the cause of your own personal work, the profession, and healthcare delivery in the United States and throughout the world every time you use the concepts covered in this text. Nurses are a powerful force and exercise their many talents to further good public policy—policy that, ultimately, must improve health care for patients, consumers, and families.

For the wide range of healthcare professionals (dentists, dietitians, pharmacists, physical and occupational therapists, physicians, physician's assistants, psychologists, and others) who may be reading this text for the first time, we encourage you to collaborate as colleagues in the 21st-century definition of "team" and integrate policymaking into your practices.

From Jeri: Finally, I want to acknowledge my forever-cheering section—my four children, their spouses and significant others, and three grandchildren. They are always there for me and provide continuous support, encouragement, and unconditional love. I love you, Kerrin, Sunny, and Heath Nethers, and George Biddle; Joan Milstead; Kevin Milstead and Gregg Peace; and Sara and Steve, and Matthew, Cynthia, and baby Colton Lott. You are a fun bunch, and you make me laugh.

From Nancy: I feel very grateful to have had this opportunity to be mentored by Dr. Jeri Milstead as she plans to step away from her role as the founding editor (for five editions!) of this text. She is a role model for whom there are not enough words to describe: Perhaps an "Energizer bunny" metaphor fits best. I wish to thank my husband, Jim, for his continuous support of all my career endeavors, including shoulder rubs when I've been using a mouse for way too many hours. I want to acknowledge my children as well: Kolton, Amanda, and Amber have been consistent cheerleaders while simultaneously acknowledging that health policy may not be the most exciting choice for light reading. I also wish to acknowledge the support and inspiration I regularly receive from colleagues and students at the Duke University School of Nursing—especially from Dr. Terry Valiga. Go Blue Devils!

With gratitude,
Jeri A. Milstead and Nancy M. Short

Contributors

Patrick H. DeLeon, PhD, MPH, JD, is distinguished professor at the Uniformed Services University of the Health Sciences (Department of Defense) in the School of Nursing and School of Medicine. He was elected to the Institute of Medicine of the National Academies of Science in 2008 and served as president of the American Psychological Association (APA) in 2000. For more than 38 years, he was on the staff of U.S. Senator Daniel K. Inouye (Democrat–Hawaii), retiring as his chief of staff. Dr. DeLeon has received numerous national awards, including the Order of Military Medical Merit; Distinguished Service Medal, USUHS; National League for Nursing Council for Nursing Centers, First Public Policy Award; Sigma Theta Tau International Honor Society of Nursing, First Public Service Award; Ruth Knee/Milton Wittman Award for Outstanding Achievement in Health/Mental Health Policy, NASW; Delta Omega Honor Society Award for Outstanding Alumnus from a School of Public Health; APA Outstanding Lifetime Contributions to Psychology Award; American Psychological Foundation Gold Medal for Lifetime Achievement in the Practice of Psychology; and Distinguished Alumni Award, University of Hawaii. Dr. DeLeon is currently the editor of *Psychological Services* and has more than 200 publications to his credit. He earned a PhD in clinical psychology, along with an MS (Purdue University), JD (Catholic University), MPH (University of Hawaii), and BS (Amherst College). Dr. DeLeon also has been awarded three honorary doctorates: PsyD (California School of Professional Psychology), PsyD (Forest Institute of Professional Psychology), and HLD (NOVA Southeastern University).

Anne Derouin, DNP, APRN, CPNP, FAANP, is assistant professor at Duke University School of Nursing. She currently serves as lead faculty for the PNP-Primary Care/MSN program at Duke University School of Nursing. She also teaches in the ABSN, DNP, and master of biological sciences programs at Duke. Dr. Derouin is on the Executive Advisory Board for the Duke–Johnson & Johnson Leadership Training program and has served as a coaching circle mentor to Duke-J&J Fellows since 2013. As a Certified Pediatric Nurse Practitioner, she has provided adolescent primary care services at community and school-based health centers affiliated with Duke's Department of Community and Family Medicine for nearly two decades. A member of the inaugural DNP program at Duke University School of Nursing, she earned an MSN/PNP-PC from Duke University and a BSN from the University of Michigan.

Dr. Derouin, who serves as the North Carolina advocacy chair for the National Association of Pediatric Nurse Practitioners (NAPNAP), is considered an adolescent clinical expert. She is active in the Society of Adolescent Health and Medicine (SAHM) and the American Academy of Nurse Practitioners (AANP) and is the co-chair for the Adolescent Special Interest Group of NAPNAP.

She has participated in pediatric, school-based health, and advanced nursing practice advocacy efforts at state and federal levels and has been selected for advocacy fellowships for several professional organizations, including the School-Based Health Alliance (formally National Assembly of School-Based Health Centers), Nurse in Washington Internship (NIWI), Shot@Life (World Health Organization's global vaccine efforts), and as a Faculty Policy Intensive Fellow for the American Association of Colleges of Nursing (AACN).

Elizabeth Ann Furlong, PhD, JD, MA, MS, BSN, RN, is associate professor emerita at Creighton University, Omaha, Nebraska. Dr. Furlong developed and taught health policy courses in a master's program in healthcare ethics at the Center for Health Policy and Ethics, in health administration, and at undergraduate and graduate levels in a school of nursing. Her doctoral dissertation focused on the policy initiation, legislative process, and eventual creation of the National Institute of Nursing Research. Dr. Furlong has been active for decades in health policy advocacy for vulnerable populations and for the nursing profession through civic engagement; in partisan political activities; and through participation on local, state, and national boards of directors of nonprofit associations and nursing and health organizations. She currently serves on the board of directors of the Association of Safe Patient Handling Professionals the Omaha Visiting Nurses Association, and the Douglas County Nursing Home Foundation. Dr. Furlong earned a JD (Creighton University, Omaha, Nebraska), a PhD and MA in political science with a major in health policy (University of Nebraska, Lincoln), an MS (University of Colorado, Denver), a BSN (Marycrest College, Davenport, Iowa), and a diploma from Mercy School of Nursing (Davenport, Iowa).

Toni Hebda, PhD, MSIS, RN-BC, CNE, is professor of nursing at Chamberlain College MSN online program and co-author of *The Handbook of Informatics for Nurses and Healthcare Professionals*, now in its sixth edition. She has presented internationally and nationally on nursing informatics, practiced as a staff nurse, taught nursing, and worked in information services. She is nationally certified in nursing informatics through the American Nurses Credentialing Center. Dr. Hebda is a member of the American Medical Informatics Association, the American Nurses Association, Sigma Theta Tau International, the American Nursing Informatics Association, and the Healthcare Information and Management Systems Society.

Dr. Hebda earned a PhD, MSIS, and MNEd from the University of Pittsburgh, a BSN from Duquesne University, and a diploma from Washington (Pennsylvania) Hospital School of Nursing. The focus of her doctoral program was on higher education. Her dissertation examined the use of computer-assisted instruction among baccalaureate programs.

Janice Kay Lanier, JD, RN, has spent the better part of her nursing career in the health policy arena. Beginning in 1981, when she was selected to participate in the competitive Ohio Legislative Service Commission Internship Program, her involvement in public policy has taken her in many different directions. Working for three state senators and staffing the Ohio Senate health committee for a year gave her a look at the inner workings of the legislative process and its players. That year convinced her of how important policymaking is to nurses and the nursing profession, so she became the director of government affairs for the Ohio Nurses Association (ONA). During her 25-plus years as a lobbyist and consultant on behalf of nursing, she was at the forefront of many initiatives, including recognition of advanced practice nursing and efforts to enact safe staffing legislation in Ohio. She also served as associate executive director of the Ohio Board of Nursing, which provided an opportunity to be involved in the regulatory side of policymaking. In 2008, she ran unsuccessfully for the Ohio House of Representatives—an experience that offered her insights into yet another aspect of public policymaking. Currently, she teaches health policy to graduate nursing students at The Ohio State University, chairs the ONA Health Policy Council, and serves on the Ohio Association of Advanced Practice Nurses Full Practice Authority Committee. She has received numerous awards in recognition of her advocacy efforts at the local, state, and national levels. Ms. Lanier earned a JD and BA in political science from The Ohio State University and a diploma from St. John's Hospital School of Nursing.

Catherine Liao, MSPH, BS, is director of government relations for Duke Health System, a position in which she is responsible for leading the implementation of a comprehensive and diversified federal government relations program working to strengthen Duke Health's identity and reputation in biomedical research, education, training, and service. Prior to joining Duke, she served for nearly six years in the Washington, D.C., Office of Congressman David Price (North Carolina-04) handling health, education, labor, and housing appropriations issues. She has worked as a research assistant at the North Carolina Institute of Medicine, assisting staff with review of federal health reform legislation and recommendations for implementation at the state level. She also completed an administrative fellowship and served in the Office of the Chief of Staff at the Durham Veterans Affairs Medical Center. Ms. Liao holds an MS in public health from the University of North Carolina's Gillings School of Global Public Health and a BA in political science from the University of North Carolina at Chapel Hill.

Jacqueline M. Loversidge, PhD, RNC-AWHC, CNS, is assistant professor of clinical nursing at The Ohio State University College of Nursing. Dr. Loversidge has been educating undergraduate and graduate students in the areas of health policy and regulation, evidence-based practice, and leadership in nursing and health care for nearly 15 years. She has extensive experience in state regulation, having held two positions on the Ohio Board of Nursing (OBN)—associate executive director and education consultant. While at OBN, she served on several National Council of State Boards of Nursing (NCSBN) committees, including the Committee on Special Projects, responsible for transformation of the paper-and-pencil NCLEX licensure examination to computer adaptive mode. Dr. Loversidge's research interests focus on advances in health professions education that have an impact on healthcare quality and safety and are informed by an evidence base. Two major areas fall under that umbrella: (1) health policy, regulation, and advocacy, including licensure and scope of practice; and (2) interprofessional education, including supporting foundations found in organizational structures and cultures. Dr. Loversidge earned a PhD in higher education policy and leadership from The Ohio State University; a master's degree with a major in nursing from Wright

State University, Dayton, Ohio; a BSN from Ohio University, Athens, Ohio; and a diploma from Muhlenberg Hospital School of Nursing, Plainfield, New Jersey.

Jeri A. Milstead, PhD, RN, NEA-BC, FAAN, is senior nurse consultant for public policy, leadership, and education. Dr. Milstead is professor and dean emerita at University of Toledo College of Nursing, where she served for 10 years; was director of graduate programs at Duquesne University (Pittsburgh, Pennsylvania) for 3 years; and was a faculty member at Clemson University (South Carolina) for 10 years. She is the founding editor and senior author of *Health Policy and Politics: A Nurse's Guide*, with copies sold in 22 countries (6 of 7 continents), and *Handbook of Nursing Leadership: Creative Skills for a Culture of Safety*. She has authored invited chapters in four other current nursing textbooks, has published in national and international journals, and was editor-in-chief of *The International Nurse* from 1995 to 2006, when the publication was retired. Dr. Milstead was a policy advisor in the Washington, D.C., office of Senator Daniel K. Inouye (Democrat–Hawaii), was president of the State Board of Nursing for South Carolina, and held leadership positions in the State Nurses Associations in Ohio, Pennsylvania, and South Carolina. She is a fellow of the American Academy of Nursing and a member of ANA/ONA and Sigma Theta Tau International. She is board certified as a Nurse Executive–Advanced by the American Nurses Credentialing Commission.

Dr. Milstead has been honored with the Mildred E. Newton Distinguished Educator award (OSU College of Nursing Alumni Society) and membership in the Cornelius Leadership Congress (ONA's "most prestigious" award), named a Local Nursing Legend by the Medial Heritage Center at OSU, and placed in the Ohio Senior Citizens Hall of Fame and the Washington Court House (Ohio) School System Academic Hall of Fame. She was named a "Transformer of Nursing and Health Care" (OSU CON Alumni Association) and a "Pioneer" in distance education and a career achievement award (Utah); she also received the Creative Teaching Award (Duquesne University) and two political activism awards. From 2005 through 2008, she was appointed to the Toledo-Lucas County Port Authority, where she chaired the port committee and was a member of a trade delegation to China. She has conducted research or consultation in the Netherlands, Jordan, Nicaragua, and Cuba.

Dr. Milstead holds a PhD in political science with majors in public policy and comparative politics from the University of Georgia; an MS and BS, cum laude, in nursing from The Ohio State University; and a diploma from Mt. Carmel Hospital School of Nursing, where she is a Distinguished Alumna and current member of the board of trustees.

J. D. Polk, DO, MS, MMM, CPE, FACOEP, is chief health and medical officer of the National Aeronautics and Space Administration (NASA) located in Washington, D.C. He is the former dean of medicine at Des Moines University (Iowa) College of Osteopathic Medicine. Prior to that, Dr. Polk was the assistant secretary (acting) for health affairs and chief medical officer of the U.S. Department of Homeland Security (DHS), assuming this post after serving as the principal deputy assistant secretary for health affairs and deputy chief medical officer. Before coming to DHS, Dr. Polk was the chief of space medicine for the NASA Johnson Space Center in

Houston, Texas. He has also served as state emergency medical services medical director for the state of Ohio and chief of Metro Life Flight in Cleveland, Ohio. He has served on the board of directors for the Red Cross of Greater Iowa, the board of directors of ChildServe of Iowa, the board of trustees for the American Public University System, the board of directors of the American Association for Physician Leadership, and has been a member of the American Osteopathic Association's Commission on Osteopathic College Accreditation. Dr. Polk is a fellow of the American College of Osteopathic Emergency Physicians and an associate fellow of the Aerospace Medicine Association.

Dr. Polk is well published in the fields of emergency medicine, disaster medicine, space medicine, and medical management. He is a clinical associate professor of emergency medicine at the Edward Via College of Osteopathic Medicine and affiliate associate professor and senior fellow in the School of Public Policy at George Mason University. He has received numerous awards and commendations, including citations from the Federal Bureau of Investigation, White House Medical Unit, Association of Air Medical Services, and U.S. Air Force, and has received the NASA Center Director's Commendation, the NASA Exceptional Service Medal, the National Security and International Affairs Medal, and the NASA Exceptional Achievement Medal.

Dr. Polk received his degree in osteopathic medicine from A. T. Still University in Kirksville, Missouri. He completed his residency in emergency medicine with the Mt. Sinai hospitals via Ohio University and completed his training in aerospace medicine at the University of Texas Medical Branch. He is board certified in both emergency medicine and aerospace medicine. Dr. Polk holds an MS in space studies from the American Military University, a master's degree in medical management from the University of Southern California's Marshall School of Business, and a master's certificate in public health from the University of New England.

Dorothy Lewis Powell, EdD, MS, ANEF, FAAN, is professor emeritus of nursing and associate dean at Duke University School of Nursing, where she founded the Office of Global and Community Health Initiatives (OGACHI). OGACHI is responsible for the development of short-term study-abroad programs across several continents for undergraduate and graduate students. She has been a dean and associate dean of nursing in higher education for more than 47 years.

Throughout her professional life, Dr. Powell has been engaged in policy-oriented endeavors, including a commitment to the poor and underserved, particularly the homeless. She has secured grants in excess of $10 million, including funding that established a nurse-managed clinic for the homeless and the acclaimed Nursing Careers for the Homeless People project in Washington, D.C. She has held local and state-level positions through the American Nurses Association, the American Association of Colleges of Nursing, as a fellow in the American Academy of Nursing, and the NLNAC Academy of Nursing Education. For a number of years, she was a member of the advisory committee for *Partners Investing in Nursing's Future*, Robert Wood Johnson Foundation, and on several Department of Health and Human Services councils. She has represented professional nursing education associations before Congress and participated in a variety of policy-advocacy conferences and meetings. Since her retirement in 2014, she has become actively involved in politics at the local and state levels, serving as precinct chair and chairman of the Durham County African American Caucus.

Dr. Powell has traveled to 47 countries conducting projects, training students, serving as a consultant, studying, planning and hosting conferences, and engaging in leisure-time activities. She has a host of current and former mentees who are excelling in practice, education, research, and policy. Dr. Powell earned an EdD in the administration of higher education from the College of William and Mary, Williamsburg, Virginia, with further study in higher education in the School of Education at Harvard University; an MS in maternal-infant nursing from Catholic University of America, Washington, D.C.; and a BSN from Hampton University (Hampton, Virginia).

Leslie Sharpe, DNP, FNP-BC, is a clinical assistant professor at the University of North Carolina at Chapel Hill (UNC-CH) School of Nursing. She serves as the lead provider and manager of Sylvan Community Health Center in North Carolina. Dr. Sharpe facilitated the opening and ongoing growth of this school-based community health center with the goal of increasing access to health care. Her faculty role with UNC-CH School of Nursing includes establishing innovative faculty practice settings in underserved communities. She educates nurse practitioners and nurses about actively engaging in advocacy efforts related to health policy and improving the health of North Carolinians. As chairperson of the North Carolina Nurses Association's Nurse Practitioner Council Executive Committee from 2011 to 2014, she represented nurse practitioners at state legislative political events and educated legislators and other stakeholders in health care about advanced practice registered nurse issues. She currently serves as the NP PAC treasurer. One of her passions is serving as a mentor for nurse practitioners in the legislative and advocacy arena; as such, she facilitates a "leadership circle" of local APRNs in the North Carolina Research Triangle area. Dr. Sharpe completed her DNP at Duke University.

Nancy Munn Short, DrPH, MBA, BSN, RN, FAAN, is associate professor at Duke University School of Nursing in Durham, North Carolina, where she has been on faculty since 2003. From 2002 to 2006, she served as an assistant dean at the school. Dr. Short received the School of Nursing's Distinguished Teaching Award in 2010 and the Outstanding DNP Faculty award in 2010, 2011, 2013, 2015, 2016, and 2017 (the DNP program began in 2009). She teaches health policy, comparative international health systems, transformational leadership, and health economics. In 2009, she was recognized as an Arnold J. Kaluzny Distinguished Alumnus by the School of Public Health. Dr. Short completed a postdoctoral fellowship as a Robert Wood Johnson Foundation Health Policy Fellow from 2004 to 2007. As a part of this fellowship, in 2005, she served as a health legislative aide for the U.S. Senate Majority Leader Bill Frist. With Darlene Curley, she served as co-chair of an AACN think tank charged with making recommendations to the board regarding ways to improve health policy education for nurses.

Dr. Short is nationally known as an advocate for public health. She has provided consultation to the University of North Carolina (UNC) Public Health Management Academy, the UNC Institute for Public Health on international issues related to distance learning, and the Johnson & Johnson Nurse Leadership Program at Duke. She is a fellow in the American Academy of Nursing.

Dr. Short served as a member of the Durham County (North Carolina) Board of Health. In 2014, she completed a two-year tenure on the board of directors of the National Association of Local Boards of Health, where she specialized in the development of performance standards for the approximately 3,000 boards of health in the United States. Under the auspices of the U.S. Department of State, she delivered leadership and quality management training to a bicommunal (Turk and Greek) program for nurses in Cyprus.

Dr. Short earned a doctor of public health degree with a major in health policy and administration at the University of North Carolina's Gillings School of Global Public Health and an MBA and BSN from Duke University.

CHAPTER 1

Informing Public Policy: An Important Role for Registered Nurses

Jeri A. Milstead and Nancy M. Short

Statutes: Written laws passed by a legislative body. Statutes differ from "common law" in that common law (also known as case law) is based on prior court decisions. Statutes may be enacted by both federal and state governments and must adhere to the rules set in the Constitution.

System (capital "S"): The U.S. healthcare delivery and finance system (usage specific to this text).

system (lowercase "s"): A group of hospitals and/or clinics that form a large healthcare delivery organization (usage specific to this text).

▶ Introduction

In 2010, the Institute of Medicine* (IOM) issued a report, *The Future of Nursing: Advancing Health, Leading Change*, that challenged nurses to work with other healthcare professionals in two ways: to learn from them and to help them learn from nurses. In this spirit of interprofessional cooperation and leadership, this text will incorporate a variety of **healthcare provider professionals (HCPs)** into the discussion of public policy, case studies, discussion points, and reader activities.

▶ How Is Public Policy Related to Clinical Practice?

It is the authors' belief that nurses and other HCPs are ideally positioned to participate in the policy arena because of their history, education, practice, and organizational involvement.

In this chapter, *policy* is an overarching term used to define both an entity and a process. The purpose of **public policy** is to direct problems to the government's attention and to secure the government's response.

The definition of public policy is important because it clarifies common misconceptions about what constitutes policy. In this text, the terms *public policy* and *policy* are interchangeable. The process of creating policy can be focused in many areas, most of which are interwoven. For example, environmental policy deals with determinants of health such as hazardous materials, particulate matter in the air or water, and safety standards in the workplace. Education policies are more than tangentially related to health—just ask school nurses. Regulations define who can administer medication; state laws dictate which type of sex education can be taught. Defense policy is related to health policy when developing, investigating, or testing biological and chemical weapons. There is a growing awareness of the need for a health-in-all-policies approach to strategic thinking about policy.

---

* The name of the Institute of Medicine was changed to the National Academy of Medicine in 2016.

Health policy directly addresses health problems and is the specific focus of this text. In general, **policy** is a consciously chosen course of action: a law, regulation, rule, procedure, administrative action, incentive, or voluntary practice of governments and other institutions. By comparison, **politics** is the process of influencing the allocation of scarce resources.

Policy as an Entity

Official government policies reflect the beliefs and values of elected members, the administration in power, and the will of the American people. Official policies provide direction for the philosophy and mission of government organizations. Some policies, known as position statements, report the opinions of organizations about issues that members believe are important. For example, state boards of nursing (government agencies created by legislatures to protect the public through the regulation of nursing practice) publish advisory opinions on what constitutes competent and safe nursing practice.

Laws (or **statutes**) are one type of policy entity that serve as legal directives for public and private behavior. Laws are made at the international, federal, state, and local levels and are considered the principal source in guiding conduct. Lawmaking usually is the purview of the legislative branch of government in the United States, although presidential vetoes, executive orders, and judicial interpretations of laws also have the force of law.

Judicial interpretation occurs in three ways: (1) through courts' interpretation of the meaning of broadly written laws that are vague regarding details; (2) by determining how some laws are applied—that is, by resolving questions or settling controversies; or (3) by interpreting the Constitution and declaring a law unconstitutional, thereby nullifying the entire statute (Litman & Robins, 1991). For example, the 1973 Rehabilitation Act prohibited discrimination against people with handicaps by any program that received federal assistance. Although this may have seemed fair and reasonable at the outset, courts adjudicated questions of how much accommodation is "fair and reasonable" (Wilson, 1989). In general, courts are idealized as being above the influence of political activity that surrounds the legislature. The court system, especially the federal court system, may also resolve conflicts between levels of government (state and federal).

Regulations and rules are another policy entity discussed elsewhere in this text. Although they often are included in discussions of laws, regulations differ from statutes. Once the legislative branch enacts a law, the executive branch of government administers that law's implementation. The executive branch consists of the president, the White House staff, multiple agencies, commissions, and departments that carry out the work of implementing and monitoring laws for the public benefit. Government agencies formulate regulations that achieve the intent of the statute. Overall, laws are written in general terms, and regulations are written more specifically to guide the interpretation, administration, and enforcement of the law. The Administrative Procedures Act, enacted in 1946, ensures a structure and process that is published and open, in the spirit of the founding fathers, so the average constituent can participate in the process of public decision making.

All these policy entities evolve over time and are accomplished through the efforts of a variety of actors or players. Although commonly used, the terms *position statement, resolution, goal, objective, program, procedure, law,* and *regulation* really are not interchangeable with the word *policy.* Rather, they are the formal expressions of policy decisions. For the purposes of understanding just what policy is, nurses must grasp policy as a process.

Policy as a Process

For purposes of analysis, policymaking comprises five processes:

- Agenda setting
- Government response (usually legislation and regulation)
- Policy design
- Implementation
- Evaluation of the policy outcomes
- Economics and finance of policy

The steps in the **policy process** are not necessarily sequential or logical. For example, the definition of a problem, which usually occurs in the agenda-setting phase, may change during fact-finding and debate. Program design may be altered significantly during implementation. Evaluation of a policy or program (often considered the last phase of the process) may propel onto the national agenda (often considered the first phase of the process) a problem that differs from the originally identified issue. For the purpose of organizing one's thoughts and conceptualizing the policy process, we will examine the policy process from a linear perspective in this text, but you should recognize that this path is not always strictly followed.

The opportunities for nurse input throughout the policy process are unlimited. Nurses are articulate experts who can address both the rational shaping of policy and the emotional aspects of the process. Nurses cannot afford to limit their actions to monitoring bills; they must seize the initiative and use their considerable collective and individual influence to ensure the health, welfare, and protection of the public and healthcare professionals.

Why You Are the Right Person to Influence Health Policy

Nursing's education requirements, communication skills, rich history, leadership, and trade association involvement, as well as our practice venues, uniquely qualify nurses to influence thought leaders and policymakers. Nursing and nurses have an ongoing impact on health and social policies. **FIGURE 1-1** illustrates some aspects of nurses' impact on the health and well-being of populations.

Advanced studies build on education and experience and broaden the arena in which nurses work to a systems perspective, including both regional health **systems** and the overall U.S. **System** of healthcare delivery and finance. Nurses not only are well prepared to provide direct care to persons and families but also act as change agents in the work environments in which they practice and the states/nations where they reside.

Nurses have developed theories to explain and predict phenomena they encounter in the course of providing care. In their practice, nurses also incorporate theory from other disciplines such as psychology, anthropology, education, biomedical science, and information technology. Integration of all

1852	**Florence Nightingale** used statistics to advocate for improved education for nurses, sanitation, and equality.
1861	**Clarissa "Clara" Barton** was a hospital nurse in the American Civil War. She founded the American Red Cross.
1879	**Mary Mahoney** was the first African American nurse in the United States and a major advocate for equal opportunities for minorities.
1903	North Carolina creates first Board of Nursing in nation and licenses the first registered nurse.
1906	**Lillian D. Wald**, nurse, humanitarian, and author. She was known for contributions to human rights and was the founder of American Community Nursing. She helped found the NAACP.
1909	The University of Minnesota bestows the first bachelor's degree in nursing.
1916	**Margaret Higgins Sanger** was an American birth control activist, sex educator, writer, and nurse. Sanger popularized the term "birth control" and opened the first birth control clinic in the United States (later evolved into Planned Parenthood).
1925	Frontier Nursing Service was established in Kentucky with advanced practice nurses (midwives).
1955	**RADM Jessie M. Scott, DSc**, served as assistant surgeon general in the U.S. Public Health Service; led division of nursing for 15 years; testimony before Congress on the need for better nursing training led to the 1964 Nurse Training Act, the first major legislation to provide federal support for nurse education during peacetime.
1966	NP role created by **Henry Silver, MD**, and **Loretta Ford, RN**.
1967	**Luther Christman, PhD**, became the first male dean of a School of Nursing (at Vanderbilt University). Earlier in his career, he had been refused admission to the U.S. Army Nurse Corps because of his gender. He was the founder of the American Association for Men in Nursing, as well as a founder of the National Student Nurses Association.
1971	Idaho statutorily recognizes advanced practice nursing.
1978	**Faye Wattleton, CNM**, was elected president of the Planned Parenthood Federation of America—the first African American and youngest person ever to hold that office. First African American woman honored by the Congressional Black Caucus.
1987	**Ada S. Hinshaw, PhD**, became the first permanent leader at the National Institute of Nursing Research at the National Institutes of Health.
1989	**Geraldine "Polly" Bednash, PhD**, headed the American Association of Colleges of Nursing's legislative and regulatory advocacy programs as director of government affairs. She became CEO of AACN in 1989 and co-authored AACN's landmark study of the financial costs to students and clinical agencies of baccalaureate and graduate nursing education.

FIGURE 1-1 Historical timeline of nurses who influenced policy. (*continues*)

1992	— **Eddie Bernice Johnson, BSN,** was the first nurse elected to the U.S. Congress (D-TX). Strong voice for African Americans and pro-nursing policies.
1996	— **Beverly Malone, PhD,** elected president of the American Nurses Association; President Clinton appointed her to Advisory Commission on Consumer Protection and Quality in the Health Care Industry and to the post of deputy assistant secretary for health within the Department of Health and Human Services.
1998	— **Lois G. Capps, BSN,** California Representative to the U.S. House from 1998–2017, where she founded the Congressional Nursing Congress.
2001	— **Major General Irene Trowell-Harris, EdD, RN, USAF (Ret.),** director of Department of Veterans Affairs, Center for Women Veterans. Instrumental in establishing fellowship for military nurses in the office of Senator Daniel K. Inouye (D-HI).
2009	— **Mary Wakefield, PhD,** became the first nurse appointed as director of the Health Resources and Services Administration. In 2015, she became the Acting Deputy Secretary for the Department of Health and Human Services. Served as Chief of Staff for U.S. Senators Quentin Burdick (D-ND) and Kent Conrad (D-ND).
2010	— **Mary D. Naylor, PhD,** a member of the Medicare Payment Advisory Commission influenced health policy with membership on the RAND Health Board, the National Quality Forum Board of Directors, and as pastchair of the Board of the Long-Term Quality Alliance.
2013	— **Joanne Disch, PhD,** influenced health policy as chair of the national board of directors for the American Association of Retired Persons and the American Academy of Nursing.

FIGURE 1-1 Historical timeline of nurses who influenced policy. (*continued*)

this information reflects the extreme complexity of nursing care and its provision within an extremely complex healthcare system. Nurses understand that partnerships are valued over competition, and that the old rules of business that rewarded power and ownership have given way to accountability and shared risk. Transformation of today's broken healthcare system will require a radical, cross-functional, futuristic change in the way people think. Observing patterns in personal behavior can be useful when working with policymakers as they try to figure out the best or most cost-effective way to address public problems. Creative ways of examining problems and innovative solutions may cause discomfort among policymakers who have learned to be cautious and go slowly. Nurses and other professionals can help officials employ new ideas to reach their policy goals by sharing stories and interpreting data to show how those data affect patients and professionals.

Communication skills are integral to the education of nurses, who often must interpret complex medical situations and terms into common, understandable, pragmatic language. Nurse education programs have formalized a greater focus on communications than is present in any other professional education program. From baccalaureate curricula through all upper levels of nurse education, major segments of nursing courses focus on individual communications and group processes. Skills include active listening, reflection, clarification, assertiveness, role playing, and other techniques that build nurse competence levels. These same skills are useful when talking with policymakers. Other chapters in this text discuss the differences in nurses' communication with patients/colleagues and with nonclinician policymakers.

Nursing care is not only a form of altruism but also incorporates intentional action (or inaction) that focuses on a person or group with actual or potential health problems. The education of nurses puts them in the position of discovering and acknowledging health problems and health System problems that may demand intervention by public policymakers. For these many reasons, accrediting agencies require policy content within nurse education programs.

Practice and Policy

Evidence and theory provide the foundation for nursing as a practice profession. Nurses stand tall in their multiple roles—provider of care, educator, administrator, consultant, researcher, political activist, and policymaker. In their daily practice, nurses spot healthcare problems that may need government intervention, although not all problems nurses and their patients face in the healthcare System are amenable to solutions by government. Corporations, philanthropy, or collective action by individuals may best solve some problems. Most nurses are employees (as are most physicians today) and must navigate the organizations in which they work. By being attuned to systems issues, nurses have developed the ability to direct questions and identify solutions. This ability is reflected in the relationships that nurses can develop with policymakers.

Nurses bring the "power of numbers" when they enter the policy arena. According to a 2017 report from the National Council of State Boards of Nursing, there are 3,913,805 registered nurses (RNs) in the United States. Collectively, nurses represent the largest group of healthcare workers in the nation.

Nurses have many personal stories that illustrate health problems and patients' responses to them. These stories have a powerful effect when a nurse brings an issue to the attention of policymakers. Anecdotes often make a problem more understandable at a personal level, and nurses are credible storytellers. By applying evidence to a specific patient situation, nurses may also bring research to legislators in ways that can be understood and can have a positive effect.

Nurses live in neighborhoods where health problems often surface and can often rally friends to publicize a local issue. Nurses are constituents of electoral districts and can make contacts with policymakers in their districts. Nurses vote. It is not unusual for a nurse to become the point person for a policymaker who is seeking information about healthcare issues. A nurse does not have to be knowledgeable about every health problem, but she or he has knowledge of a specific patient population as well as a vast network of colleagues and resources to tap into when a policymaker seeks facts. The practice of nursing prepares the practitioner to work in the policy arena. The public policy process (**FIGURE 1-2**), after all, involves the application of a decision-making model in the public sector.

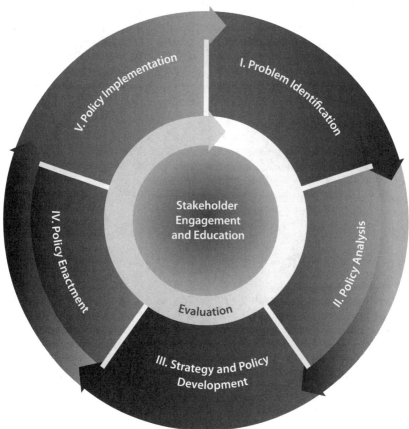

FIGURE 1-2 The policy process.

Reproduced from Centers for Disease Control and Prevention. (2012). Overview of CDC's Policy Process. Atlanta, GA: Centers for Disease Control and Prevention, U.S. Department of Health and Human Serivces. Retrieved from https://www.cdc.gov/policy/analysis/process/

All facets of nursing practice and patient care are highly regulated by po-litical bodies. State boards of nursing and other professional regulatory boards exert much influence in interpreting the statutes that govern nursing. Scope of practice is legislated by elected members but then defined in the **rules and reg-ulations** by boards. Because each state and jurisdiction defines the practice of nursing differently, there is wide variation in the nursing scope of practice across the specific states. A fear expressed by many boards is that their decisions may interfere with Federal Trade Commission (FTC) rules that restrict monopoly practices. In 2014, the FTC published a policy paper addressing the regulation of the **advanced practice registered nurse (APRN)** that includes five key findings with important implications for policymakers:

1. APRNs provide care that is safe and effective.
2. Physicians' mandatory supervision of and collaboration with advanced nurse practice is not justified by any concern for patient health or safety.
3. Supervision and collaborative agreements required by statute or regulation lead to increased costs, decreased quality of care, fewer innovative practices, and reduced access to services.

4. APRNs collaborate effectively with all healthcare professionals without inflexible rules and laws.
5. APRN practice is "good for competition and consumers" ("FTC Policy Paper," 2014, p. 11).

Professional nurses who are knowledgeable about the regulatory process can more readily spot opportunities to contribute or intervene prior to final rule making.

Organizational Involvement

Professional organizations bring their influence to the policy process in ways that a single person may not. There are a myriad of nurse-focused organizations, including those in specialty areas, education-related organizations, and leadership-related organizations. For example, the American Nurses Association, National League for Nursing, and Sigma Theta Tau International state a commitment to advancing health and health care in the United States and/or on a global scale, as noted in their mission statements and goals, and offer nurses opportunities to develop personal leadership skills. The Oncology Nurses Society, American Association of Critical Care Nurses, American Association of Nurse Anesthetists, Emergency Nurses Association, and many other specialty organizations focus on policies specific to certain patient populations and provide continuing education. Participating on committees within trade associations provides opportunities to learn about the organization, its mission, and its outreach efforts in more depth.

Professional associations afford their members experiences to become knowledgeable about issues pertinent to the organization or the profession. These groups can expand a nurse's perspective toward a broader view of health and professional issues, such as at the state, national, or global level. This kind of change in viewpoint often encourages a member's foray into the process of public policy. Some nurses are experienced in their political activity. They serve as chairs of legislative committees for professional organizations, work as campaign managers for elected officials, or present testimony at congressional, state, or local hearings; a few have run for office or hold office.

Political activism is a major expectation of most professional organizations. Many organizations employ professional lobbyists who carry those organizations' issues and concerns forward to policymakers. These sophisticated activists are skilled in the process of getting the attention of government and obtaining a response. Nurses also have an opportunity to voice their own opinions and provide information from their own practices through active participation in organizations. This give-and-take builds knowledge and confidence when nurses help legislators and others interpret issues.

Taking Action

Nurses cannot afford to limit their actions in relation to policy. Instead, nurses need to share their unique perspectives with bureaucrats, agency staff, legislators, and others in public service regarding what nurses do, what nurses and their patients need, and how their cost-effectiveness has long-term impacts on health care in the United States.

Many nurses are embracing the whole range of options available in the various parts of the policy process. They are seizing opportunities to engage in ongoing, meaningful dialogues with those who represent the districts and states and those who administer public programs. Nurses are becoming indispensable sources of information for elected and appointed officials, and they are demonstrating leadership by becoming those officials and by participating with others in planning and decision making. By working with colleagues in other health professions, nurses often succeed in moving an issue forward owing to their well-recognized credibility and the relatively fewer barriers they must overcome.

Addressing Nursing Shortages

Nurses can bring research and creativity to efforts geared toward solving public policy issues such as the nursing shortage and the most efficacious use of RN and APRNs. Aiken and colleagues have reported repeatedly that hospitals with higher proportions of baccalaureate-prepared nurses demonstrate decreased patient morbidity and mortality (Aiken et al., 2003, 2012, 2014; Van den Heede et al., 2009; Wiltse-Nicely, Sloane, & Aiken, 2013; You et al., 2013). Aiken's research includes studies in the United States and in nine European countries. Although the National Council of State Boards of Nursing has stated that it is not ready to support legislation or regulation that requires a bachelor of science in nursing (BSN) degree as the entry level into practice as a registered nurse, the marketplace is moving in a different direction. Many healthcare agencies are limiting new hires to those with a BSN and have developed policies that require RNs with associate's degrees or diplomas to complete a BSN within 5 years of employment. Academic institutions have expanded or created RN-to-BSN programs in response to the demand from the accrediting agency for Magnet status, the American Nurses Credentialing Center.

Second-degree nurse education programs, reminiscent of similar programs initiated during World War II, have flourished at the bachelor's and master's degree levels. These programs were created to accept applicants with college degrees in fields other than nursing and provide students with an opportunity to graduate with a degree in nursing in an abbreviated time period; graduates are eligible to sit for the National Council Licensure Examination (NCLEX-RN) to become registered nurses. These popular programs provide new avenues that address the nurse shortage.

Perhaps the greatest potential for change in the education of nurses will be the effect of the IOM (2010) report, *The Future of Nursing: Leading Change, Advancing Health*. Developed under the aegis of and funded by the Robert Wood Johnson Foundation, this report explicitly recognized that nurses (the largest healthcare workforce in the United States) must be an integral part of a healthcare team. Its authors emphasize four key messages (IOM, 2010, pp. 1–3):

1. Nurses should practice to the full extent of their education and training.
2. Nurses should achieve higher levels of education and training through an improved education system that promotes seamless academic progression.
3. Nurses should be full partners with physicians and other healthcare professionals in redesigning health care in the United States.

4. Effective workforce planning and policymaking require better data collection and an improved information infrastructure.

A consortium of professional organizations has moved forward together to address common problems. The Josiah Macy Jr. Foundation (2014) developed recommendations that support working together in five areas: (1) engagement, (2) innovative models, (3) education reform, (4) revision of regulatory standards, and (5) realignment of resources.

▶ Healthcare Reform at the Center of the Public Policy Process

Starting with the Harry Truman administration in the 1940s, every U.S. president's administration has struggled to reform the healthcare System to meet the needs of all U.S. residents. President Barack Obama declared early in his administration that a major priority would be health care for all, and in 2010, the Patient Protection and Affordable Care Act (commonly known as the ACA and "Obamacare") was established, a huge first for the United States. Seven years after the passage of the ACA, however, more than one-third of U.S. residents were unable to identify that Obamacare and the ACA were one and the same (Advisory Board, 2017).

The Affordable Care Act was being debated and amended as this text was being revised; no one can predict how health care for the nation will be addressed by the Trump administration. Public uncertainty about personal coverage and methods of financing care are major issues; the former solutions may not fit new program designs. Most care providers recognize the problems inherent in offering care to the uninsured and underinsured. The disparities in care seen in low-socioeconomic groups and vulnerable populations (e.g., children, the elderly) and groups with specific health concerns (e.g., persons with diabetes, smokers) present enormous challenges. Nurses have proffered solutions that have been taken seriously by major policy players.

Expanding the historical boundaries of nursing will require skills in negotiation, diplomacy, assertiveness, expert communication, and leadership. Sometimes physician and nurse colleagues are threatened by these behaviors, and it takes persistence and certainty of purpose to proceed. Nurses must speak out as articulate, knowledgeable, caring professionals who contribute to the whole health agenda and who advocate for their patients and the community. All healthcare professions have expanded the boundaries of practice from their beginnings. Practice inevitably reflects societal needs and conditions; homeostasis is not an option if the provision of health care is to be relevant.

▶ Developing a More Sophisticated Political Role for Nurses

In addition to being clinical experts, nurses are entrepreneurs, decision makers, and political activists. Many nurses realize that if they are to control practice and move the profession of nursing forward as major players in the healthcare arena, they must be involved in the legal decisions about the health and welfare of the public—decisions that often are made in the governmental arena.

For many nurses, political activism used to mean letting someone else get involved. Today's nurses often tune in to bills that reflect a particular passion (e.g., driving and texting), disease entity (e.g., diabetes), or population (e.g., childhood obesity). Although this activity indicates a greater involvement in the political process, it still misses a broader comprehension of the whole policymaking process that provides many opportunities for nurse input before and after legislation is proposed and passed.

Nurses who are serious about political activity realize that the key to establishing contacts with legislators and agency directors is to forge ongoing relationships with elected and appointed officials and their staffs. By developing credibility with those active in the political process and demonstrating integrity and moral purpose as client advocates, nurses are becoming players in the complex process of policymaking.

Nurses have learned that by using nursing knowledge and skill, they can gain the confidence of government actors. Personal stories drawn from professional nurses' experience anchor altruistic conversations with legislators and their staffs, creating an important emotional link that can influence policy design. Nurses' vast network of clinical experts produces nurses in direct care who provide persuasive, articulate arguments with people "on the Hill" (i.e., U. S. congressional members and senators who work on Capitol Hill) during appropriations committee hearings and informal meetings.

Nurses regularly participate in formal, short-term internship programs with elected officials and in bureaucratic agencies. Most of these internships were created by nursing organizations convinced of the importance of political involvement. Interns and fellows learn how to handle constituent concerns, how to write legislation, how to argue with opponents yet remain colleagues, and how to maneuver through the bureaucracy. They carry the message of the necessity of the political process to the larger profession, although the rank-and-file nurses still are not active in this role.

Nurses who have been reluctant to become active in the political arena cannot afford to ignore their obligations any longer. Each nurse counts, and collectively, nursing is a major actor in the effort to ensure the United States' healthy future. Many nurses have already expanded their conception of what nursing is and how it is practiced to include active political participation. The process is similar at the federal or state level: Identify the problem and become part of the solution.

Working with the Political System

Many professional nurses and APRNs develop contacts with legislators, appointed officials, and their staffs. Groups that offer nurse interaction include the House Nursing Caucus and Senate Nursing Caucus (their membership shifts with the election cycle). Members hold briefings on the nurse shortage, patient and nurse safety issues, vaccination, school health, reauthorization of legislation (e.g., the Emergency Medical System, the Ryan White Act), preparedness for bioterrorism, and other relevant and pertinent issues and concerns.

Nurses must stay alert to issues and be assertive in bringing problems to the attention of policymakers. It is important to bring success stories to legislators and officials—they need to hear what good nurses do and how well they practice. Sharing positive information will keep the image of nurses positioned within an affirmative and constructive picture. Legislators must run for office (and U.S. representatives do so every 2 years), so media coverage with a local nurse who is pursuing noteworthy accomplishments is usually welcomed.

▶ Conclusion

Healthcare professionals must have expert knowledge and skills in change management, conflict resolution, active listening, assertiveness, communication, negotiation, and group processes to function appropriately in the policy arena. Professional autonomy and collaborative interdependence are possible within a political system in which consumers can choose access to quality health care that is provided by competent practitioners at a reasonable cost. Professional nurses have a strong, persistent voice in designing such a healthcare system for today and for the future.

The policy process is much broader and more comprehensive than the legislative process. Although individual components can be identified for analytical study, the policy process is fluid, nonlinear, and dynamic. There are many opportunities for nurses in advanced practice to participate throughout the policy process. The question is not *whether* nurses should become involved in the political system, but *to what extent*. Across the policy arena, nurses must be involved with every aspect of this process. By knowing all the components and issues that must be addressed in each phase, the nurse in advanced practice will find many opportunities for providing expert advice. APRNs can use the policy process, individual components, and models as a framework to analyze issues and participate in alternative solutions.

▶ Discussion Points

1. Identify a problem you have encountered in school or in practice (e.g., "My patients all have dental problems and have no means of paying for dental care"). Discuss how the diagram of the policy process (Figure 1-2) can help inform how you approach finding a solution to this problem. Reflect on which level of government might address this problem and why. Identify the stakeholders in this issue.

2. Discuss the role of research in nursing/healthcare practice as it affects health policy. What has been the focus over the past century? What is the pattern of nursing research vis-à-vis topic, methodology, and relevance? To what extent do you think the current focus on evidence-based practice has influenced research? Cite examples.

3. Trace the amount of federal funding appropriated for nursing or HCP research over specific year(s). Do not limit your search to federal health-related agencies; that is, investigate departments (e.g., commerce, environment,

transportation), military services, and the Department of Veterans Affairs. Which funding opportunities exist for nurse scientists/HCP scientists?

4. Read books and articles about the changing paradigm in healthcare delivery systems. Discuss the change in nursing or another healthcare profession as an occupation versus a profession.

5. Consider a thesis, graduate project, or dissertation on a specific topic (e.g., clinical problems, healthcare issues) using the policy process as a framework. Identify policies within public agencies and determine how they were developed. Interview members of a government agency's policy committee to discover how policies are changed.

6. Review official governmental policies. Which governmental agency is responsible for developing the policy? For enforcing the policy? How has the policy changed over time? What are the consequences of not complying with the policy? What is needed to change the policy?

7. Identify nurses and healthcare professionals who are elected officials at the local, state, or national level. Interview these officials to determine how the nurses and HCPs were elected, what their objectives are, and to what extent they use their nursing knowledge in their official capacities. Ask the officials if they tapped into nurses groups during their campaigns. If so, what did the nurses and HCPs contribute? If not, why?

8. Discuss the fluidity among the major components of the policy process. Point out how players move among the components in a nonlinear way. How can this knowledge facilitate entrance into the policymaking process?

9. Watch television programs in which participants discuss national and international issues. Analyze the patterns of verbal and nonverbal communication, pro-and-con arguments, and other methods of discussion used on the program. Position your analysis within the framework of gender differences in communication and utility in the political arena.

10. List ways in which healthcare professionals can become more knowledgeable about the policy process. Choose at least three activities in which you will participate. Develop a tool for evaluating the activity and your knowledge and involvement.

11. Select at least one problem or irritation in a clinical area, and brainstorm with other healthcare professionals or graduate students on how to approach a solution. Who else could you bring into the discussion who could become supporters? Discuss funding sources—be creative.

12. Attend a meeting of the state board of your health profession or a professional convention. Identify issues discussed, resources used, communication techniques, and rules observed. Evaluate the usefulness of the session to your practice.

13. Discuss which skills (e.g., task, interpersonal) and attitudes are required for the nurse in the policy arena. Who is best prepared to teach these skills, and which teaching techniques should be used? How will the skills be evaluated? Develop a worksheet to facilitate planning. Discuss at least five strategies for helping nurses integrate these skills into their practices.

14. Convene a group of healthcare professionals and discuss common problems, potential solutions, and strategies to move forward.

🔍 CASE STUDY 1-1: *The Addiction Epidemic*

You are an acute care nurse practitioner who works in an urban emergency room (ER). You see many people who come to the ER who have overdosed (OD) on heroin. Emergency medical services personnel may administer a drug that might reverse the overdose such as naloxone (Narcan). You may see three ODs during each 12-hour shift; some of these patients are admitted to the hospital, and others are sent home with a consultation for psychiatric followup. You are becoming hardened to the issue and have begun to question what you can do to address this epidemic.

Discussion Points

1. You hear that the state health director is convening a task force. List four actions you can take to be invited to participate in this task force.
2. Which other healthcare professionals should be included on the task force?
3. Which state agencies and regulatory boards could add value to the discussion?
4. Which information/experience could the APRN use to lead a discussion about widespread addiction?
5. Identify three issues that might be brought up at a meeting that could derail a focus on public safety. Which tactics can the nurse use to bring the discussion back to the issue of safety?
6. Which design tactics could be considered when writing a policy to address this issue?
7. How can information about this issue be disseminated within the profession and to those outside the profession?

References

Advisory Board. (2017, February 7). Many Americans think repealing Obamacare won't repeal the ACA, survey finds. Retrieved from https://www.advisory.com/daily-briefing/2017/02/09/many-americans-think-repealing-the-aca#

Aiken, L. H., Clarke, S. R., Cheung, R. B., Sloane, D. M., & Silber, J. H. (2003). Educational levels of hospital nurses and surgical patient mortality. *Journal of the American Medical Association, 290*(12), 1617–1623.

Aiken, L. H., Cimotti, J. P., Sloane, D. M., Smith, H. L., Flynn, L., & Neff, D. E. (2012). Effects of nurse staffing and nursing education on patient deaths in hospitals with different work environments. *Medical Care, 49*(12), 1047–1053.

Aiken, L. H., Sloane, D. M., Bruyneel, L., Van den Heede, K., Griffiths, P., Busse, R., . . . Sermeus, W. (2014). Nurse staffing and education and hospital mortality in nine European countries: A retrospective observational study. *Lancet, 383*(9931), 1824–1830.

Centers for Disease Control and Prevention. (2012). Overview of CDC's policy process. U.S. Department of Health and Human Services. Retrieved from https://www.cdc.gov/policy/analysis/process/docs/cdcpolicyprocess.pdf

FTC policy paper examines competition and the regulation of APRNs. (2014). *American Nurse, 46*(3), 11.

Institute of Medicine (IOM). (2010). *The future of nursing: Leading change, advancing health.* Washington, DC: National Academies Press.

Josiah Macy Jr. Foundation. (2014). Publications. Retrieved from http://www.macyfoundation.org/publications/publications/aligning-interprofessional-education

Litman, T. J., & Robins, L. S. (1991). *Health politics and policy* (2nd ed.). Albany, NY: Delmar.

National Council of State Boards of Nursing. (2017). Active RN licenses. Retrieved from http://ncsbn.org/6161.htm

Patient Protection and Affordable Care Act of 2010. (2010). Pub. L. No. 111-148, 124 Stat. 119.

Van den Heede, K., Lesaffre, E., Diya, L., Vleugels, A., Clarke, S. P., Aiken, L. H., & Sermeus, W. (2009). The relationship between inpatient cardiac surgery mortality and nurse numbers and educational level: Analysis of administrative data. *International Journal of Nursing Studies, 46*, 796–803.

Wilson, J. Q. (1989). *American government institutions and policies* (4th ed.). Albany, NY: Delmar.

Wiltse-Nicely, K. L., Sloane, D. M., & Aiken, L. H. (2013, June). Lower mortality for abdominal aorta aneurysm repair in high volume hospitals contingent on nurse staffing. *Health Systems Research, 48*(3), 972–991.

You, L.-M., Aiken, L. H., Sloane, D. M., Liu, K., He, G-P, Hu, Y., . . . Sermeus, W. (2013). Hospital nursing, care quality, and patient satisfaction: Cross-sectional survey of nurses and patients in hospitals in China and Europe. *International Journal of Nursing Studies, 50*(2), 154–161.

CHAPTER 2

Agenda Setting: What Rises to a Policymaker's Attention?

Elizabeth Ann Furlong

KEY TERMS

Contextual dimensions: Studying issues in the real world, in the circumstances or settings of what is happening at the time.
Iron triangle: Legislators or their committees, interest groups, and administrative agencies that work together on a policy issue that will benefit all parties.
Streams: Kingdon's classic research on agenda setting noted a streams metaphor—the concept of the interaction of public problems, policies, and politics that couple and uncouple throughout the process of agenda setting.
Window of opportunity: Limited time frame for action.

▶ Introduction

This chapter emphasizes the agenda-setting aspect of policymaking by using exemplar case studies at local, state, and national levels. Agenda setting is the process of moving a problem to the government's attention so that solutions can be considered. Registered nurses (RNs), advanced practice registered nurses (APRNs), and other interprofessional healthcare workers (IPHCWs) can apply the knowledge from these case studies to the many current concerns they face. The author acknowledges the older dates of many of the references cited in this chapter. These classic political science references on agenda setting are retained in this chapter to further the historical knowledge of the nurse policy advocate. Agenda setting can happen in legislative settings and in private organizations.

The local example in this chapter demonstrates what can be done in the latter venue. By seeking and obtaining a grant from a national organization, nurse leaders are initiating and furthering a new policy practice in a health organization. The outcomes of this new agenda policy can have potential implications for furthering agenda setting at governmental levels.

FIGURE 2-1 illustrates the various levels of the political agenda:

- Agenda universe: All ideas that could possibly be brought up and discussed in a society.
- Systemic agenda: All issues that are commonly perceived as meriting public attention within the legitimate jurisdiction of the existing governmental authority.
- Institutional agenda: Items that have risen to the attention of a governing body.
- Decision agenda: Items about to be acted on by a governing body.

APRNs and other IPHCWs, as well as policymakers and citizens, are interested in the best public policies to address society's concerns. Early political science researchers mainly studied the later steps of policymaking—implementation and evaluation—to gain an understanding of public policy and knowledge that could be used by policymakers to create better public policies. Although all stages of the policy process have been studied, the need for more research on the earlier parts of policymaking—agenda setting, policy formulation, and policy design—has been the subject of more discussion in recent times (Bosso, 1992a; Ingraham, 1987; May, 1991). Research interest in these latter areas grew during the 1980s and 1990s and continues into the 21st century.

As noted earlier, this chapter presents examples of agenda setting at the local, state, and national levels. The first example demonstrates how nurse and interprofessional health leaders are changing practice interventions at the organizational level with use of a grant. By seeking and obtaining a grant from a national organization, nurse leaders can initiate new practices in a health organization. The outcomes of this new agenda policy can have potential implications for furthering agenda setting at governmental levels. Changing policies and processes in the delivery of healthcare services in an ambulatory health center in a nonprofit

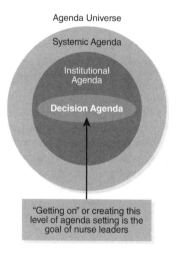

FIGURE 2-1 Levels of the political agenda.

health organization is not only a policy end unto itself but also has implications for other nurse leaders to set such agendas in their respective organizations.

APRNs and other IPHCWs also need to learn how issues get on legislative agendas. The state-level example presented in the second case study involves a nurse practitioner bill that was passed in Nebraska. The first national example in this chapter focuses on an event that had just occurred as this text was being written. The second national-level case study is a classic national legislative example; research and analysis for this second national example were performed by this author. Following that analysis, those same theories are applied to the Nebraska nurse practitioner bill.

⌕ *CASE STUDY 2-1:* A Local Example

Policies can be changed in organizations as well as legislatively. This first example demonstrates nurse and interprofessional health leaders changing practice interventions with use of a grant. Specifically, they are setting an agenda in an ambulatory health center, with this planning and intervention facilitated by a grant.

Two departments in Omaha Creighton University's College of Nursing and the Center for Interprofessional Practice, Education, and Research are furthering interprofessional health care and education by their 2016 receipt of a $50,000 grant from the National Center for Interprofessional Practice and Education (*Blue News* [daily e-newsletter, Creighton University], 2016). The grant at Creighton, titled "Accelerating Interprofessional Community-Based Education and Practice," will assist in developing a nurse practitioner–led interprofessional team to be utilized in Creighton's healthcare-affiliated system, Catholic Health Initiative (CHI). In addition to the grant, both Creighton University and CHI donated $25,000 to the endeavor. Dean Catherine Todero of the College of Nursing noted, "Nurse practitioners are increasingly taking lead roles in a number of clinical and educational health care situations" (*Blue News*, 2016). This grant will further the practice, education, and research of a nurse practitioner–led interprofessional team for a national agency.

⌕ *CASE STUDY 2-2:* A Nurse Practitioner– Initiated Bill in the Spring 2014 Nebraska Unicameral Legislature

An example of agenda setting in 2014 was an effort by the Nebraska Nurse Practitioners (NNP), a state nursing association, to find a state senator who would introduce a bill into the Nebraska unicameral legislative session to eliminate the Integrated Practice Agreement (IPA) from the Nurse Practitioner Practice Act (Nebraska Legislature, 2014). The public hearing for the bill was held on January 31, 2014; the sponsoring state senator's goal was for the bill to emerge from the seven-member Health and Human Services Committee with support from all or most of the members (Senator S. Crawford, personal communication, January 2014).

(continues)

🔍 *CASE STUDY 2-2: A Nurse Practitioner–Initiated Bill in the Spring 2014 Nebraska Unicameral Legislature* *(continued)*

Prior to the bill's introduction, the NNP had to undergo review by the Nebraska Credentialing Review (407) Program. This state-level review program had been created to evaluate current Nebraska health professionals who are seeking to expand their scope of practice or to evaluate the scope of practice of a new type of provider (Nebraska Department of Health and Human Services, n.d.). As part of its review, the NNP submitted extensive documentation to three review bodies—an ad hoc Technical Review Committee appointed by the director of the Nebraska Division of Public Health, a second review by the State Board of Health, and a third review by the director of the Division of Public Health. These reviews represented input from the Department of Health and Human Services (DHHS) about possible concerns for Nebraskans in either public health or safety. Although the recommendations at the three levels are advisory, they serve to inform state senators when considering and voting on proposed legislation (D. Wesley, lobbyist, personal communication, June 2013). The NNP proposal received support at the first two levels; at the second level, the vote was 12–5 to eliminate the IPA requirement (Whitmire, 2013). There also were recommendations with this second vote to (1) have practice requirements for the new graduate nurse practitioner (NP) and (2) have ongoing competency evaluations of all NPs. At the third level of review, the director and chief medical director of the DHHS were strongly opposed to the NNP proposal (Ruggles, 2013).

APRNs in Nebraska set the agenda with four goals in mind:

- Decrease barriers to their full scope of practice
- Provide more and needed access to health care (especially primary care and mental health care) in rural parts of the state
- Meet the emerging primary healthcare needs associated with an increased Nebraska population having health insurance because of the Affordable Care Act
- Decrease the exodus of APRNs to contiguous states that did not have such IPA agreements (Sundermeier, 2013/2014)

In seeking passage of this bill, Nebraska NPs wanted to join the 17 other states and the District of Columbia that had facilitated full scope of practice availability for nurse practitioners. As noted by Bobrow and Dryzek (1987), this case study underscores the importance of **contextual dimensions** furthering agenda setting. As noted previously, there were four important contexts in setting this agenda topic at this time in this state.

This agenda, which was based on evidence-based practice studies and the promotion of all nurses working to their full potential, is also advocated by the National Academy of Medicine (Institute of Medicine, 2010). By providing legislative language to a state senator to introduce a bill, APRNs set the agenda in Nebraska.

A variety of strategies were implemented to further the agenda goal. This chapter's author served as chair of the Nebraska Nurses Association's Legislative Advocacy and Representation Committee (LARC). This committee worked in unison and collaboratively with the NNP, its lobbyist, the NNA lobbyist, and the sponsoring state senator to serve as the lead strategists and voices. APRNs used public media to promote their perspectives. For example, following a negative review from the Nebraska DHHS, one APRN educated the public via an op-ed article about APRNs in the state's largest newspaper (Holmes, 2013). She noted several of the previously made arguments as support for why APRNs wanted the IPA eliminated.

The bill passed by a 43–0 vote during the last day of the 2014 unicameral session. However, the governor vetoed the legislation, and there was not time for the unicameral legislature to enact an override.

In early 2015, the bill was reintroduced, passed, and signed by the new governor on March 5, 2015 (Lazure, Cramer, & Hoebelheinrich, 2016). Other factors facilitating its passage included (1) education regarding APRN capabilities along with advocacy during the campaigns of 17 new state senators; (2) obtaining commitments from both gubernatorial candidates that they would not veto the bill if reintroduced in 2015; (3) ongoing advocacy by the earlier noted nursing groups; and (4) interprofessional health groups that both supported the bill and said they would testify at a public hearing. Nebraska is now one of 21 states in which nurse practitioners have full practice authority (Pohl, Thomas, Barksdale, & Werner, 2016).

Before presenting two national case studies, the reader should take note of some salient concepts. Congress may pass a law that directs an agency to take action on a certain subject and set a schedule for the agency to follow in issuing rules. More often, an agency surveys its area of legal responsibility and then decides which issues or goals have priority for rulemaking. A few of the many factors that an agency may consider are presented here:

- New technologies or new data on existing issues
- Concerns arising from accidents or various problems affecting society
- Recommendations from congressional committees or federal advisory committees
- Petitions from interest groups, corporations, and members of the public
- Lawsuits filed by interest groups, corporations, states, and members of the public
- Presidential directives
- "Prompt letters" from the Office of Management and Budget (OMB)
- Requests from other agencies
- Studies and recommendations of agency staff (https://www.federalregister .gov/uploads/2011/01/the_rulemaking_process.pdf)

🔎 *CASE STUDY 2-3:* The Veterans Health Administration Ruling on APRN Practice

In December 2016, the U.S. Department of Veterans Affairs (VA) announced its final rule regarding APRN practice within the Veterans Health Administration national health system. The decision allows nurse practitioners, certified nurse–midwives, and clinical nurse specialists to practice without physician supervision. This change will facilitate broader access to health care within the VA system (American Association of Colleges of Nursing [AACN], 2016). During 2016, nurses nationally were encouraged to post advocacy messages to the appropriate webpage (https://www.va.gov/orpm) for changing such rules and regulations. This use of the media was an example of promoting advocacy by the four professional associations representing APRNs, the American Nurses Association, and other nursing groups at national and state levels. By the time the Final Rule was released in May 2016, more than 179,734 comments had been posted (J. Thew, personal communication, 2017). This large number of comments reflects advocacy behaviors of nurses.

🔎 *CASE STUDY 2-4:* The National Center for Nursing Research Amendment

A classic example of agenda setting was the initiation of federal legislation in 1983 that increased the funding base for nursing research. An amendment to the 1985 Health Research Extension Act, which created the National Center for Nursing Research (NCNR) on the campus of the National Institutes of Health (NIH), was the focus of this national example of agenda setting.

Creation of the NCNR came about because a group of nurse leaders wanted to create a national institute of nursing within the NIH. To help pass the legislation in 1985, a political compromise was made with congressional legislators to create a center instead of an institute (a lesser agency in the hierarchy). In 1993, however, the NCNR was turned into an institute, and today the agency continues as the National Institute of Nursing Research (NINR). The discussion here regarding the NCNR amendment focuses on the agenda setting and policy formulation that occurred from 1983 to 1985. Achievement in getting the NINR funded was an especially notable accomplishment because no other health profession has such an institute.

The Influence of National Nurse Groups

The creation of the National Center for Nursing Research on the campus of the National Institutes of Health in Bethesda, Maryland, was a policy victory for national nurse organizations. Although nurses' groups traditionally have not been considered strong political actors, these groups recognized the importance of political activity to bring about public policies that enhanced patient care (Warner, 2003). In the last decade of the 20th century, nurse groups were just emerging as actors in policy networks; however, "a full cadre of nurse leaders who are knowledgeable and experienced in the public arena, who fully understand the design of public policy, and who are conversant with consumer, business and provider groups [did] not yet exist" (DeBack, 1990, p. 69). In a study of national health organizations that play a key role in the health policymaking area (Laumann, Heinz, Nelson, & Salisbury, 1991), no nurse organizations were cited. APRNs are well aware of this absence because state legislative and regulatory activity affects their professional practice on a daily basis.

Research on the NCNR amendment has been important because it studied political actors who were not generally studied (e.g., nurse interest groups); this research contributes to public policy scholars' knowledge of all actors in policy networks. Laumann et al. (1991) acknowledged that "we may even run a risk of misrepresenting the sorts of actors who come to be influential in policy deliberation" (p. 67). The significance of policy research becomes obvious when the Schneider and Ingram (1993a) model of social construction of target populations in policy design is applied to nurse interest groups. For example, how nurses were viewed by policymakers—the social construction of nurses as a target population—influenced not only the policy in which nurses were interested but also the passage of the total NIH reauthorization bill.

Dohler (1991) compared health policy actors in the United States, Great Britain, and Germany and found that it is much easier to have new political actors in the United States because there are multiple ways to become involved. Dohler has written of the great increase in new actors since 1970. Baumgartner and Jones (1993) also described multiple paths of access to becoming involved.

▶ Overview of Models and Dimensions

Several researchers have developed models of agenda setting and policy formulation (Baumgartner & Jones, 1993; Cobb & Elder, 1983), alternative formulation, and policy design (Schneider & Ingram, 1993a). Data analysis reveals the importance of the Schneider and Ingram (1993a) model of the social construction of target populations and of the classic Kingdon (1995) model for an understanding of the agenda-setting process for the amendment described in Case Study 2-4 to the NIH-reauthorizing legislative bill. Analysis of this legislation over the period of a decade also underscores the importance of Dryzek's (1983) classic definition of policy design. An analysis of the legislation supported the importance of studying the contextual dimension that has been advocated by Bobrow and Dryzek (1987), Bosso (1992a), DeLeon (1988–1989), Ingraham and White (1988–1989), May (1991), and Schneider and Ingram (1993b). The value of other models—institutional, representational communities and an institutional approach, and the congressional motivational model—is addressed as well, as these models contribute to an understanding of this example. These findings are discussed in detail in this analysis. For example, during the study of interest groups opposed to this legislation, this researcher noted two occurrences of an **iron triangle** in the early 1980s, in which legislators and their staff and agency bureaucrats worked with interested parties to resolve issues (**FIGURE 2-2**).

Kingdon Model

One model that served as an explanatory focus for this research was the Kingdon (1995) model, which explains how issues get on the political agenda and, once there, how alternative solutions are devised (**FIGURE 2-3**). The four important

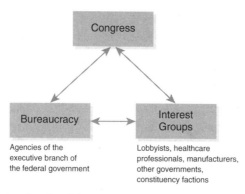

FIGURE 2-2 Iron triangle of politics.

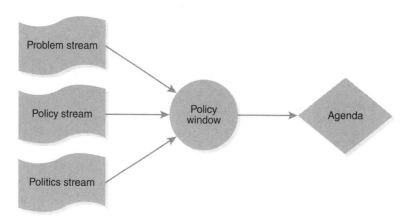

FIGURE 2-3 Kingdon model.

concepts of this model are the three **streams** (problem, policy, and politics) and the **window of opportunity**. A problem stream can be marked by systematic indicators of a problem, by a sudden crisis, by feedback that a program is not working as intended, and by the release of certain important reports. A practical application for APRNs and other IPHCWs is that they can be attentive to these indicators and maximize such opportunities to get an issue on the agenda. A policy stream relates to those policy actors and communities who attach their solutions (policies) to emerging problems. This concept also relates to the actual policy being promoted: APRNs and other IPHCWs can be attentive to identifying problems and framing their solutions to such concerns. The third stream of Kingdon's model is the political stream, which consists of the public mood, pressure group campaigns, election results, partisan or ideological distributions in Congress, and changes in administrations. Other factors include congressional committee jurisdictional boundaries and turf concerns among agencies and government branches.

APRNs and other IPHCWs need to be constantly attentive to all these political factors, which can be integrated with the fourth concept, the window of opportunity. This window opens when the three streams become integrated at a time that is favorable to solve a problem with the preferred policy and with the least resistance.

Interview data and a review of the literature showed many ways in which the Kingdon model explained the agenda setting for the NCNR legislation. For example, for the problem stream, the following were variables: (1) the need for nursing research was recognized by many (e.g., Rep. Madigan [Republican–Illinois], legislative staffers, and national nurse leaders); (2) data were available regarding the financial disparity in research funding for nurses; and (3) an Institute of Medicine (IOM) report (Cantelon, 2010) on this problem was released in 1983. There were two variables for the political stream: (1) the policy would be valuable for Rep. Madigan's re-election and (2) the policy proposal was an important way for the Republican party to secure increased votes from women. In terms of the policy stream, it was sound public policy. The window of opportunity opened with the release of the 1983 IOM report in conjunction with the election cycle, the singular presence of many national nurse leaders who were knowledgeable about both policy and politics, and a U.S. representative who initiated the idea for this bill—all these factors came together quickly and at an opportune time. In summarizing these findings in relation to the Kingdon model, this example validated the importance of the political and problem streams.

Ultimately, the NCNR amendment was passed without meeting the policy stream processes described by Kingdon, in that it did not go through a softening-up phase. This concept refers to several revisions being made to a particular policy as compromises are made and negotiations take place. As stated, the NCNR amendment was articulated once and moved forward; there was no tweaking or change in the legislation's language.

Professional nurses and other IPHCWs may be able to apply the Kingdon model to ongoing priority practice issues with which they are concerned. For example, APRNs and other IPHCWs can be attentive to the three streams (policy, problem, and political) and recognize the existence of a window of opportunity in which to move their agenda forward. APRNs and other IPHCWs also need to be aware that taking part in political activity in regulatory agencies could be an ideal way to problem solve. Case Study 2-3, for example, addressed changes to a Final Rule and regulations within the VA system for three types of APRNs. Another example occurred in the early part of the 21st century when nurse practitioners encountered increased difficulty in having mail-order pharmacies recognize and fill their prescriptions (Edmunds, 2003). Two nurse practitioners from New York and South Carolina addressed this problem stream by working with the Food and Drug Administration and the Federal Trade Commission. The NPs recognized that working through regulatory agencies was the best initial solution for solving this problem (Edmunds, 2003).

Importance of Contextual Dimensions

Some authors, notably Bobrow and Dryzek (1987), Bosso (1992a), DeLeon (1988–1989), Ingraham and White (1988–1989), May (1991), and Schneider and Ingram (1993b), have emphasized the need to analyze the political context in which policies get on the agenda, alternatives are formulated, and policies are put into effect. Although neither a definitive nor an exhaustive list, five contextual dimensions are suggested by Bobrow and Dryzek (1987) for studying the success or failure of any designed policy:

- Complexity and uncertainty of the decision–system environment
- Feedback potential
- Control of design by an actor or group of actors
- Stability of policy actors over time
- Stirring the audience into action

DeLeon (1988–1989) writes that sometimes researchers, because of their unstructured environment, have chosen to study approaches and methodologies that may meet scientific rigor better, but in doing so, come "dangerously close to rendering the policy sciences all-but-useless in the real-life political arenas" (p. 300).

DeLeon (1988–1989) notes that it is nearly impossible for researchers to "structure analytically the contextual environment in which their recommended analyses must operate" (p. 300). Whether analyzing the 1983 case study or the 2014–2015 case study, APRNs and other IPHCWs must analyze the context in which they find themselves, apply theory, and evaluate the outcome later for theory application. Researchers and advocacy activists today must work in a world characterized by great social complexity, extreme political competition, and limited resources. Of these writers, Bosso and May are especially strong in their advocacy of this contextual approach to the study of public policy. Bosso (1992b) echoes DeLeon's concern:

> In many ways, the healthiest trend is the admission, albeit a grudging one for many, that policymaking is not engineering and the study of policy formation cannot be a laboratory science. In policy making, contexts do matter, people do not always act according to narrow self-interest and decisions are made on the basis of incomplete or biased information. (p. 23)

For many healthcare professionals, this "messy" process is very uncomfortable. Nevertheless, data from congressional documents, archival sources, and personal and telephone interviews highlight the importance of the political context to all aspects of policy design for the NCNR—how the policy arrived on the agenda, how policy alternatives were formulated, the legislative process, implementation, and redesign of the legislation eight years later, resulting in new legislation within two years to accomplish the original goal (Bobrow & Dryzek, 1987; Bosso, 1992b; DeLeon, 1988–1989; Ingraham & White, 1988–1989; May, 1991; Schneider & Ingram, 1993b).

Examples of Political Contextual Influence

Sixteen variables are analyzed here in regard to their contribution to the 1985 passage of the NCNR and the 1993 change of the NCNR to the NINR (**TABLE 2-1**).

TABLE 2-1 Variables Contributing to Passage of Legislation Creating the National Center for Nursing Research

Partisan political conflict between legislators	Influenced the initial agenda setting of the amendment and the legislative process throughout the two years. Opposition to Rep. Waxman's (Democrat–California) NIH bill in the spring and summer of 1983 resulted in Rep. Madigan's initiating a substitute policy. An impetus for Rep. Madigan's bill was a perception that Rep. Waxman yielded too much power with NIH legislation. As noted by two congressional staffers, this was an example of partisan conflict.
Election cycle	A U.S. representative's concern with his re-election chances influenced the initial agenda setting because of the congressional perception that nurses were a target population who could help his re-election chances. Several respondents noted that this was an important factor in the initial decision for this type of public policy
Bipartisan negotiation—presence versus absence	Bipartisan negotiations between Rep. Waxman and Rep. Madigan in early fall 1983 resulted in a firm resolve during the 97th and 98th Congresses to stay with the proposed NINR policy and during the 99th Congress to accept a compromise on the NCNR. Another example of bipartisan negotiation was the early committee work by Rep. Madigan, Rep. Broyhill (Republican–North Carolina), and Rep. Shelby (Democrat–Alabama) to forge a simple bipartisan four-line amendment. The bipartisan effort of these three representatives smoothed the way for passage of this amendment by the subcommittee.
Interest-group unity	Unity by nurse groups was considered by many interviewees to be a crucial factor in the bill's passage, and this unity also was important in explaining why no other policy alternatives were pursued. Because the decision to support Rep. Madigan was officially made by the Tri-Council (the American Nurses Association [ANA], the National League for Nursing [NLN], the Association of Nurse Executives, and the American Association of Colleges of Nursing) in the summer of 1983, and although other policy alternatives were considered after that point, the priority of presenting a united front with Rep. Madigan was maintained by nurse organizations.
Non-interest-group unity	Prior disunity by the American Association of Medical Colleges had disillusioned Rep. Madigan and increased his interest in initiating the NINR policy with the nurse providers' groups.

(continues)

TABLE 2-1 Variables Contributing to Passage of Legislation Creating the National Center for Nursing Research *(continued)*

Partisan conflict between the White House and an interest group	The White House and nursing organizations (which had generally supported Democratic presidential and vice presidential candidates) had an influence on this legislation's history. The 1984 campaign support by the ANA for Democratic candidates was the reason for the Republican presidential veto of a NINR amendment and the NIH bill.
Ideological and partisan conflicts over current issues	Concerns about fetal tissue research and animal rights research caused much difficulty in the early 1980s. Concerns about immigration laws and immigrants with human immunodeficiency virus (HIV) infection raised concerns in the 1990s and affected compromises and passage of the bills. These issues, although not directly addressed in the NINR amendment, had a major effect on the bill's legislative history.
Federal or state budget deficit concerns	There was opposition to the creation of new federal entities because of the deficit concern, and President Ronald Reagan consistently used this argument as a reason not to create an NINR.
Timing of passage during the president's "lame-duck" term	The NIH bill with the NCNR amendment was passed in 1985, when President Reagan was beginning his second term. The number of Republican members of Congress, the lack of any constraint to vote along party lines that was reflected in the 1985 legislative vote, and the ability to override the president's veto were all factors. The timing of this vote in President Reagan's lame-duck term helped the bill's passage.
History of legislators with administrative agencies	Rep. Waxman's attempts to exert control over NIH was a factor in Rep. Madigan's initiation of NIH legislation during the summer of 1983. Data support the perspective that, of all administrative agencies, the NIH consistently was regarded positively by members of Congress, and this positive perception was reflected in ample funding levels on a consistent basis. Contrary to this usual positive regard was the negative situation between Rep. Dingell (Democrat–Michigan) and the NIH. Rep. Dingell had "captured" letters sent by NIH officials to research scientists asking them to lobby their congressional representatives for increased funding—an example of the internal workings of an iron triangle. Rep. Dingell reminded NIH officials that this activity violated law.

The relationship of Congress, administrative agencies, and the Office of Management and Budget	NIH officials became anxious when the OMB dictated that NIH develop a last-minute revised budget to honor a 1980 promise to fund 5,000 new grants yearly. This mandated division of NIH's economic pie contributed to NIH officials not wanting new research entities on their campus that would further erode existing programs and projects. A second similar budgetary crisis occurred at NIH in spring 1985 that, again, caused much consternation for NIH officials and research scientists.
Internal political dynamics and relationships in Congress	Rep. Waxman was a member of the Congressional class of 1974, when the dynamic in Congress was a decentralization of power with a large new congressional class. (A congressional class refers to that cohort of officials elected in a certain year.) The data show that Rep. Waxman was interested in gaining more power and control over NIH. Although his committee had authorizing power over the NIH, it did not have the greater power of the Appropriations Committee, which was responsible for funding. However, through his ability to authorize legislation, Rep. Waxman had leverage to gain more power. Rep. Waxman's attempt to micromanage the NIH resulted in Rep. Madigan's initiating a substitute policy.
Communication between the White House and Congress	President Reagan publicly vetoed the legislation in 1984, although he could have allowed its passage quietly by not signing the bill. The veto was intended to alert Congress to expect conflict the following year if the bill's provisions were not changed. An example of the negative relationship between the White House and Congress can be seen with the congressional override vote in 1985. Members of Congress (and many members of the president's political party) felt betrayed over their work on this legislation and over what they thought their communication had been with the president about passing this policy and putting it into effect. This sense of betrayal spurred their work in securing the veto override.
International politics	During the fall of 1985, the Senate waited until the Geneva Summit was finished before beginning the veto-override vote. This was done to keep President Reagan from losing any credibility regarding his leadership ability during the summit meeting because the Soviet leader would be aware of the veto override.

(continues)

TABLE 2-1 Variables Contributing to Passage of Legislation Creating the National Center for Nursing Research   *(continued)*

The skills and abilities of an interest group	In the early 1980s, many factors influenced the ability of nurse interest groups to promote this policy once it was on the agenda: (1) the formation of the Tri-Council, (2) a special interest in public policy by the executive director of the NLN, (3) the anticipated need to reauthorize the Nurse Education Act, (4) the policy orientations of many deans of nursing education programs, (5) a combination of people who saw the need, (6) much networking by nurses, (7) the presence of highly motivated people who were interested in furthering the nursing profession, (8) nurses appointed to positions within the White House, (9) more nurses working on Capitol Hill, and (10) the study conducted by Dr. Joanne Stevenson (personal communication, 1990) on nurse researchers' inability to obtain NIH grants.
The wit of "all politics is personal" and the importance of personal relationships	Data revealed the importance of personal relationships in getting the idea on the agenda, in obtaining strategic information, in sharing needed information, and in making requests. For example, strategic networking at certain cocktail parties helped with the legislation's acceptance, as did carpooling with selected political actors. Savvy nurse leaders facilitated other nurses in meeting with legislators and legislative aides in these settings so nurses could lobby effectively. The importance of congressional staffers to the initiation and passage of legislation must be emphasized: Several interviewees spoke of the importance of certain staffers in their tenacity to ensure that the NCNR amendment was passed. Clearly, the adage that "all politics is personal" influenced the legislation at various points.

Control and Stability Factors

Two of Bobrow and Dryzek's (1987) five contextual dimensions were in evidence and contributed to the success of this policy, both because the NCNR was passed as legislation in 1985 and because the NCNR became the National Institute of Nursing Research in 1993. The two criteria—namely, the control of design by an actor or group of actors and the stability of policy actors over time—were related in this instance.

Once this policy was on the agenda and once nurses were united, the nurse interest groups were committed to the legislation. The nurse interest groups showed unity in working with Representative Madigan and staying the course. Although other policy alternatives were discussed, they were never vigorously pursued by the nurse interest groups. Once the compromise on the NCNR was made in 1985, the nurse interest groups found the deal acceptable because they knew they had a "foot in the door" and because they planned to accomplish their original design (i.e., a nursing institute rather than a nursing center) at a later date.

The second dimension, stability of policy actors, also relates to the nurse interest groups. These groups of nurse leaders were stable for over a decade and kept tenaciously to their goal. Although the policy arrived on the formal agenda because of Rep. Madigan's actions, a very unchanging group of nurse actors worked for more than 10 years to see that the original policy design eventually was enacted (i.e., change from the NCNR to the NINR).

According to May (1991), regardless of how one defines policy design, there is the "emphasis on matching content of a given policy to the political context in which the policy is formulated and implemented" (p. 188). This statement describes the contextual dimension of how this public policy arrived on the formal agenda. Rep. Madigan was going to introduce substitute legislation for Rep. Waxman's NIH bill. Rep. Madigan's NINR amendment was based on an appraisal of which policy content would best work in that political context.

Schneider and Ingram Model

In addition to emphasizing the role of the political context in agenda setting, Schneider and Ingram (1991, 1993a, 1993b) specifically push for empirical research that studies the social construction of target populations (those groups affected by the policy). They propose that one can best understand agenda setting, alternative formulation, and implementation of policy by knowing how elected officials perceive different target populations—in other words, by knowing the "social construction" (i.e., images, symbols, and traits) of such populations.

In their beginning work in this area, Schneider and Ingram proposed a theory in which the continuum of target populations is categorized as the advantaged, contenders, dependents, and deviants. Their model suggests that pressure to initiate beneficial policy that helps those groups will be seen positively, whereas groups who are seen negatively will receive punitive policy. Schneider and Ingram argue that groups whose members are viewed positively include the "advantaged" and the "dependents," whereas the negatively perceived groups are the "contenders" and the "deviants." This is just a beginning categorization—Schneider and Ingram call for more empirical research in this area to refine their theory. In particular, they admit that their theory is currently lacking in three areas: (1) definitions of target populations and social constructions; (2) an explanation of how social constructions influence public officials in choosing agendas and designs of policy; and (3) an explanation of how policy agendas and designs influence the political orientations and participation patterns of target populations.

Schneider and Ingram's proposed theory, together with Kingdon's research, provide the best explanation for understanding the process of the NCNR legislation. Schneider and Ingram (1991, 1993a, 1993b) write that one can best understand agenda setting, alternative formulation, and policy implementation by knowing how elected officials see different target populations and by knowing the social constructions of such populations. In the case study, the NCNR policy was initiated by Rep. Madigan because of the social construction of this target nurse population. Proposing public policy for this target population would help him pass his substitute NIH legislation. Nurses, as a target population, were positioned on the continuum as positively viewed groups. Although Schneider and Ingram acknowledge that their emerging theory needs empirical testing to refine and define several of its components, this author found it to be of explanatory value and extreme importance in explaining the outcomes with the NCNR legislation.

Mueller (1988) wrote: "Politicians must be convinced that they will gain from new policies—either through political success or through program effectiveness" (p. 443). The selection of nurses as a target population at a time when congressional members, especially Republicans, needed the female vote to win re-election contributed to a convincing argument for potential political success for the nurses.

▶ Summary Analysis of a National Policy Case Study

"No data are ever in themselves decisive. Factors beyond only the data help decide which policy is formulated or adopted by the people empowered to make the decision to form policy" (James, 1991, p. 14). In this quote, James is referring to data in a problem stream as described by Kingdon. The accuracy of this quote was evident in this nursing research described in Case Study 2-4, as Schneider and Ingram's theory of the "social construction of target populations," together with Kingdon's model and the contextual dimension, explained the policy process.

The contextual dimension influenced all aspects of the policy, from agenda setting in 1983 through policy redesign in 1991, and later with the passage of the amended legislation in 1993 that accomplished the original 1983 goal. The importance of studying the political context was demonstrated by the 16 contextual dimensions that influenced this legislative policy process.

Of particular explanatory value in the early agenda setting and policy-alternative formulation for this legislation were Schneider and Ingram's model and Kingdon's model. The particular amendment was pursued because of application of the "social construction of target populations"; that is, the target population of nurses was chosen because nurses would help Rep. Madigan's and other Republican members of Congress's chances for re-election. Notably, Kingdon's theory adds to further understanding of this legislation. Within Kingdon's model, neither the problem stream nor the policy stream was decisive in driving the legislative process; rather, the political stream played the key role. The factors making up the political stream (re-election chances for Rep. Madigan and other Republican congressional representatives, partisan ideology in Congress, the public mood about gender issues, and turf concerns between government agencies) all strongly influenced the placement of this issue on the national agenda. The hypotheses supported by this empirical research include the notions that policy is more likely to be initiated for those target populations who are positively viewed by members of Congress; issues are more likely to reach the formal agenda when the political stream factors are related to positively viewed target populations; and the policy process is best understood in a contextual perspective.

▶ Theory Application to the Nebraska Nurse Practitioner Case Study

Although this chapter has emphasized this author's research into a national policy case study on agenda setting, the same theories can also be applied to the

Nebraska state case study. The national case study's agenda setting was initiated by a U.S. representative. In contrast, in the state case study, NPs initiated and set the agenda (i.e., by seeking a state senator to introduce a bill, LB916).

In the Nebraska case, NPs were knowledgeable about the problem, policy, and political streams as well as the window of opportunity. Further, NPs knew the context of many variables within Nebraska and the nation that have affected the progression of such bills, both in Nebraska and in other states. Variables include the 2010 IOM report, evidence-based research on the quality and safety of nurse practitioner care, the 54,000 uninsured Nebraskans, the Affordable Care Act, whether the unicameral legislature passed a modified Medicaid expansion bill during its sessions, the political conservatism of the state, and the structure of the unicameral legislature as a short 60-day session in even-numbered years (J. Sundermeier, personal communication, December 2013). Specifically, the problem stream incorporated two variables: (1) NPs in Nebraska did not meet the goal of the IOM report (i.e., were not working to their full scope of authority) and (2) more Nebraskans, especially those living in rural areas, could have enhanced access to health care if NPs had this full scope of authority. Nurse practitioners selected a policy stream proposal that was being furthered by the IOM report (i.e., work to one's full authority).

Finally, NPs were aware of the key political variables: (1) the modified Medicaid expansion bill that did not pass in 2013, which led to an increase in the number of uninsured people in the state; (2) the political conservatism of state; (3) the short 60-day session (which means a prioritization of bills for passage by the state senators); and (4) the pushback against their position by the Nebraska Medical Association (NMA). In January 2014, the strategy of the NMA was to delay action on LB916 by seeking another study in addition to the thorough review conducted under the Nebraska Credentialing Review (407) Program, which lasted for many months during 2013 (D. Wesley, personal communication, January 28, 2014). A delaying tactic during proposed agenda setting, instead of direct opposition, is a common strategy employed by opponents to a policy (D. Wesley, personal communication, January 28, 2014).

All the variables listed in this state case study for the three streams eventually converged into a window of opportunity for NPs, who saw the bill finally being introduced in January 2014. As this example suggests, the Kingdon model continues to facilitate policy analysis for a range of policies (Kingdon, 2001; Lieberman, 2002). Further, the social construction theory (used in the analysis of the NCNR national case study) was as relevant in 2014 in Nebraska with LB916 as it had been decades earlier in the NCNR/NINR development. Nurse practitioners in Nebraska continued to struggle with the social construction perception of NPs versus physicians and hospital administrators and the amount of power each of these provider groups holds. For example, the Nebraska Hospital Association took a neutral stance on the NP bill (D. Wesley, personal communication, January 28, 2014).

In addition to taking on the specific role of setting the agenda (i.e., introducing and shepherding a bill through a legislative body), APRNs and other healthcare providers supported such agenda setting by their colleagues in other ways. For example, this writer served in her third year as Chair of the Legislative Advocacy and Representative Committee (LARC) of the Nebraska Nurses Association (NNA). Both LARC and the NNA were fully supportive of the NNP and followed the strategies of the NP advocacy plan. LARC, representing the NNA, provided verbal and written testimony during the late January 2014 public hearing, and timely email messages were prepared by LARC and sent to all NNA members to encourage them to engage in appropriate advocacy with the respective Health and Human Services Committee senators who were considering this bill. Another way this writer furthered the agenda-setting goals of the NNP was by her membership in a League of Women Voters (LWV) chapter in a large Midwestern city and education of LWV members on this bill. These LWV civic activists were encouraged, after their evaluation of the bill, to also advocate as citizen consumers. This writer utilized her participation in the monthly AARP Advocacy Forum in the largest city in Nebraska to enlist other lay and consumer advocacy activists for their lobby assistance.

LB916 passed the third and final vote (final reading) on April 17, 2014, with a 43–0 passage vote (six senators were either not present or abstained from voting). This was the last day of the unicameral session. On April 22, 2014, the governor vetoed the bill, citing a rationale based on input from the physician director of the Nebraska Health and Human Services Department. Because April 17 was the last day of the legislature, it was not possible to have an override of the veto. The Nebraska Nurse Practitioner Association planned to reintroduce the bill in the spring of 2015. As noted earlier in this chapter, the bill passed in 2015.

Even though sound policy ideas may be presented to policymakers and the appropriate legislative process may be followed, not all ideas will take hold and not all solutions proposed will come to fruition. In Nebraska, it is not unusual for a proposed policy bill to move through as many as three or more unicameral sessions before it is passed; passage the first time around is unusual. Each session is two years, so achieving success in passing legislation calls for tenacity by policy advocates. Persistence and long-term planning are integral and critical to policymaking.

▶ Conclusion

For professional nurses and IPHCWs, these four case studies contribute to an understanding of agenda setting by illuminating the importance of the Schneider and Ingram model, the Kingdon model, and the contextual dimensions of policy initiation, development, implementation, and redesign. Specifically, they illustrate how these models can be used to analyze the creation of a local grant to study the practice and education of a nurse practitioner–led interprofessional health team; a state law facilitating full practice authority for NPs; a Final Rule and regulation that facilitate the full practice authority of NPs in the national VA system; and the National Institute for Nursing Research.

▶ Discussion Points

1. How does the Kingdon model explain the NCNR getting on the political agenda?
2. How does the Kingdon model apply to the Nebraska case study?
3. How can APRNs and other IPHCWs become aware of factors in the problem stream to which Kingdon alluded? Which problems are you concerned about in your specific profession?

4. What are examples of policy streams that APRNs and other IPHCWs could be advancing relative to their practice?

5. How can APRNs and other IPHCWs become involved in the political stream? How are you involved?

6. How can APRNs and other IPHCWs anticipate windows of opportunity? Given your profession, for which signals will you specifically be observant?

7. According to Schneider and Ingram, to which of the four target populations does your specific health provider group belong? Discuss the relevance to agenda setting.

8. What are ways that APRNs and other IPHCWs can network with congressional members and their staffers?

9. How can APRNs and other IPHCWs promote unity among themselves and with other healthcare providers?

10. How can all healthcare providers support one another and further some of the IOM goals?

11. Which current contextual dimensions can promote APRNs' and other IPHCWs' practices?

12. How can APRNs and other IPHCWs best use the Kingdon model and the Schneider and Ingram model?

13. Given your specific health profession, which policy do you recognize that needs to be on the agenda at the local, state, or national level? What can you do to begin that process?

References

American Association of Colleges of Nursing. (2016, December 13). VA ruling on APRN practice: A breakthrough for veterans health care. Message posted on the American Association of Colleges of Nursing Listserv: web@aacn.nche.edu

Baumgartner, F. R., & Jones, B. D. (1993). *Agendas and instability in American politics*. Chicago, IL: University of Chicago Press.

Blue News. (2016, September 28). College of Nursing, CIPER earn prestigious national grant. Daily e-newsletter, Creighton University.

Bobrow, D. B., & Dryzek, J. S. (1987). *Policy analysis by design*. Pittsburgh, PA: University of Pittsburgh Press.

Bosso, C. J. (1992a). Designing environmental policy. *Policy Currents*, 2(4), 1, 4–6.

Bosso, C. J. (1992b). *Policy formation: Current knowledge and practice*. Paper presented at the American Political Science Association meeting (pp. 1–30), Chicago, IL.

Cantelon, P. (2010). *National Institute of Nursing Research history book*. Washington, DC: NIH.

Cobb, R. W., & Elder, C. D. (1983). *Participation in America: The dynamics of agenda-building* (2nd ed.). Baltimore, MD: Johns Hopkins University Press.

DeBack, V. (1990). Public policy: Nursing needs health policy leaders. *Journal of Professional Nursing*, 6(2), 69.

DeLeon, P. (1988–1989). The contextual burdens of policy design. *Policy Studies Journal*, 17(2), 297–309.

Dohler, M. (1991). Policy networks, opportunity structures, and neo-conservative reform strategies in health policy. In B. Main & R. Mayntz (Eds.), *Policy networks: Empirical evidence and theoretical considerations* (pp. 235–296). Frankfurt, Germany: Campus Verlag.

Dryzek, J. S. (1983). Don't toss coins in garbage cans: A prologue to policy design. *Journal of Public Policy*, 3(4), 345–368.

Edmunds, M. (2003). Advocating for NPs: Go and do likewise. *Nurse Practitioner*, 28(2), 56.

Holmes, L. (2013, December 14). Give nurse practitioners more rein [in The Public Pulse Letters to the Editor]. *Omaha World Herald*, p. 4b.

Ingraham, P. W. (1987). Toward more systematic consideration of policy design. *Policy Studies Journal, 15*(4), 611–628.

Ingraham, P. W., & White, J. (1988–1989). The design of civil service reform: Lessons in politics and rationality. *Policy Studies Journal, 17*(2), 315–330.

Institute of Medicine (IOM). (2010). *The future of nursing: Leading change, advancing health.* Retrieved from http://www.nationalacademies.org/hmd/Reports/2010/The-Future-of-Nursing -Leading-Change-Advancing-Health.aspx

James, P. (1991). Bravo to the nursing emphasis on policy research. *Reflections, 17*(1), 14–15.

Kingdon, J. W. (1995). *Agendas, alternatives, and public policies.* New York, NY: Harper Collins College.

Kingdon, J. W. (2001). A model of agenda-setting, with applications. *Law Review, MSU-DCL, 2,* 331.

Laumann, E. O., Heinz, J. P., Nelson, R., & Salisbury, R. (1991). Organizations in political action: Representing interests in national policy making. In B. Marin & R. Mayntz (Eds.), *Policy networks: Empirical evidence and theoretical considerations* (pp. 63–96). Frankfurt, Germany: Campus Verlag.

Lazure, L., Cramer, M., & Hoebelheinrich, K. (2016). Informing health policy decision makers: A Nebraska scope of practice case study. *Policy, Politics, & Nursing Practice, 17*(2), 85–98.

Lieberman, J. M. (2002). Three streams and four policy entrepreneurs converge: A policy window opens. *Education and Urban Society, 34,* 438–450.

May, P. J. (1991). Reconsidering policy design: Policies and publics. *Journal of Public Policy, 11*(2), 187–206.

Mueller, K. J. (1988). Federal programs to expire: The case of health planning. *Public Administration Review, 48*(3), 719–725.

Nebraska Department of Health and Human Services. (n.d.). Credentialing review (407) program. Retrieved from http://dhhs.ne.gov/pages/reg_admcr.aspx

Nebraska Legislature. (2014). LB916—Eliminate integrated practice agreements and provide for transition-to-practice agreements for nurse practitioners. Retrieved from http:// nebraskalegislature.gov/bills/view_bill.php?DocumentID=21963

Pohl, J., Thomas, A., Barksdale, D., & Werner, K. (2016, October 26). Primary care workforce: The need to remove barriers for nurse practitioners and physicians. *Health Affairs* Blog.

Ruggles, R. (2013, December 11). A setback for key health players. *Omaha World Herald, 149*(58), p. 1.

Schneider, A., & Ingram, H. (1991). *The social construction of target populations: Implications for citizenship and democracy.* Paper presented at the annual meeting of the American Political Science Association, Washington, DC.

Schneider, A. L., & Ingram, H. (1993a). How the social construction of target populations contributes to problems in policy design. *Policy Currents, 3*(1), 1–4.

Schneider, A., & Ingram, H. (1993b). Social construction of target populations: Implications for politics and policy. *American Political Science Review, 87*(2), 334–347.

Sundermeier, J. (2013/2014). Nebraska nurse practitioners move forward. *Nebraska Nurse, 46*(4), 5.

Warner, J. R. (2003). A phenomenological approach to political competence: Stories of nurse activists. *Policy, Politics, and Nursing Practice, 4*(2), 135–143.

Whitmire, T. (2013). Nebraska nurse practitioners. *Nebraska Nurse, 46,* 9.

Online Resource

https://www.regulations.gov/ The types of regulations that can be found on this site include Proposed Rules and Rules, as well as Notices from the Federal Register. Documents such as Public Comments and Supporting and Related Materials are often associated with these regulations, and can also be found on this site. This is an interactive site allowing pre-decision participation in regulations formulation.

CHAPTER 3

Government Response: Legislation

Politics: Playing the Game

Janice Kay Lanier

Politics is the art of problem solving.

—**Jonah Goldberg**, Editor-at-Large, *National Review Online*

© Visions of America/Joe Sohm/Photodisc/Getty

or reshaping a particular Congressional district occurs when a state's population totals either increase or decrease to the extent that a new district must be added or an existing district eliminated. The process for doing that may differ from state to state, but the reconfiguration can have significant political implications for future elections. State legislatures are also made up of population-based districts that may be reconfigured based on census data. Frequently the districts are drawn with little regard for geographic considerations. Instead, political factors are the most compelling reasons for how a district is configured. Concentrating the voting strength of a minority party into as few districts as possible while giving the other party a majority in as many districts as possible is known as gerrymandering.

Executive order: An order or directive issued by the president or governor directed at an executive branch agency that has the force and effect of law during the tenure of the issuing chief executive. An executive order cannot conflict with existing law or the Constitution but can direct the agency to use its discretion when implementing a particular program or policy.

Lame-duck session: The weeks immediately following a November general election when an outgoing legislative body attempts to speed its priorities through the legislative process. Legislative activity can be particularly vigorous if control of the legislative or executive branch of government will change when the newly elected individuals take office in January.

Legislation: The bills considered by legislators that, if approved, become laws.

Legislative language: The legal terminology and technical format that federal and state governments require when legislators propose to enact new laws or revise existing ones.

Legislator: An elected individual who serves in the state legislature or the U.S. Congress. These officials make decisions regarding bills and resolutions pending before the legislative body to which they have been elected.

Legislature: The legislative body made up of individuals authorized to enact laws.

Lobbyist: An individual who works to influence legislators and other governmental decision makers. A professional lobbyist is required to register with the body being lobbied.

Political action committees (PACs): Formal organizations that exist to engage in a process through which candidates for political office are endorsed and otherwise supported. They must adhere to state and/or federal laws in carrying out its activities.

Special interest group: An organized group with a common cause that works to influence the outcome of laws, regulations, or programs.

Super-majority: While many legislative actions can be taken based on a simple majority vote, certain actions, including overriding a presidential or gubernatorial veto, require that the legislative body achieve a two-thirds vote of its members; the latter is termed a super-majority.

▶ Introduction

It is not possible to separate politics from policymaking, whether the policy decisions are made in the public sector, the private sector, or at home. "Politic" is defined as being wise or shrewd, while "politics" is defined as methods, opinions, or scheming (Goldman, 2000) or the process for influencing the allocation of scarce resources (Chaffee, 2014, p. 307). Regardless of the definition used, many nurses and other healthcare professionals see "politics" as a negative term and perceive "playing politics" as a reason for not getting involved in political advocacy. That position means the expertise and insights that nurses and others possess by virtue of their hands-on experiences in caring for patients are not reflected in the policies that come out of Washington, D.C., state capitals, or boardrooms.

Because of the contributions nurses could and do make to the decision making that occurs in a variety of boardrooms, a coalition was formed to encourage more nurses to become members of policymaking boards. The Nurses on Boards Coalition (2016), which is made up of 24 nursing organizations plus strategic healthcare leadership and corporate partners, set a goal to have 10,000 nurses serving on corporate, health-related, and other boards by 2020. Such participation by nurses will help the public see the breadth of expertise nurses bring to the table and help develop a cadre of experienced nurses who can share their knowledge with other members of the nursing profession.

Some may believe involvement in policymaking is self-serving, concerned only with advancing selfish professional interests. Actually, the ultimate point in participating in policymaking is to improve patient outcomes. Focusing on "politic" (wisdom) rather than "politics" (influence) may make joining in the policy debate more relatable and palatable. This chapter provides insights into the processes that determine how policy is made and offers some opportunities to reflect on why certain outcomes occur but others do not. It will help readers find their way through the political maze by providing a basic understanding of some of the "rules of the game"—that is, how laws are made and who is on the field of play.

Before embarking on that journey, a word is in order about one of the most obvious displays of politics—elections. Elections matter, sometimes in ways that are not obvious on the surface. Never has that been more evident than in the aftermath of the 2016 presidential election. Trying to analyze what happened given the unprecedented nature of the campaign will occupy political scientists and others for years to come. Whether clear answers will emerge from a retrospective review remains to be seen, but it is certainly undeniable that the 2016 election will have lasting implications on many levels.

Clearly, election results determine who will hold office, who will be the president or governor, and who will be in the Senate or the House of Representatives. Will one party control two elected branches of government (legislative and executive), or will power be shared? Will the party in control have enough members to form a **super-majority** that allows it to ignore the concerns of the minority party, or will various perspectives be heeded so that bipartisan policies eventually emerge from the legislative process? Generally, some of these questions can be answered immediately after the votes are counted or shortly after the newly elected officials take office. For others, the answers emerge over time.

Elections matter on another level, too. As the newly elected Trump administration began to take shape, much rhetoric focused on the future of significant policy positions taken by the Obama administration as well as on the future of Medicare and Medicaid. Obamacare was in the headlines as Republicans saw their opportunity to finally repeal a law that had long been a thorn in their sides. Before the Republican majority had even been sworn in, debate began to rage about how to make the changes: repeal and replace Obamacare immediately, repeal immediately and replace later, or repeal later after a replacement strategy has been determined. Out of those discussions, held behind closed doors, one revelation emerged that seemed particularly telling. Moderate Republicans expressed concerns about the plan to repeal Obamacare within a year of Donald Trump's inauguration as well as the plan to revise the long-standing Medicare and Medicaid programs. Because of all the technicalities associated with repeal or revision of these programs (e.g., changes in insurance), putting the changes into play—that is, implementing the changes—would run up against the next election cycle in 2018. Inevitable implementation problems might not bode well for the majority party's ability to maintain its current stranglehold on both Houses of Congress (Ferris & Wong, 2016).

The most telling insight that this peek behind closed doors offers is the realization (for better or worse) that policymakers are not necessarily focused on how real people will be affected by changes to Obamacare or Medicare and Medicaid but rather on how the changes will affect their own re-election chances. While some may find this focus disturbing, it demonstrates not just that election results do matter but also that even the threat of an upcoming election cycle affects what policymakers are willing or able to do. Awareness can be used in developing strategies for appealing to what really matters to policymakers. Being shrewd or "politic" is the takeaway lesson here. Timing is everything.

This chapter offers insight into the subtle rules governing political participation and sets out the options available to nurses for finding their way through the political maze. To navigate this environment successfully, the nurse must first have a basic understanding of how laws are made and who the participants in the lawmaking process are.

▶ Process, People, and Purse Strings

Process: How a Bill Really Becomes a Law

No one would presume to play a game of football without knowing the basic rules. Likewise, even simple board games, such as checkers or Monopoly, have rules that one must follow to have a chance of winning. Lawmaking is no different. In many ways it is a game, admittedly with very high stakes, and there is a process that determines what must happen for an idea, concept, or concern to become part of the U.S. Code or state statutes.

Most students complete a government course in high school. Although diagrams depicting how a bill becomes a law are important, they are also very rudimentary. There is much more to the process than can be neatly depicted on a chart. It is also important to realize that although the process may seem straightforward, it can be circumvented when the will of the party in control determines it is expedient to do so. For example, recent use of **executive orders** by the U.S. President and some governors is a non-legislative strategy that affects public policy in limited but significant ways. Parliamentary procedure maneuvers, filibusters, internal rule changes governing chamber proceedings, a **lame-duck session**, changes to committee appointments, and **Christmas tree bills** are all tactics or opportunities used to achieve one's legislative goals expeditiously. Whether these tactics engender good public policy has been the subject of much debate among political scientists; however, regardless of the debate, nurses must be aware of these options so that they do not become the unwitting victims of a clever strategic move.

The Federal Process

Bills are ideas that a **legislator** has determined need to be enacted into law. These ideas can come from many sources: the legislator's own experiences; issues brought forward by **constituents**, a **special interest group**, or a **lobbyist** on behalf of their clients; and not infrequently as a result of tragic events that trigger a public outcry for a new or amended law (e.g., school shootings that intensify the debate over gun control). Once the concept is drafted into the proper **legislative language**, it is introduced into the House of Representatives or Senate, depending on the chamber to which the bill's chief sponsor belongs. Each bill is numbered sequentially, and it retains this number throughout the process.

Many bills are introduced during a legislative session, but few receive much attention in the form of committee consideration. Fewer still actually become law.

Committee Consideration

Once introduced, a bill is referred to a standing committee for further consideration. These standing committees are generally subject-matter focused, such that bills related to health care go to a health committee, finance issues to a banking committee, farm-related matters to an agriculture committee, and so on. Standing committees at the federal level tend to be permanent; at the state level, they can be configured differently over time depending on the vision of the leadership of the party in power at the beginning of each new legislative session. Subcommittees consider particular bills in greater detail. Bills are amended (revised) or "marked up" (voted on after being revised) in committee and subcommittee. Hearings offer affected parties (i.e., special-interest groups) opportunities to state their positions. A bill that emerges from committee may bear little resemblance to the original proposal, often because of the input received at a hearing.

Committee hearings are important, but they often appear to be more chaotic than productive, at least to the average observer. Much of the real business of lawmaking occurs behind the scenes, but one must also participate in the defined committee processes to earn a place at the more informal behind-the-scenes tables.

EXHIBIT 3-1 How to Find Legislation

Go to https://www.congress.gov
Select "Legislation" and search on a topic such as "health care"
Example: H.R. 315 is the 315th bill introduced in the 115th Congress.
   H.R.315—115th Congress (2017–2018) To amend the Public Health Service Act to distribute maternity care health professionals to health professional shortage areas identified as in need of maternity care health services.
Sponsor: Rep. Burgess, Michael C. [R-TX-26] (Introduced 01/05/2017)
Cosponsors: (2)
Committees: House—Energy and Commerce
Latest Action: 01/05/2017 Referred to the House Committee on Energy and Commerce. (All Actions)
Tracker: This bill has the status Introduced

Committee chairs (appointed by the political party in the majority) are extremely influential, particularly with respect to the subject areas that are the focus of the committee's work. Chairs determine which bills will be heard and when, and they establish the procedural framework under which the committee operates. The chair's position on an issue can determine the fate of a bill from the outset. Because of the extent of their power and influence, committee chairs are able to raise large sums of money from special-interest groups to support their re-election—and re-election is always an important consideration for lawmakers. The House and Senate leaders (elected by their colleagues) determine who will be named committee chairs. Certain committees are seen as more prestigious than others, so being named the chair of one of those committees is very important to an ambitious legislator. "Ranking members" are the appointed committee leaders for the political party in the minority.

Not surprisingly, political considerations play a role in this entire process. Being aware of the dynamics that are the foundation of the overall committee process helps ensure more effective representation by those who want to influence the outcome of the committee's work.

Floor Action

If a bill is able to garner committee approval, it goes to the full chamber for a vote. The timing for scheduling a vote, as well as various attempts to amend the bill or delay the vote, are integral parts of the lawmaking process. Much maneuvering occurs backstage, and the ability to influence these less public interactions is as important as the words or concepts being debated. Again, people's relationships and politics determine the ultimate results. To be effective in one's efforts to influence outcomes, one must be aware of these relationships and take them into account. Once a bill is approved in either the House or Senate, legislators begin the process again in the other chamber.

Conference Committee

Seldom does a bill complete the journey through the second chamber without change, which means the originating chamber must agree to the new version of the bill. Without agreement, a bill will be referred to a conference committee made up of representatives from the House and Senate; they reconcile the differences in the two bills and ask their respective chambers to support the conference committee report. If agreement cannot be reached, the bill dies.

Chief Executive Signature

If the House and Senate reach agreement, the bill goes to the chief executive (president or governor), who must sign the bill before it can become law. If the chief executive vetoes the bill, it goes back to the **legislature** for a potential veto override, which requires a two-thirds majority of both chambers.

All this must happen within a single legislative cycle—2 years (a biennium). It is not surprising that it often takes several years for a particular legislative issue to finally become law, especially when powerful interest groups are on opposite sides of the proposal.

TABLE 3-1 Congressional Structure

Senate	House of Representatives
100 members, 2 from each state.	435 members based on a state's population. The number of representatives apportioned to each state changes every 10 years after the national census data are obtained. Drawing and redrawing congressional **district** lines is a very political process that each state implements according to its own laws.
6-year terms, with one-third up for re-election every 2 years, and no limit on the number of terms that can be served.	2-year terms, with no limit on the number of terms that can be served.
The vice president is the Senate leader, but a president pro tempore is elected each session by the majority party.	The majority party elects the Speaker of the House.

State legislatures typically follow the bicameral (two-chamber) structure of the federal government (**TABLE 3-1**). The exception is Nebraska, which has a unicameral body.

The number of legislators may vary from state to state, as may the length of the term in office for the senators. Some states (but not the federal government) have adopted laws that limit the number of consecutive terms a legislator may serve in any one chamber. These term limits were adopted to deal with legislators who served multiple years in their respective chambers. Their re-election was seldom challenged, and voters became convinced that policymaking would be better served by changing their lawmakers on a more regular basis.

Not surprisingly, term limits have had unintended consequences, some of which have changed the dynamics within the legislature and affected policy-making in general. Relationship and leadership development, which takes time, have been short-circuited. Ambitious lawmakers frequently seek leadership positions without the time-in-office foundations in place needed to be effective in these roles. Institutional memory has been lost with term limits, as has the depth of understanding of the complexity of the issues legislators must address. The interest in developing long-term solutions to challenging problems has been replaced with a more incremental immediate approach that focuses on short-term solutions rather than on the underlying cause of the problems. These realities affect the strategies adopted by interest groups seeking a legislative solution to their problem or concerns.

Although there may be subtle differences between the state and federal law-making processes, the political dynamics that affect the ultimate outcome of any policymaking initiative are quite similar regardless of the venue.

People: Players in the Game

One might believe that the only players in the lawmaking game are the elected officials—that is, the senators and representatives representing their respective states or districts. Although they are certainly integral to the process, many other individuals are keys to successfully achieving one's legislative goals. In sports and other games, those who take game playing seriously spend time learning the strengths and weaknesses of the people on the field or at the table with them. They study game film and read scouting reports and use other resources to minimize surprises and help define their own strategies. That same attention to detail should apply to policymaking, but it is often sadly neglected.

Many people cannot identify their federal, state, or local elected officials. Although many can name the president of the United States, few will be able to say with assurance who represents them in the halls of **Congress** and fewer still can name their state senators or representatives. Every nurse should know the identity of his or her U.S. senators and congressional representative. It is equally or more important, however, for nurses to also know their state representative and senator because so much professional regulation occurs at the state level. Technology has made it easy to learn the identity of lawmakers at every level by simply going to federal or state government websites and entering ZIP code data. These sites also provide brief biographical information, photos, and other pertinent and helpful background material.

Why is this important? Politics is at heart a "people process." As in other people-centered endeavors, the relationships among and between people determine outcomes in the political process. To have even the most basic conversation with elected officials, one must know who they are and what they care about.

Legislative Aides

In addition to knowing elected officials, one must make an effort to know staff members—aides and others—who often control access to their bosses and influence how various issues are perceived and prioritized. At the federal level, every legislator determines how his or her office will be staffed—usually using a chief of staff, legislative directors, press secretary, and legislative assistants/aides (LAs) (**TABLE 3-2**). Federal lawmakers also maintain local or district offices with a small staff presence at each site. On the state level, the number of aides can vary, but as state legislatures have become more than part-time endeavors, the use of aides has increased. Typically, state officials have at least one aide who is usually a generalist, whereas the aides at the federal level are more issue focused.

Regardless of whether an aide is in Washington, D.C., or at any of the statehouses across the country, elected officials rely on aides for the details and nuances associated with specific legislative initiatives. Aides delve more deeply into the issues and work closely with other aides in developing strategies and alternative concepts that they then present to their legislators for consideration.

Although communicating with legislators is important, nurses should not underestimate the importance of aides and other staff members, who may provide the last word to a legislator regarding the issue or concern. Including aides and other staff members in communications and making special efforts to respectfully integrate them into the entire process is a tactic that is likely to yield positive results.

TABLE 3-2 Federal Staffing Patterns

Staff Member	Role
Chief of staff	Senior staff person; answers directly to the member.
Administrative assistant	Oversight responsibilities for staff.
Legislative directors	Responsible for day-to-day legislative activities.
Press secretary	Responsible for press releases and public relations.
Legislative assistants/ aides (LAs)	Responsible for specific legislative areas/issues—for example, health, agriculture, or Social Security. LAs have more than one area of responsibility. They provide staff assistance to the member at committee hearings, write policy briefs, and prepare the member's statements and witness questions. They may help draft bills by working in concert with the legislative council.
Committee staff	Support the work of congressional committees. Separate staffs are allocated to the majority and minority parties, with a larger number serving the majority party. These individuals' focus usually is narrower than that of the legislator's personal staff, and they usually are older and more experienced. They plan the committee agenda, coordinate schedules, gather and analyze data, draft committee reports, and so on.

Lobbyists

Although nurses may not know the identity of specific lobbyists, it is important to understand which role lobbyists play in the policymaking process and how their influence affects the game of politics. No bill becomes law without lobbyists' input. Lobbying is the act of influencing—the art of persuading—a governmental entity to achieve a specific legislative or regulatory outcome. Although anyone can lobby, lobbyists are most often individuals who represent special-interest groups and are looked to as the experts by lawmakers who need information and a rationale for supporting or not supporting a particular issue.

The role of lobbyists has become even more critical as the complexity of **legislation** has increased. For example, the 1914 law creating the Federal Trade Commission was a total of 8 pages and the Social Security Act of 1935 totaled 28 pages, but the Financial Reform bill (conference version) of 2010 contained 2,319 pages (Brill, 2010). Legislators, who are often pressed for time and/or newly elected to the legislature, rely on lobbyists' expertise to help them understand what they are voting for or against. When the 21st Century Cures Act became law late in 2016, Senate disclosure records showed that more than 1,400 lobby-ists worked on that legislation, which became a Christmas tree bill as the 114th Congress raced toward adjournment. Ultimately, the act included a wide range of provisions that addressed everything from Food and Drug Administration reform to substance abuse and the related mental health crisis to hospital readmission penalty revisions (Muchmore, 2016).

A brief review of one year of lobbyist activity (**TABLE 3-3**) provides insights regarding the emphasis some healthcare-sector associations place on lobbying to further or protect their own interests. Taking a longer-term view, from 1998 to 2016, the U.S. Chamber of Commerce spent $1,304,320,680 on its lobbying efforts. During that same time frame, the American Medical Association (AMA) spent $347,122,500 on lobbying, the American Hospital Association (AHA) spent $311,163,263, and the Pharmaceutical Research & Manufacturers of America (PHARMA) spent $305,515,300. The American Nurses Association (ANA), by comparison, spent $18,583,260 over this period, significantly less than other healthcare-related organizations (Center for Responsive Politics, 2016b).

Former lawmakers, their staff members, and executive agencies' staff members often become lobbyists after leaving public service. These so-called revolving-door lobbyists have unparalleled access, connections, and insights that serve their clients well. While ethics laws prohibit this kind of employment for a period of time immediately after leaving public service, these individuals may serve as consultants while waiting out their legally imposed hiatus. The number of revolving-door lobbyists working for a particular organization can be indicative of how much an organization values its lobbying efforts. In a world where these numbers matter, the gap between nursing organizations' spending and that of other health-sector entities cannot be ignored.

On September 18, 1793, President George Washington laid the cornerstone for the U.S. Capitol. While the shovel, trowel, and marble gavel used for the ceremony are still displayed, repeated efforts to locate the cornerstone itself have been unsuccessful.

At times, policymaking seems as shrouded in mystery as the location of the Capitol's cornerstone. That's why you need an experienced partner (a.k.a. lobbyist) to help you unravel the mystery.

—A pitch for Capitol Tax Partners, a lobbying firm

Purse Strings: "Show Me the Money"

Game playing comes with a price in both athletic venues and legislative arenas. Not only are significant sums of money spent by special-interest groups in support of their lobbying efforts, but money is also critical to election and re-election campaigns. The role money plays in the policymaking process causes concern and discomfort for many nurses and other healthcare professionals. It is where the notion of "politics," with all of its unfavorable connotations, is on full display, and it is the reason many nurses (and others) consider political participation to be something to avoid.

TABLE 3-3 Lobbying the Federal Government in 2016

Entity	Total Spent*	Number of Lobbyists and Revolvers**	Entity	Total Spent*
American Medical Association	$15,290,000	24/5 revolvers	4/6 revolvers	14—Health issues; Medicare and Medicaid; education; veterans affairs; pharmacy
American Nurses Association	$854,973	5/1 revolvers	1/2 revolvers	3—Health issues; Medicare and Medicaid; federal budget and appropriations
American Association of Nurse Practitioners	$401,207	4/0 revolvers	2/5 revolvers	3—Federal budget and appropriations; health issues; veterans affairs
American Psychological Association	$865,647	14/5 revolvers	5/8 revolvers	12—Health issues; Medicare and Medicaid; federal budget and appropriations; law enforcement and crime; veterans affairs
American Association of Nurse Anesthetists	$830,000	6/4 revolvers	2/2 revolvers	6—Medicare and Medicaid; veterans affairs; education; health issues; insurance
American Society of Anesthesiologists	$660,000	6/0 revolvers	4/8 revolvers	5—Health issues; veterans affairs; Medicare and Medicaid; science and technology; federal budget and appropriations
American Academy of Physician Assistants	$420,000	4/0 revolvers	1/4 revolvers	1—Health issues

Data from Center for Responsive Politics. (2016b). Influence & lobbying. Retrieved from http://www.opensecrets.org/influence

* Costs include salaries, retainers, and expenses that lobbyists incur as part of their jobs. They could also include developing materials to support an initiative, or studies/surveys commissioned to support or refute a position.

** Revolvers (revolving-door lobbyists) are individuals who have served as elected officials or government agency or lawmaker staff members.

The amount of money that flows to and through the legislative process has raised serious questions as to whether the whole process is for sale to whoever has the deepest pockets. Unfortunately, winning an election or re-election, even at the local level, can be a very expensive proposition, costing millions of dollars. In the 2016 election, campaigning for the average U.S. Congress House seat cost $1 million, while campaigning for the average U.S. Senate seat cost tens of millions of dollars. Pennsylvania had the most expensive U.S. Senate race, with expenditures exceeding $46 million; the most expensive House seat race was in District 08 in Maryland, where the costs exceeded $20 million (Center for Responsive Politics, 2016a). The cost of getting elected means incumbents and challengers must focus their efforts on raising money during three of every five workdays (Zakaria, 2013, p. E8). The most likely sources from which to obtain the needed dollars are wealthy individuals and special-interest groups that are willing to invest in these decision makers. The return on the investment must be beneficial—otherwise, the money invested in political campaigns would not continue to increase.

In fact, this spending trend is likely to continue due to the U.S. Supreme Court decision in *Citizens United v. Federal Election Commission* (2010), which basically allows unlimited spending by corporations and unions during campaigns, provided these efforts are not coordinated with an individual's campaign. In its *Citizens United* ruling, the Supreme Court struck down the 2002 federal campaign finance law prohibiting unions and corporations from spending money directly advocating for or against candidates. The First Amendment was the basis for the Court's decision. The League of Women Voters has voiced its support of legislation that would require disclosure of the sources of such spending.

Not only has the amount of money flowing to campaigns increased dramatically, but the source of those dollars (who has the deep pockets) also has changed and is expected to change even more in the future. For the first time, the 2014 midterm elections saw more money going into campaigns but fewer people contributing. Spending by outside groups constituted 14.9% of all spending, which was an increase of almost 5% compared with 2010 (Center for Responsive Politics, 2016b). Although the number of **527 committees** has increased, contributions from these entities have varied over time (**TABLE 3-4**).

According to the Federal Elections Commission, as of November 28, 2016, the healthcare sector had contributed $236,399,000 to campaigns during the 2016 election cycle, with approximately 60% of that total going to Republican candidates. (The top overall sector was finance, insurance, and real estate, which contributed $962,165,528 to candidates in the 2016 elections.) Physicians and other healthcare professionals are traditionally the largest source of federal campaign contributions within the healthcare sector; however, comparing the dollars coming from physician-related entities as opposed to nursing organizations reveals that the amount contributed by nursing is significantly less than the amount given by physician groups (**TABLE 3-5**). The only nursing organization listed among the top 20 healthcare-sector contributors during the 2016 elections was the American Association of Nurse Anesthetists, coming in at number 13. Other nursing organizations making contributions included the American Nurses Association, the American Association of Nurse Practitioners, and the American College of Nurse-Midwives

TABLE 3-4 527 Committee Fund Raising and Expenditures, 2010, 2014, and 2016

Entity: 2016	Receipts/Expenditures
Democrat/liberal	$31,645,812/26,647,731
Republican/conservative	$13,651,784/15,104,108
Women's issues	$10,029,733/9,863,780
Health professionals	$987,693/800,491
Hospitals and nursing homes	$40,524/22,520
Entity: 2014	**Receipts/Expenditures**
Democrat/liberal	$27,130,578/23,342,697
Republican/liberal	$26,876,343/30,501,588
Women's issues	$17,368,505/17,157,633
Health professionals	$1,475,284/1,546,829
Hospitals and nursing homes	$57,424/43,961
Entity: 2010	**Receipts/Expenditures**
Democrat/liberal	$24,151,559/26,806,934
Republican/conservative	$67,679,617/64,666,600
Women's issues	$9,374,595/10,876,045
Health professionals	$1,147,486/1,945,807
Hospitals and nursing homes	Not reported

Data from Center for Responsive Politics. (2016b). Influence & lobbying. Retrieved from http://www.opensecrets.org/influence

TABLE 3-5 Political Contributions by Physician Groups, 2015–2016

Organization	Amount Contributed
Cooperative of American Physicians	$1,945,015
American Society of Anesthesiologists	$1,926,150
American Medical Association	$1,878,563
American Association of Orthopedic Surgeons	$1,671,575

Data from Center for Responsive Politics. (2016a). Health sector: PAC contributions to federal candidates. Retrieved from http://www.opensecrets.org/pacs/sector.php?txt=H01&cycle=2016

(Center for Responsive Politics, 2016a). Nurses' willingness to pay this price remains an open question.

Although it may be distasteful, success in the halls of Congress and at state-houses is integral to the advancement of nurses' legislative agenda. That agenda includes measures intended to advance the profession itself as well as efforts to promote societal values that are committed to better patient outcomes. Nurses want their issues advanced successfully, and that expectation comes with a price tag that nurses must expect to pay.

▶ Playing the Game: Strategizing for Success

Continuing the game-playing analogy, why are some teams more successful than others? If all the players know how to play the game, why are some consistent winners and others are not? Why are the legislative agendas of some groups adopted seemingly with minimal opposition, whereas others find it hard to get a place at the policy table? In athletic contests, the skill of the players, the expertise of the coaching staff, the financial investment of the team owners/supporters, and team chemistry all contribute to success on the field. Those same factors also determine success at the policymaking table.

Skill of the Players

Knowing the process and people, along with understanding how money affects the policymaking dynamics, is a start, but it is not sufficient to ensure success. To move to the next level, nurses and others must learn to think politically, to play politics, and to strategize with the political consequences and realities always at the forefront. In other words, they must apply their critical thinking skills in the policymaking context.

As political scientists have noted, politics underlies the process through which groups of people make decisions. It is the basis for the authoritative allocation of value. Simply put, politics is the effort and strategies used to shape a policy choice in all group relationships.

When one "plays politics," one is considered to be shrewd or prudent in practical matters, tactful, and diplomatic; playing politics is also seen as being contrived in a shrewd way, or being expedient. When one thinks like a politician, it means he or she is looking beyond the issue itself and considering other forces and factors that affect what is likely to work and what has no chance of success. Deciding which of several policy options will lead to the greatest benefits and the fewest costs, in a world where re-election is a key consideration and media are a relentless presence, means the best solution may not be the path ultimately chosen. The scenario in Case Study 3-1 provides an example of what thinking politically might look like.

🔍 CASE STUDY 3-1: Workplace Safety

Emergency department (ED) nurses have expressed concern about workplace safety, with many experiencing physical attacks on a routine basis. Many employers have been reluctant to report assaults to law enforcement because of the bad publicity it might engender. Nurses and others in psychiatric settings have similar concerns, as do nurses working in home health.

Professional organizations representing these individuals, particularly ED nurses, formed a coalition to strategize about how to protect their members. Before the coalition had finished its work, the issue came to a head when an agitated family member assaulted a nurse, resulting in severe injuries to the nurse. Local media picked up the story, and a state legislator, who was a member of the minority party and facing a difficult re-election, was surprised to learn that although teachers and law enforcement officials are part of a "protected class," attacking healthcare workers was a misdemeanor rather than a felony offense. For protected workers, the same assault carries the more stringent criminal designation that includes possible incarceration. The legislator decided to take on this issue, in part because he thought it might help his re-election efforts and because nurse organizations had supported his candidacy in the past.

Which factors must the politically savvy nurse consider if this issue is to move successfully from concept to legislation to law?

Clearly, success at the policy table involves more than the language of the proposal itself. Timing and the general political climate are key, unity is important, and quid pro quo is the reality in the statehouse halls. Politically savvy nurses must be willing to take risks but should be smart when doing so (**EXHIBIT 3-2**). In other words, they should enter the policy arena fully prepared for the challenges they will face.

- Issues always have at least two sides, and maybe more, that are reasonable depending upon one's point of view and experiences.
- Listen to what people are saying with an analytical ear. Critical thinking is not just for the practice setting. Apply theories and concepts about policymaking to the issues being considered. Use therapeutic communication techniques.
- Utilize a variety of sources; do not just rely on those that are consistent with your own ideology. Most sources have a bias, so broaden your reading and listening to get a more complete perspective and perhaps move a bit closer to the truth. Always consider the source of the information provided.
- Connect with others who are involved in the policymaking side of the profession. Share what you learn with colleagues.

▶ Thinking Like a Policymaker

Coaching Staff: Mentoring and Support

Given all the subtle factors that affect success on Capitol Hill or in state legislatures and the role money plays in the process, how can an individual hope to have sufficient knowledge or time to make a difference in the policymaking aspects of the profession? How can that nurse ever play the game effectively? Fortunately, the American Nurses Association (ANA) and its state constituent associations, as well as specialty nursing groups, can provide their members with the tools they need to be successful. The success of these organizations' efforts in the legislative arena depends in large part on their members' involvement with and understanding of the importance of an effective legislative presence on behalf of the profession in Washington, D.C., and in statehouses across the country. Many of these organizations offer opportunities for their members to come to Washington or to state capitals for lobbying days, which include briefings on both the issues and the ways to be effective spokespersons for the profession. These organizations know that it is the individual nurse—the so-called grassroots lobbyist—who has the most impact on the decisions made by elected officials. In fact, grassroots lobbying is seen by some as the most effective of all lobbying efforts (deVries & Vanderbilt, 1992).

Grassroots lobbyists are constituents who have the power to elect officials through their vote. When constituents have expertise and knowledge about a particular issue (such as nurses in healthcare policymaking), they are especially valuable resources for their elected officials. Although issues debated in Washington, D.C., are national in scope, members of Congress are still concerned about how those issues are perceived back home. The connections established by a nurse constituent with his or her lawmakers at the federal, state, and local levels may provide timely access and a listening ear at key points during the policymaking process.

Some professional organizations have established liaison or key-person programs that match members with their elected officials, train them to be effective in the grassroots lobbying role, and provide periodic updates and information to help the nurses communicate in a timely manner with relevant messages targeted to the specific official. In turn, grassroots lobbyists establish ongoing connections with their elected officials that transcend specific legislative initiatives and communicate regularly with the sponsoring nursing organizations regarding what they learn through their interactions.

Coaching and mentoring nurses who are willing to engage in these kinds of supported liaison relationships will benefit both the individual nurse and the organizations doing the coaching. The nurse can markedly increase a legislator's understanding of nursing and the role nurses play in health care. With increased understanding, the legislator is more apt to be supportive of the profession's legislative agenda.

Investment: Time and Money

A vision without resources is an hallucination.

—**Thomas Friedman**

How much are nurses willing to pay in both time and money to support the political activities of professional organizations? Are there sufficient human and financial resources available to make the vision of success a reality, or is it destined to be a hallucination? What does that payment look like?

Far too few nurses—only approximately 6% of all nurses (Haylock, 2014, p. 613)—pay the membership fees needed to support the activities of nursing organizations, including maintaining an effective presence at statehouses or on Capitol Hill. Many of these organizations must rely primarily on busy volunteers to do the essential work of tracking legislative action or regulatory proposals in a timely manner. They cannot afford paid staff, even on a part-time basis. As a consequence, the everyday work of developing key relationships and being seen as a nursing expert cannot or does not happen. If more nurses were to become members of professional nursing organizations, the necessary resources would significantly increase, as would nursing's overall influence at the policy table.

Although the convergence of politics and money is not always pretty, ignoring the importance of financial contributions in moving a legislative agenda forward is naïve at best. Refusing to address this factor will ultimately undermine efforts to advance the positive aspects of the nursing profession's agenda.

Some nurse organizations have established **political action committees (PACs)** that enable them to make contributions to political candidates and office holders who are supportive of nurses' legislative agenda. The money comes from the organization's members, so it again relies on the small number of nurses who belong to one of these organizations The amount of money raised for PAC purposes by nursing organizations pales in comparison to the amounts that other healthcare sector entities are able to contribute.

In addition to political contributions, special-interest groups may improve their chances for successful policymaking by endorsing candidates who are running for elective office. Candidates who want to demonstrate their appeal to the overall electorate prize these endorsements; this is particularly true for endorsements issued by nursing organizations such as ANA on the federal level and state constituent associations of ANA on the state level. This level of political activity occurs through the associations' PACs and must adhere to requirements set out in federal and state election laws. The endorsement process requires significant membership involvement, which is difficult for small nursing organizations to mount successfully.

Both money and human resources are critical when considering the level of investment by the members of the nursing profession. Nurses account for the largest segment of the healthcare workforce, but far too few invest in their profession through membership in professional organizations. These low numbers significantly affect the amount of tangible and intangible resources available to associations for their work in the political arena. The strength of nurses lies in their numbers, and that strength is enhanced when nurses support the work of their professional associations through their dues and volunteerism.

Team Chemistry: Getting Along With One Another

Even with skilled players, strong support systems, and sufficient resources, a team will not succeed without an often elusive quality: team chemistry. Divisiveness has long plagued the nursing profession, and it remains an issue today. Disunity within the profession is a certain road to defeat and fuels the opposition's fire. Opponents are well aware of the potential impact that a united nursing profession could have on health policy decisions and other important issues. Nurses' numbers alone are formidable. For that reason, competing interests subtly and purposefully poke at the hot spots that typically divide nurses (e.g., educational preparation, union versus non-union debates). Nurses' tendency to align themselves within specialty practice groups and to lobby or get involved only when an issue directly relevant to that particular group is being considered is encouraged without consideration of a broader perspective. Political astuteness would dictate that nurses recognize when they are being kept off balance by subversive divisive messages encouraged by those who benefit from nursing's disunity and ignore the discordant rhetoric. Further, all nurses should have a basic understanding or awareness of the legislative initiatives of specialty groups. They should actively support the initiatives of their colleagues or, at a minimum, refrain from opposing the cause publicly. Concerns should be shared privately and diligent efforts made to find a compromise position outside of the public eye.

▶ Conclusion

Nurses with an understanding of how the policymaking process works can contribute to the political work of the organizations to which they belong and ultimately benefit the patients for whom they care. Such contributions are consistent with the obligations set forth in the profession's social policy statement and its code of ethics. *Nursing's Social Policy Statement* notes the connection between policymaking and the delivery of health care and the effect on the well-being of society. "Individual and inter-professional involvement is essential" (ANA, 2010, p. 7). An essential feature of professional nursing is to "influence social and public policy to promote social justice" (p. 9). The *Code of Ethics for Nurses* (ANA, 2015) repeatedly emphasizes the role nurses play in promoting, advocating, and striving to protect the health, safety, and rights of the patient, which extends to statehouses, boardrooms, and other arenas in which this advocacy can affect public policy. Moreover, the *Future of Nursing* report issued by the Institute of Medicine in 2010 states that "nurses should be full partners with physicians and other healthcare professionals, in redesigning health care in the United States" (p. S-3). This role will be played out, in part, in the health policy context, where nurses should participate in, and sometimes lead, decision making and be engaged in healthcare reform–related implementation efforts. To be ready to assume this responsibility, nurse education programs should include course content addressing leadership-related competencies for all nurses. These competencies include a firm grounding in politics and policymaking processes.

There is no substitute for visibility in the legislative arena. Showing up is what political activism is all about. "If you are not at the table, you are on the menu" is a sentiment frequently echoed in many policymaking venues. For too long, nurses have been on the menu rather than active participants in shaping public policy around health care. Simply watching the game and complaining about policy decisions will not change outcomes. Nurses must become convinced that they do have something valuable to contribute, that they have the ability and the time to do it, and that advocacy in the policy arena is not an option but a non-negotiable professional responsibility.

▶ Discussion Points

1. Watch the HBO movie *Iron Jawed Angels*. Which political considerations were at play in efforts to win voting rights for women?
   a. To what extent have Americans today become complacent with respect to the importance of voting?
   b. Describe the similarity of the fight waged by suffragettes and the one nurses have waged to gain recognition of advanced practice.
   c. Discuss with colleagues how complacency imperils future professional advances for nursing.
2. Respond to the following statement in the context of the Patient Protection and Affordable Care Act (ACA), taking into consideration the results of the 2016 election and its immediate aftermath as the Republican majority jockeyed to enhance its power and promote its philosophical beliefs.

   > The suppliers of legislative benefits are legislators, and their primary goal is to be re-elected. Thus, legislators need to maximize their chances for re-election, which requires political support. Legislators are assumed to be rational and to make cost–benefit calculations when faced with demands for legislation. However, the legislator's cost–benefit calculations are not the cost–benefits to society of enacting particular legislation. Instead, the benefits are the additional political support the legislator would receive from supporting legislation and the lost political support they would incur as a result of their action. When the benefit to legislators (positive political support) exceeds their costs (negative political support) they will support the legislation. (Feldstein, 2006, p. 10)

   a. Consider how the cost–benefit analysis depicted in the statement affected efforts to repeal/replace the ACA.
   b. Discuss how the cost–benefit analysis depicted in the statement did or did not affect decisions made by states about whether to expand Medicaid eligibility as allowed by the ACA but put in jeopardy by

Republican control of both the legislative and the executive branches of the federal government.

c.   Discuss how the cost–benefit analysis depicted in the statement did or did not affect decisions made by Congress to maintain or modify the Medicare and Medicaid programs.

3.   The mission of state boards of nursing is the protection of the public by the regulation of nursing practice.

a.   Compare the regulations in your state with those of at least one other state to determine the extent that APRNs have legal authorization to practice within the full scope of their education and experience.

b.   Develop a proposal to change at least one regulation in your state's nurse practice act. Which tactics would you use to persuade board members that your plan will positively affect nurses and the public?

c.   Identify groups that might oppose your proposal and create responses that defend your position.

4.   Create a worksheet that requires use of the state and federal government websites to identify one's own elected officials, party affiliation, committee appointments, and other relevant background information. Use this worksheet to plan your involvement in the political arena.

References

American Nurses Association (ANA). (2010). *Nursing's social policy statement*. Washington, DC: Author.

American Nurses Association (ANA). (2015). *Code of ethics for nurses*. Washington, DC: Author.

Brill, S. (2010). On sale: Your government. *Time, 176*(2), 28–33.

Center for Responsive Politics. (2016a). Health sector: PAC contributions to federal candidates. Retrieved from http://www.opensecrets.org/pacs/sector.php?txt=H01&cycle=2016

Center for Responsive Politics. (2016b). Influence & lobbying. Retrieved from http://www.opensecrets.org/influence

Chaffee, M. (2014). *Science, policy, and politics*. In D. Mason, J. Leavitt, & M. Chaffee (Eds.), *Policy and politics in nursing and health care* (6th ed., pp. 307–315). St. Louis, MO: Elsevier Saunders.

Citizens United v. Federal Elections Commission. (2010). 130 S. Ct. 876.

deVries, C. M., & Vanderbilt, M. (1992). *The grassroots lobbying handbook*. Washington, DC: American Nurses Association.

Feldstein, P. (2006). *The politics of health legislation: An economic perspective* (3rd ed., pp. 27–84). Chicago, IL: Health Administration Press.

Ferris, S., & Wong, S. (2016, December 2). Republicans raise red flags about speedy Obamacare repeal. Retrieved from http://www.thehill.com./policy/healthcare/308490-republicans-raise-red-flags-about-speedy-obamacare-repeal

Goldman, J. (2000). *Webster's new world dictionary*. Cleveland, OH: Wiley.

Haylock, P. (2014). *Professional nursing associations: Meeting the needs of nurses and the profession*. In D. Mason, J. Leavitt, & M. Chaffee (Eds.), *Policy and politics in nursing and health care* (6th ed., pp. 609–617). St. Louis, MO: Elsevier Saunders.

Institute of Medicine. (2010). *Future of nursing report: Leading change, advancing health*. Washington, DC: National Academies Press.

Muchmore, S. (2016, December 5). Add-ons ensure Cures Act easy lame-duck passage. *Modern Healthcare, 46*(49), 10.

Nurses on Boards Coalition. (2016). Improving the health of communities and the nation. Retrieved from http://nursesonboardscoalition.org/

Zakaria, F. (2013, August 4). Washington is failing everyone except lobbyists. *Columbus Dispatch*, p. E8.

CHAPTER 4

Government Response: Regulation

Jacqueline M. Loversidge

Recognition: A form of credentialing that denotes a government authority has ratified or confirmed an individual's credentials.

Registration: A form of credentialing that denotes enrolling or recording the name of a qualified individual on an official agency or government roster.

Regulations (rules): Orders or directives that provide details or procedures to operationalize a federal or state law (statute). A law directs an agency or government to develop and implement regulations/rules to achieve the purpose(s) of that law. Rules have the force and effect of law.

▶ Introduction

Regulation of the U.S. healthcare delivery system and of healthcare providers exists to protect the interests of public safety, but regulatory structures are extraordinarily complex. The vastness of the industry, the manner of healthcare financing, and the proliferation of laws and regulations that govern practice and reimbursement contribute to that complexity.

This chapter focuses on major concepts associated with the regulation of healthcare professionals. Understanding licensure and credentialing processes and their impact on nursing is essential. Understanding how regulations affect the healthcare system and individual providers empowers nurses and other providers to advocate on behalf of the profession and consumers.

All healthcare professionals are licensed by state government agencies. Practice-specific boards or commissions (e.g., the Ohio Board of Nursing) or multiprofessional boards (e.g., Michigan's Department of Licensing and Regulatory Affairs) are executive-branch regulatory agencies that govern each profession with the goal of protecting the public. State practice-specific board processes are similar from state to state but vary to some extent because their laws are determined by individual state legislatures, and their regulations are determined by the specific agency.

▶ Regulation Versus Legislation

The legislative and regulatory processes operate in parallel. Both are public processes and equally powerful; however, their processes differ in important ways. Legislation is shaped by elected lawmakers—for example, state legislators or members of the U.S. Congress. Laws are written in general terms to assure applicability over time and to establish public policy. Regulations emerge from the law's rule-making authority and shape details of implementation.

The legislative process is the first step in this two-layer process. Lawmakers introduce bills and shepherd them through the complex legislative process. The process begins when one or more (usually not more than two) legislators from the same house sponsor introduction of a bill during a legislative or congressional session. Bills may address issues of interest to the sponsoring legislator or of concern to the sponsor's constituents. Bills can be amended, substituted, or "die" at any number of points during the session. Checks and balances are built into the process; bills must be scrutinized by both houses and successfully navigate through committees during which testimony is heard. If they are passed by both houses and signed by the president or governor, they are enacted ("enrolled") and become law. Bills must pass during the session in which they are introduced; otherwise, they "die," with the docket for that congressional session or state general assembly being cleared, and the bill must be reintroduced in a subsequent session.

The terms *legislation, act, law,* and *statute* are synonyms. *Legislation* also refers to both a bill-in-progress and a law that has been enacted. When referring to laws regulating professions, the term **practice act** is used.

Once signed into law, statute implementation is generally the responsibility of an administrative agency. Administrative agencies execute their responsibilities by enforcing both law and regulations. **Regulations (rules)** enable reasonable implementation of the law. Note the terms *regulation* and *rule* are also used interchangeably. Whereas law is written in broad language, regulations are detailed and specify how the law will be put into practice. An administrative agency's authority to write and implement regulations is established in the laws that create the agency.

> Example: Nurse practice acts (NPAs) generally require the **board of nursing (BON)** to write rules with criteria that applicants must meet to be eligible to sit for licensure examinations and for issuing licenses. Rules amplifying that provision of law include specific eligibility criteria and application procedures, designate approved examinations (e.g., NCLEX for registered nurses [RNs] and licensed practical nurses [LPNs] or national certifying examinations for APRNs), and include renewal procedures and fees.

The regulatory and legislative processes differ in other ways. Rule making is not dependent on legislative session schedules, so rules may be promulgated (written) at any time by an administrative agency. Also, regulations adhere to **administrative procedures act (APA)** requirements; some states require evaluation and revision of regulations on a predictable schedule to assure regulations reflect the current environment.

Like lawmaking, regulation promulgation is a public process and is described in greater detail later in this chapter. The rule-making process, like lawmaking, also includes structures to assure checks and balances. For example, a nonbiased government body, such as Ohio's legislative Joint Committee on Agency Rule Review (JCARR), may be charged with oversight; it reviews all administrative regulations to assure that (1) the filing administrative agency does not exceed its statutory authority and (2) proposed regulations do not encroach on other laws or regulations.

If an administrative agency finds its regulations are inadequate to serve the needs of the public, and if the law does not support the additional rule-making authority it needs, it may seek statutory modification to add a section in the law that allows additional rule-making authority. To do so requires the agency to seek law change through the full legislative process. For nursing, this may include what is known as opening the nurse practice act.

Both laws and regulations have the same force and effect of law. Therefore, even though regulations are written by a government agency rather than a legislative body, regulations carry great weight because their origin stems from the law that provided the agency with its rule-making authority.

From here forward, the term *law* will be used instead of *legislation*, but *regulation* and *rule* will be used interchangeably. There are uses for which the term *rule* is preferable (e.g., rule-making authority).

▶ Health Professions Regulation and Licensing

Definitions and Purpose of Regulation

Regulation, as defined in *Black's Law Dictionary*, means "control over something by rule or restriction" (Garner, 2014, p. 1475). Health professions regulation is needed as a mechanism to protect the interests of public safety. There is extraordinary diversity and variability in health professions education programs—and, therefore, in licensure and other forms of credentialing. Laypersons cannot judge the competency of a health professional or determine whether that professional's practice meets acceptable and prevailing standards. For these reasons, because of the potential risk for harm and because of the intimate nature of nursing and health care, states protect the public by establishing laws to regulate the profession (Russell, 2012). Health professions regulation seeks to safeguard the public by acting as gatekeeper for entry into the health professions and by providing for ongoing maintenance of acceptable standards of practice for those professions. Practice acts, and the rules promulgated from those practice acts, constitute government regulatory oversight of professions.

Practice acts vary by state, but most include the same basic elements (Russell, 2012):

- Creation of a agency/board that serves as the decision-making body
- Definitions, standards, and scopes of practice
- Scope of the board's power and authority and its composition
- Standards for educational programs
- Types of titles, licensure, and certification
- Title protection
- Licensure requirements
- Grounds for disciplinary action, including due process (remedies) for the licensee charged with violation of the practice act or regulations

Requirements for mandatory continuing education and/or competency requirements for licensure and relicensure are also found in practice acts.

The board's rule-making authority is specified in the practice act as one of its "powers and duties." This rule-making authority generally includes categories such as initial licensing requirements, standards of practice, delegation standards, requirements for prelicensure registered nurse (RN) and licensed practical nurse/licensed vocational nurse (LPN/LVN) educational programs, advanced practice registered nurse (APRN) standards and requirements for practice and prescribing, disciplinary procedures, and standards for continuing education or competence.

It cannot be presumed that silence of the law on an issue implies legislative intent for the BON to write a rule. When there is no prior statutory authority to address an issue, the legislative process must be initiated to allow the agency authority to promulgate new, specific regulations.

> Example: An APRN with prescribing authority petitions the BON to clarify whether prescriptive authority for Schedule II controlled substances is within the scope of practice for the APRN. The board's staff refers the APRN to a provision in the statute that allows the APRN to "prescribe drugs and therapeutic devices" as long as the APRN practices in collaboration with a physician and in a way consistent with the nurse's education and certification. The staff concludes that the phrase "prescribe drugs and therapeutic devices" may include Schedule II controlled substances if permitted in the APRN–physician collaboration agreement. No specific language is found in the law that authorizes the prescribing of Schedule II controlled substances, but neither is it specifically prohibited.
>
> The medical board, which monitors BON opinions regarding potentially overlapping areas of practice, reads the BON's opinion and requests a state attorney general's opinion. The attorney general concludes that the BON may not extend the scope of practice of the APRN through either opinion or regulation. The expressed will of the legislature must be sought using the legislative process.
>
> Subsequently, the BON seeks a legislative sponsor to introduce a bill permitting APRNs to specifically prescribe Schedule II controlled substances.

Not all state boards of nursing are granted statutory authority to express formal opinions; some must rely on the specific language in the practice act and regulations, the official opinions of an attorney general's office, or court decisions.

History of Health Professions Regulation

Physicians were the first healthcare professionals to gain legislative recognition for their practice. Most states had physician licensing laws in place by the early 1900s. Nursing soon followed suit. North Carolina was the first state to establish a regulatory board for nurses in 1903, and by the 1930s, state licensing had been enacted in 40 states (Hartigan, 2011). Physician scopes of practice are broad; they are unlimited in many states. Historically, this has been problematic for nursing and other nonphysician healthcare providers seeking to define their unique scope, particularly in areas that may overlap with physicians' services. The history of nursing regulation has been characterized by efforts to accommodate this medical preemption (Safriet, 1992).

Early nursing regulation was permissive (voluntary). Systems were developed that allowed nurses to register with a governing board—hence the title "registered nurse." In some states, nurses were registered by the medical board before separate boards of nursing were established. **Registration** is a minimally restrictive form of state regulation and does not usually require entrance qualification (e.g., examination). Between the 1930s and 1950s, states enacted mandatory licensure laws (NPAs) requiring practicing nurses to obtain licensure with the state regulatory agency. These early NPAs defined nursing as a dependent practice focused on physician order implementation. The American Nurses Association model definition, published in 1955, laid the groundwork for NPAs to define independent functions for nurses, although the model reaffirmed prohibitions against medical diagnosis and prescribing (Hartigan, 2011).

Over time, BONs began establishing licensure criteria and administering licensure examinations. The early licensure examinations were BON-constructed paper-and-pencil examinations, performance examinations, or a combination. During that time, BONs also independently established examination passing standards. Statutory authority to regulate schools of nursing and establish requirements for school structure, faculty, and curricula were added to NPAs. Because interstate mobility was becoming more common, states developed *reciprocity* agreements with other states. The **National Council of State Boards of Nursing (NCSBN)** Nurse Licensure Compact has since replaced reciprocity. Not all states participate in the compact, and this complex process should not be confused with the obsolete two-state reciprocal arrangements (Hartigan, 2011; NCSBN, 2014b).

By the 1940s, the need for a standardized licensure exam had become apparent. In 1944, the State Board Test Pool Examination (SBTPE) was established by the National League for Nursing (NLN). The SBTPE assured standardization and relieved state BONs of the burdens associated with writing and grading the examination. Over the years, questions about potential for conflict of interest were raised. Although individual BONs set their own passing standards, authority for the creation and control of the examination had been absorbed by a professional association (the NLN). This relationship set up conflicts between governmental regulation and professional self-regulation, which should be separate and independent. Concurrently, BON leaders created a forum in which they could meet and discuss matters of common interest, although that forum was structured as a council of the American Nurses Association (ANA). This created additional conflict between BONs' prescribed governmental duty to establish licensure standards and professional associations' rights and responsibilities to remain independent of governmental influence.

In 1978, the NCSBN was formed, with the assistance of a Kellogg Foundation grant, to address these issues. NCSBN is autonomous and represents the states' interests rather than those of professional nursing organizations (Hartigan, 2011).

History of Advanced Practice Registered Nurse Regulation

In the 1960s, the birth of two federal entitlement programs, Medicare and Medicaid, increased the number of individuals with access to government-subsidized health care. At the same time, a shortage of primary care physicians was predicted, particularly in rural areas. A window of opportunity opened, and the first formal nurse practitioner (NP) programs were begun, with the goal to increase access to primary care in the rural areas where physicians were unlikely to locate.

In 1971, Idaho became the first state to legally recognize diagnosis and treatment as part of the scope of nurse practitioners. APRN (nurse practitioner) regulation in Idaho was accomplished through a joint agreement between the state boards of nursing and medicine. The Idaho model set a precedent for other states to include some form of joint nursing and medical board oversight for APRN regulation. The joint regulation model compensated for the broad definitions of medical practice but was a compromise because advanced practice nursing was still considered to constitute "delegated medical practice," requiring some medical board oversight (Safriet, 1992). The struggle to define APRNs' scope of practice and determine the necessity of medical board oversight continues in some states.

Both the ANA and the NCSBN have proposed model rules and regulations for the governing of advanced practice nursing. The actual practice acts are inevitably a product of individual states' political forces, so titles, definitions, criteria for entrance into practice, scopes of practice, reimbursement policies, and models of regulation are state specific. Since 1988, *The Nurse Practitioner* has published a map and summary of annual survey data from each state's BON and nursing organizations relative to the legislative status of advanced practice nursing. Significant advances have been made in many states, particularly regarding independent APRN practice without direct physician supervision. In 2017, 15 states/jurisdictions report that NPs are regulated solely by a BON and have both independent scope of practice and prescriptive authority without physician supervision, delegation, consultation, or collaboration. In 10 states, NPs are regulated by a BON, have full autonomous practice and prescriptive authority, but additionally must complete a postlicensure/certification supervision period or engage in a collaboration or mentorship. In the remaining states, NPs are regulated either solely by a BON or in combination with BON oversight (Phillips, 2017).

Methods of Professional Credentialing

Various methods are used to credential health professionals. The method accepted in a particular state is determined by the state government and based on at least two variables: (1) the potential for public harm if safe and acceptable standards of practice are not met and (2) the profession's degree of autonomy and accountability for decision making. Historically, government agencies have been encouraged to select the least restrictive form of regulation to achieve public protection (Pew Health Professions Commission, 1994).

Today, four methods are used in the United State for credentialing and regulation of individual providers. These are described next, beginning with the most restrictive method and progressing to the least restrictive method.

Licensure

A license is "a privilege granted by a state. . . the recipient of the privilege then being authorized to do some act. . . that would otherwise be impermissible" (Garner, 2014, p. 1059). **Licensure** is the most restrictive method of credentialing. Anyone who practices within the defined scope must obtain the legal authority to do so from the appropriate administrative state agency. Licensure serves as a barrier to those who are unqualified to perform within a specific scope of practice. Licensure also protects the monetary interests of those who are licensed to perform certain acts by limiting economic competition with unlicensed individuals.

Licensure implies competency assessment at the point of entry into the profession. Applicants for licensure must pass an initial licensing examination, then comply with continuing education requirements or undergo competency assessment by the regulatory body that provides oversight for that profession. Because competency is unique to the individual professional and specialty, it is difficult to measure; most licensing agencies require mandatory continuing education in lieu of continued competency assessment for license renewal. Licensure offers the public the greatest level of protection by restricting use of a specific title and a scope of practice to professionals who meet these rigorous criteria and hold a current valid license. Unlicensed persons cannot identify themselves by the title identified in law (e.g., medical assistants cannot hold themselves out as nurses), and they cannot lawfully perform any portion of the scope of practice, unless their own practice act allows them to provide such services because of overlap.

Licensees are held accountable to practice according to provisions in law and rule and to adhere to legal, ethical, and professional standards. A licensee holds greater public responsibility than an unlicensed citizen. Therefore, disciplinary action may be taken against licensees who have violated law or rule. Notably, a revocable license means that the legal authority (e.g., a BON) may divest the licensee of the license if it is deemed that the license holder has violated law or regulations and that it is in the best interest of the public. Health professions are largely regulated by licensure because of the high risk of potential for harm to the public if unqualified or unsafe practitioners are permitted to practice.

Registration

Registration is the "act of recording or enrolling" (Garner, 2014, p. 1474). Registration provides for a review of credentials to determine compliance with criteria for entry into a profession and permits the individual to use the title "registered." Registration provides title protection but does not preclude individuals who are not registered from practicing within the scope of practice, so long as they do not use the title "registered" or misrepresent their status.

Registration does not necessarily imply that prior competency assessment has been conducted. Some state laws may have provisions for removing incompetent or unethical providers from the registry or for "marking" the registry when a complaint is lodged against a provider. However, removing the person from the registry does not assure public protection, because the individual may practice without use of the title. An exemplar is the states' Nurse Aide Registry, which tracks individuals who have met criteria to be certified for employment in long-term care settings; this registry was required by the Omnibus Budget Reconciliation Act of 1987.

Certification

A certificate is "an official document stating that a specified standard has been satisfied" (Garner, 2014, p. 275). In nursing, **certification** usually refers to the *voluntary* process requiring completion of a specialty-focused education program, competency assessment, and practice hours. This type of certification in nursing is granted by proprietary professional nursing organizations and attests that the individual has achieved a level of competence in nursing practice beyond entry-level licensure.

Certification awarded by proprietary organizations does not have the force and effect of law. However, the term *certification* may also be used by state government agencies as a regulated credential; states may offer a "certificate of authority" or an otherwise-titled certificate to practice within a prescribed scope of practice. In this case, certification is required by law for practice in the specific role. For example, an APRN may need to hold a certificate as a nurse practitioner from a proprietary organization to qualify for a certificate of authority from a state BON to practice as an NP in that state. Most states have enacted regulations requiring nationally recognized specialty nursing certification for an APRN to be eligible to practice in the advanced role.

Astute consumers may ask whether a provider is certified as a means of assessing competency to practice. Employers also use certification as a means of determining eligibility for certain positions or as a requirement for internal promotion.

Recognition

Recognition is "confirmation that an act done by another person was authorized. . . the formal admission that a person, entity, or thing has a particular status" (Garner, 2014, p. 1463). Official recognition is used by several boards of nursing as a method of regulating APRNs and implies the board has validated and accepted the APRN's credentials for the specialty area of practice. Criteria for recognition are defined in the practice act and may include requirements for certification.

Professional Self-Regulation

Self-regulation occurs within a profession when its members establish standards, values, ethical frameworks, and safe practice guidelines exceeding the minimum standards defined by law. This voluntary process plays a significant role in the regulation of the profession, equal to legal regulation in many ways. Professional standards of practice and codes of ethics exemplify professional self-regulation. National professional organizations set standards for specialty practice. By means of the certification process, these organizations determine who may use the specialty titles within their purview. Documentation of continuing education and practice competency or reexamination is usually required for periodic recertification. Standards are periodically reviewed and revised by committees of the membership to assure they reflect current practice.

Although professional organizations develop standards of practice, they have no legal authority to require compliance by certificate holders. Administrative licensing agencies retain that authority but look to prevailing professional standards of practice when making decisions about what constitutes safe and competent care. Legal regulation and professional self-regulation are two sides of the same coin, working together to fulfill the profession's contract with society.

Regulation of Advanced Practice Registered Nurses

The evolution of APRN practice across the United States has been inconsistent because the U.S. Constitution gives states the right to establish laws governing professions and occupations. As a result, titles, scopes of practice, and regulatory standards are unique to each state. To bring some uniformity to the education and regulation of advanced nursing practice, the NCSBN convened an Advanced Practice Task Force in 2000, at the behest of its BON membership, and invited the American Association of Colleges of Nursing (AACN) to join in a consensus-building process. Together they developed the *Consensus Model for Regulation: Licensure, Accreditation, Certification, and Education (LACE)*. The LACE report proposed definitions of APRN practice, titling, and education requirements. It also described an APRN regulatory model, identified APRN roles/population foci, and offered strategies for implementation (APRN Joint Dialogue Group, 2008). This model served as the basis of BON regulation of advanced practice nursing for some years. In 2016, however, the NCSBN convened an APRN Roundtable to consider revisions in education, certification, and other factors and issues currently facing APRN regulation (NCSBN, 2016).

APRN regulation is also dependent on relationships between national nursing organizations and their affiliate certifying organizations (e.g., the ANA and the American Nurses Credentialing Center [ANCC]). Together these organizations play important roles in shaping APRN preparation and practice. The certifying organizations are nongovernmental bodies that develop practice standards and examinations to measure the competency of nurses in an area of clinical expertise. BONs require APRNs to hold a graduate degree in nursing and national certification in the specialty area relevant to their educational preparation. BONs also establish rules allowing acceptance of national APRN certification examination results according to predetermined criteria. The NCSBN guidelines (2002) continue to serve state BONs in determining those criteria.

Historically, the courts have held that state boards may not abdicate their authority by passively accepting examinations from independent bodies without having conducted a thorough evaluation of the examination's regulatory sufficiency and legal defensibility (NCSBN, 1993). The basis for regulatory sufficiency and legal defensibility of licensure or certification examinations includes two elements: (1) the ability to measure entry-level practice, based on a practice analysis that defines job-related knowledge, skills, and abilities; and (2) development of examinations using psychometrically sound test construction principles.

▶ The State Regulatory Process

The 10th Amendment of the U.S. Constitution specifies that all powers not specifically vested in the federal government are reserved for the states. One of these powers is the duty to protect its citizens (police powers). This power is translated in the form of states' authority and interest in regulating the professions to protect the health, safety, and welfare of its citizens. Administrative agencies are given referent power, through their legislatively enacted practice acts, to promulgate (write) regulations and enforce both the laws and the regulations for which they are responsible. These administrative agencies have been called the "fourth branch" of government because of their significant power to execute and enforce the law.

Boards of Nursing

Nurse practice acts vary by state, but all NPAs include the major provisions, or elements, discussed earlier in this chapter. Provisions included in NPAs focus on a central mission—protection of the public safety.

There are 60 boards of nursing (BONs) in the United States, including those in the 50 states, the District of Columbia, and the U.S. territories; each of these is known as a *jurisdiction*. Each BON is a member of the NCSBN. Some states have separate boards for licensing RNs and LPNs/LVNs. Several states regulate RNs and/or LPNs/LVNs through multiprofessional boards, which have jurisdiction over a variety of licensed professionals such as physicians, nurses, and dentists. As members of the NCSBN, BONs represent the interest of public safety by providing oversight of the construction and administration of the National Council Licensure Examinations (NCLEX). BONs are allowed the privilege of using these examinations and meet to discuss and act on matters of common interest (NCSBN, 2008).

Composition of the Board of Nursing

Boards of nursing are generally composed of licensed nurses and consumer members. In most states, the governor appoints members. An exception is North Carolina, where board members are elected by nurses licensed to practice in the state. Some NPAs designate specific board member representation—for example, from advanced practice nursing or nursing education, and in the case of joint boards, representation from LPNs/LVNs in addition to RNs/APRNs. In other states, criteria for appointment comprise only licensure and state residency.

Nurses interested in serving as board members may look to their professional associations to secure endorsements or ask for support from their state district legislators. Knowing the composition of the board and its vacancy status allows professional organizations to influence the representation on the board.

Board Meetings

Most state administrative procedures acts (APAs) require boards to post public notice of meetings and make agendas available, usually 30 days prior to the meeting. State government agencies must comply with open meeting ("sunshine") laws, which permit the public to observe and/or participate in board meetings. Board meetings may vary in their degree of formality. Public participation is usually permitted, but open dialogue between board members and the public is generally limited. Opportunities to address the board may be scheduled on the meeting agenda (e.g., during an "open forum" time) and may require advance notification of the individual's name, topic, and the organization represented (if applicable). Boards may go into closed executive session for reasons specified in the state's administrative procedures act (e.g., to obtain legal advice, conduct contract negotiations, and discuss disciplinary or personnel matters). Boards must comply with APA regulations regarding subject matter that may be discussed in an executive session and report out of executive session when the public session resumes.

Board meeting participants include board members (appointed or elected), board staff (employees of the board), and legal counsel for the board. Legal counsel advises the board on matters of law and jurisdiction. Some boards may have "staff" counsel, but many state boards receive advice only from an assigned representative of the state attorney general's office, known as an assistant attorney general (AAG).

All voting is a matter of public record, and board action occurs only in open public session. When board members vote, they must take into account implications for the public welfare and safety, the legal defensibility of the outcome of the vote, and the potential statewide impact of the decision. The board must act only within its legal jurisdiction.

BONs may publish action summaries of board meetings in their newsletters, in addition to articles written by board members and staff that explain law and rule. BON newsletters typically include disciplinary actions taken against licensees during board meetings. The nature of the offense is included in some states' newsletters. Some states mail newsletters to licensees, but many BONs now make newsletters available only electronically.

Monitoring the Competency of Nurses: Discipline and Mandatory Reporting

Licensed nurses are accountable for knowing the laws and regulations governing nursing in the state of licensure and for adhering to legal, ethical, and professional standards of care. Some state regulations include standards of practice; other states may refer to professional or ethical standards established by professional associations. Employing agencies also define standards of practice through policies and procedures, although these are separate from, in addition to, and superseded by the state's NPA and regulations.

Most NPAs include provisions for mandatory reporting that require employers to report violations of the NPA or regulations to the BON. Licensed nurses also have a moral and ethical duty to report unsafe and incompetent practice to the BON. In addition, the public may file complaints against licensees with BONs. The NPA provides the BON with authority to investigate complaints against licensees and potentially take action on the license, including the license or certificate to practice as an APRN. State APAs assure that licensees subject to disciplinary action are provided due process. When a nurse is found, through the administrative processes, to have violated provisions of the NPA or regulations, the BON can take action on the license; these actions may include a reprimand, fine, suspension, suspension of license with stay (i.e., probation), permanent revocation of license, or any other action permitted by the NPA.

A nurse who holds a multistate license (i.e., a license that permits a nurse to practice in more than one state in accordance with a multistate compact agreement) is held accountable for knowing and abiding by the laws and regulations of the state of original licensure as well as the compact state in which the nurse practices. Multistate regulation is discussed in more detail later in this chapter. Nurses with multistate licenses should be aware that ignorance of the law in any state of licensure and/or practice does not excuse misconduct.

Changing the Rules
Revising or Instituting New State Regulations

State agencies exercise their authority and duty to promulgate regulations amplifying their laws by following the state's administrative procedures act. The administrative procedures act of each state specifies the rule-making process, including requirements for public notification and for providing an opportunity for public comment. State rule-making processes differ. For example, some states designate government commissions or committees as the authorities for review and approval of regulations, whereas other states submit regulations to the general assembly or to committees of the legislature. Nevertheless, all state rule-making processes share some common elements:

- Public notice that a new regulation or modification of an existing regulation has been proposed
- Opportunity to submit written comment or testimony
- Opportunity to present oral testimony at a rules hearing
- Agency filing of the rule in final form
- Publication of the final regulation in a state register or bulletin

Public comment may be very influential in determining the final outcome. The administrative agency drafting the regulation has discretion in determining which amendments are made and may make amendments based on public input prior to final filing.

The time frame for implementation of new or revised regulations varies according to the state's administrative procedures act. Generally, effective dates are within 30 to 90 days of publication of the final regulation. In some states, the agency is required to prepare a fiscal impact statement, providing an estimate of the costs that will be incurred as a result of the rule, both to the agency and to the public.

Board Rule-Making Processes

BONs make regulatory decisions using methods similar to those used by other public officials in executive-branch agencies. When drafting new rules or revising existing rules, BONs examine matters of public safety and issues administering existing regulations, invite comment from stakeholders (in particular, nursing organization representatives), and may seek counsel from BON advisory committees or task forces. Leveraging participation opportunities early in the rule-drafting process is important, in addition to providing testimony during formal hearings. It is also imperative to appreciate that the process becomes complex when it is confounded by the perspectives, values, and ethics of a variety of stakeholders.

Because rule making involves dealing with both political complexities and content issues, BONs may use policy design or process models to facilitate decision making. Using a process model that is both familiar in nursing and adaptable to the health policy arena—for example, evidence-based practice (EBP)—can facilitate a BON's rule making because it provides an organized framework for problem solving.

The South Dakota BON has successfully used an evidence-informed health policy (EIHP) model to analyze one of its policies (Damgaard & Young, 2017). The EIHP model is adapted from Melnyk and Fineout-Overholt's (2015) EBP model and is a paradigm and problem-solving approach to health policy decision making. Like EBP, EIHP combines the use of evidence with issue expertise and stakeholder values and ethics to inform and leverage policy discussion and negotiation. The hoped-for outcome is the best possible health policy agenda and improvements (Loversidge, 2016b). Using the term *informed* rather than *based* shifts the focus of evidence to its realistic uses in policy arenas, which include informing and influencing stakeholders, as well as mediating dialogue; it also acknowledges the complexity of multiple factors, relationships, and rapidly shifting priorities inherent in the political process (Loversidge, 2016a).

Since EIHP is a full-cycle process model, it can facilitate decision making throughout the phases of regulation promulgation, rollout, implementation, and evaluation. The model includes three components and seven steps, summarized in **TABLE 4-1**. In particular, it makes use of the **PICOT** question. As used in health policy, the "P" part of this question—Population of interest—generally focuses

TABLE 4-1 Loversidge's Evidence-Informed Health Policy Model: Components and Steps

Components of EIHP	Steps of EIHP
▪ *External evidence:* Includes best research evidence, evidence-informed relevant theories, and best evidence from opinion leaders, expert panels, and other relevant sources. ▪ *Issue expertise:* Includes data from sources such as professional and healthcare associations/organizations and government agencies; also includes professions' understanding/experience with the issue; may include other data resources. ▪ *Stakeholder values and ethics:* Considers the values and ethics of healthcare providers, policy shapers, healthcare consumers, and others.	▪ *Step 0:* Cultivate a spirit of inquiry in the policy culture or environment. ▪ *Step 1:* Identify the policy problem; ask a policy question in the form of a PICOT question. ▪ *Step 2:* Search for/collect relevant/best evidence. ▪ *Step 3:* Perform critical appraisal of the evidence. ▪ *Step 4:* Integrate best evidence with issue expertise and stakeholder values and ethics; the result will be the desired health policy decision/change. ▪ *Step 5:* Contribute to the health policy development/implementation process. ▪ *Step 6:* Frame the policy change for dissemination. ▪ *Step 7:* Evaluate the effectiveness of the policy change and disseminate findings.

Data from Loversidge, J. M. (2016b). An evidence-informed health policy model: Adapting evidence-based practice for nursing education and regulation. *Journal of Nursing Regulation, 7*(2), 27–33.

on the consumer. The "I" (Intervention) refers to the policy change. "C" is the Comparison—the current policy or lack thereof. The "O" component describes the anticipated Outcome after policy implementation (Loversidge, 2016b). "T" is the Time needed to implement the policy.

Monitoring State Regulations

Administrative agencies promulgate hundreds of regulations each year. In this rapidly changing healthcare environment, conflicts related to definitions and scopes of practice, right to reimbursement, and requirements for supervision and collaboration may occur. Regulations that affect nursing practice may be implemented by a variety of agencies. Knowing which agencies regulate health care, healthcare delivery systems, and professional practice, and monitoring legislation and regulations proposed by those agencies, is important for safeguarding practice. Chief among the agencies that should be tracked are the health professions licensing boards, state agencies that govern licensing and certification of healthcare facilities, agencies that administer public health services (e.g., public health, mental health, and alcohol and drug agencies),

EXHIBIT 4-1 Questions to Ask When Analyzing Regulations

1. Which agency promulgated the regulation?
2. What is the source of the agency's authority (the law that provides the agency's rule-making authority)?
3. What is the intent or rationale of the regulation, and is it clearly stated?
4. How does the regulation affect the practice of nursing? Does it constrain or limit practice?
5. Is the language in the regulation clear or ambiguous? Can the regulation be interpreted in different ways? Discuss the advantages of language that is clear versus ambiguous.
6. Are there definitions to clarify terms?
7. Are any important points omitted?
8. Is there sufficient lead time to comply with the regulation?
9. What is the fiscal impact of the regulation?

and agencies that govern federal/state contribution program reimbursement (e.g., Medicare and Medicaid).

In particular, APRNs should be aware of regulations that mandate benefits or reimbursement policies and lobby for their inclusion as potential recipients of these benefits or funds. Several states have instituted open-panel legislation, known as "any willing provider" and "freedom of choice" laws. These bills mandate that any provider who is authorized to provide the services covered in an insurance plan must be recognized and reimbursed by the plan. Conversely, insurance companies and business lobbyists oppose this type of legislation. As managed care contracts are negotiated, APRNs must ensure their services are given fair and equitable consideration. Other important areas for nurses include worker's compensation participation and liability insurance laws.

In summary, agencies that may potentially promulgate regulations that could have implications for APRN and RN practice or reimbursement should be monitored. **Exhibit 4-1** provides some key questions to consider when analyzing a regulation for its impact on nursing practice.

Serving on Boards and Commissions

One way to actively participate in the regulatory process is to seek appointment to the state BON or to other health-related boards or commissions. Appointments to boards and commissions should be sought strategically. It is important to select an agency with a mission and purpose consistent with your own interests and expertise. Because most board appointments are gubernatorial or political appointments, it is important to obtain endorsements from legislators, influential community leaders, and professional associations. Individuals seeking appointment are more likely to acquire endorsements if they have an established history of service to the professional community.

Letters of support should document the appointment candidate's primary area of practice and contributions to professional and community service.

Delineate involvement in local, state, and national organizations. A letter from the employer is recommended, as both an indication of the employer's willingness to support time away from work to fulfill the responsibilities of the position during the term of office and as an endorsement of the candidate's professional merit. A personal letter from the appointment candidate should include the rationale for volunteering to serve on the particular board or commission, evidence of a good match between the individual's expertise and the board or commission purpose, and expression of clear interest in public service. A specific application form may be required (often found on the governor's website), and a résumé or curriculum vitae should be attached.

Appointment decisions take into account the individual's potential contributions to the work of the board or commission. This kind of public service requires a substantial time commitment, so it is wise to speak to other board members or the executive director/agency administrator to determine the extent of that commitment.

▶ The Federal Regulatory Process

The federal government has become a central factor in health professions regulation. A number of forces have influenced this trend; however, the advent of the Medicare and Medicaid programs was especially significant. Federal initiatives that have grown from these programs include cost containment (prospective payment), consumer protection (combating fraud and abuse) (Jost, 1997; Roberts & Clyde, 1993), and the initiatives and programs written into the Patient Protection and Affordable Care Act (ACA) and the Health Care and Education Reconciliation Act of 2010 (U.S. Department of Health and Human Services [DHHS], 2014).

In July 2001, the Centers for Medicare and Medicaid Services (CMS) replaced the former Health Care Financing Administration (HCFA). As a result of its reformulation, this agency now provides increased emphasis on responsiveness to beneficiaries, providers, and quality improvement. Three business centers were established as part of the reform: Center for Beneficiary Choices, Center for Medicare Management, and Center for Medicaid and State Operations (CMS, 2014). In 2003, President George W. Bush signed the Medicare Prescription Drug, Improvement, and Modernization Act (MMA) into law. The act created a prescription drug benefit for Medicare beneficiaries and established the Medicare Advantage program (O'Sullivan, Chaikind, Tilson, Boulanger, & Morgan, 2004), effectively providing seniors with prescription drug benefits and more choice in accessing health care.

As the Medicare program has evolved, the practice of APRNs has likewise been influenced by changes in Medicare reimbursement policy. In 1998, when Medicare reimbursement reform was enacted, APRNs won the right to be directly reimbursed for provision of Medicare Part B services that, until that time, had been provided only by physicians. In addition, the reform lifted the geographic location restrictions that had limited patient access to APRNs. More recent revisions to the required qualifications, coverage criteria, billing, and payment for Medicare services provided by APRNs are specific, depending on whether the APRN is a certified registered nurse anesthetist (CRNA), nurse practitioner (NP), certified nurse-midwife (CNM), or clinical nurse specialist (CNS). Reimbursement for

APRNs has generally improved; for example, NP services are now paid at 80% of the lesser of the actual charge or 85% of the fee schedule amount a physician is paid (U.S. DHHS, CMS, 2016). However, APRNs continue to lobby for reimbursement at 100% of the amount paid to physicians.

Relationships between the state and federal regulatory systems are highly dynamic. Responsibilities once assumed by the federal government have been shifted to the state level; administration and management of the Medicaid and welfare programs are examples. The perspective that states are better equipped to make decisions about how best to assist their citizens, coupled with a public sentiment that generally seeks to diminish federal bureaucracy and its accompanying tax burden, have been instrumental in moving the placement of authority to the states. However, although states have primary authority over regulation of the health professions, federal policies continue to have a significant effect on healthcare workforce regulation. For example, policies related to reimbursement and quality control over the Medicare and Medicaid programs are promulgated by the U.S. Department of Health and Human Services and administered through its financing agency, CMS.

The Veterans Health Administration, the Indian Health Service, and the uniformed armed services are also regulated by the federal government. Large numbers of health professionals, many of whom are nurses/APRNs, are employed by these federal agencies and departments. Federally employed health professionals must be licensed in at least one state/jurisdiction. These individuals are subject to the laws of the state in which they are licensed and the policies established by the federal system in which they are employed. However, the state of licensure need not correspond with the state in which the federal agency or department resides, because practice that occurs on federal property is not subject to state oversight. This status reflects the fact that the Supremacy Clause of the U.S. Constitution, Article VI, Paragraph 2, establishes that federal laws generally take precedence over state laws (Legal Information Institute, n.d.). State laws in conflict with federal laws cannot be enforced.

The Commerce Clause of the U.S. Constitution limits the ability of states to erect barriers to interstate trade (Gobis, 1997). Courts have determined that the provision of health care constitutes interstate trade under antitrust laws, which in turn sets the stage for the federal government to preempt state licensing laws regarding the practice of professions across state boundaries if future circumstances make this a desirable outcome for the nation. The impact of technology on the delivery of health care—for example, telehealth—allows providers to care for patients in remote environments and across the geopolitical boundaries defined by traditional state-by-state licensure. This raises the question as to whether the federal government would have an interest in interceding in the standardization of state licensing requirements to facilitate interstate commerce. If this occurred, the federal government would be in the position of usurping what is presently the state's authority.

Licensing boards have an interest in avoiding federal intervention and are beginning to identify ways to facilitate the practice of telehealth while simultaneously preserving the power and right of the state to protect its citizens by regulating health professions at the state level. One approach to nursing regulation that addresses this conundrum is **multistate regulation**, which is discussed later in this chapter.

Federal Rule Making

The federal regulatory process is established by the federal administrative procedures act. In this process, a Notice of Proposed Rulemaking (NPRM) is published in the *Federal Register*, a public, daily federal government publication containing current executive orders, presidential proclamations, rules and regulations, proposed rules, notices, and sunshine act meetings. The NPRM includes information about the substance of intended regulations and information about public participation in the regulatory process, including procedures for attending meetings or hearings and for providing comment. The agency writing the rules is mandated to consider all public comments, and amendments to draft regulations may be made based on public input if warranted. The agency publishes final regulations in the rules and regulations section of the *Federal Register*. Rules become effective 30 days after they are filed in final form by the agency and published in the *Federal Register* (**FIGURE 4-1**).

Emergency Regulations

Provisions for promulgating emergency regulations are defined at both the state and the federal levels. Emergency regulations are enacted if an agency determines that the public welfare is in jeopardy and the regulation will serve as an immediately enforceable remedy. Emergency regulations usually take effect upon their date of publication, are generally temporary, and are effective for a limited time period (usually 90 days), with an option to renew them. Emergency regulations must be followed with permanent regulations that are promulgated in accordance with the usual APA requirements.

Locating Information

Each state government periodically publishes a document containing notices, proposed regulations, final regulations, and emergency regulations. The publication cycle for this document—usually called the State Register or State Bulletin—can be obtained by accessing the state legislative printing office/website or the state legislative information system office/website. Federal regulatory information is available online: the National Archives manages the Code of Federal Regulations (CFR) website and the U.S. Government Publishing Office oversees the eCFR website.

Because state and federal agencies promulgate numerous regulations, it is in one's best interest to belong to at least one national professional organization, most of which employ professional lobbyists who track legislation, monitor agencies' rule making, and report to their membership. Some state organizations employ such lobbyists; many others do not have the financial resources to do so. Specialty organizations' newsletters and journals and legislative subscription and monitoring services and bulletins can be relied upon to summarize proposed regulation content and track status progress.

Providing Public Comment

Regulatory agencies provide a small window of opportunity for public comment. Most comment periods last 30 days from the date of publication of

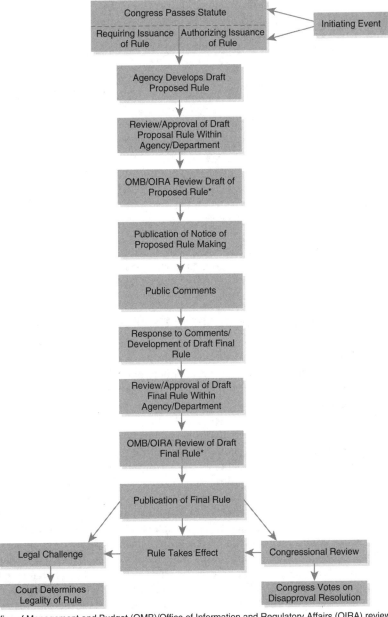

* The Office of Management and Budget (OMB)/Office of Information and Regulatory Affairs (OIRA) reviews only significant rules and does not review any rules submitted by independent regulatory agencies.

FIGURE 4-1 The federal rule-making process.

Reproduced from Carey, M. P. (2013, June 17). The federal rulemaking process: An overview. *Congressional Research Service Report RL32240*. Retrieved from http://www.fas.org/sgp /crs/misc/RL32240.pdf the proposed regulation. However, longer comment periods are sometimes permitted if the agency anticipates the issue will draw strong public interest or involves controversy.

Public rule hearings are held by the agency proposing the regulation. Public agencies must comply with administrative procedures act regulations regarding public hearings. Federal agencies are generally required to hold hearings when a numeric threshold is reached (i.e., a certain number of individuals or agency/organization representatives make requests to offer testimony). Written comments received by the agency are made a part of the permanent record and must be considered by the agency's board or commission members prior to publication of the final regulation. A final regulation can be challenged in the courts if the judge determines the agency did not comply with the administrative procedures act or ignored public comments.

The *Federal Register* provides agency contact information on its website, making it feasible for the public to provide comment on proposed regulations. Only written comments are included in the public record, although agencies may permit oral comments if time is short. Instructions for submitting electronic comments or written submissions by mail, hand delivery, or courier are generally included on the filing agency's *Federal Register* webpage. Comments received after the comment period posted in the *Federal Register* is closed can be legitimately disregarded by the agency.

Strengths and Weaknesses of the Regulatory Process

The regulatory process is somewhat more well ordered than the legislative process in that it is directed by state or federal administrative procedures acts. These procedures guarantee opportunities for comment and public input. The regulatory process also includes built-in delays and time constraints that slow the process of developing and implementing regulations. However, administrative agencies are able to exert a great deal of control over the rule-drafting process. Agency staff have an interest in assuring the final regulation has sufficient detail that it can be reasonably enforced. It is possible that agency staff, although skilled regulators, may not be knowledgeable about a regulation's impact from the practitioners' point of view. If the agency did not invite stakeholders to assist with the original drafting of the regulation, then public input during the comment period is especially important.

In addition to enforcement, administrative agencies may have legislative authority to interpret regulations. Sometimes regulations may be misinterpreted by agency staff or board members, resulting in the imposition of a new meaning that is not aligned with the original intent of the regulation. These interpretations may be published as opinions, interpretive statements, and/or declaratory rulings of the board. Opinions of the attorney general or court may also misinterpret the original legislative intent, but the judicial branch of government is more likely to apply sound legal standards to its fact-finding and conclusions of law. Regardless, official opinions carry the force and effect of law even if they are not promulgated as regulations, according to the administrative procedures act.

Regulation in a Transforming Healthcare Delivery System

In the United States, the healthcare delivery system is undergoing a period of significant and rapid change. Evidence of system shifts began in 1995, when the Pew Health Professions Commission (1994) published a sweeping report that stimulated new thinking about existing regulatory systems. The report suggested that the system, based on a century-old model structured with separate health professions agencies regulating individual health professionals with potentially overlapping scopes of practice, was out of sync with the nation's healthcare delivery systems and financing structures. The Pew Health Professions Commission suggested that major reform was needed and asked states to review regulatory processes with the following questions in mind (Dower & Finocchio, 1995, p. 1):

■ Does regulation promote effective health outcomes and protect the public from harm?
■ Are regulatory bodies truly accountable to the public?
■ Does regulation respect consumers' rights to choose their own healthcare providers from a range of safe options?
■ Does regulation encourage a flexible, rational, and cost-effective healthcare system?
■ Does regulation allow effective working relationships among healthcare providers?
■ Does regulation promote equity among providers of equal skill?
■ Does regulation facilitate professional and geographic mobility of competent providers?

The Pew Task Force on Health Care Workforce Regulation challenged state and federal governments to respond to the complex health professions education and regulation issues identified in the report. Report recommendations addressed the use of standardized and understandable language, standardization of entry-to-practice requirements, assurance of initial and continuing competence of healthcare practitioners, and redesign of professional boards, including creation of super-boards in which the majority of members are consumer representatives. The report also called for better methods of assessing the achievement of objectives and improved disciplinary processes (Pew Health Professions Commission, 1995). Some of these changes have already been implemented in regulatory agency structures, such as standardization of entry-to-practice requirements, but redesign of professional boards has been slow to change.

Following the 1995 Pew report, the Institute of Medicine (IOM)—now known as the National Academy of Medicine—issued a number of reports related to safety in healthcare systems, known as the Quality Chasm Series. Several of these reports made recommendations with regard to regulation. For example, in its first report, *To Err Is Human*, the IOM called for licensing and certification bodies to pay greater attention to safety-related performance standards and expectations for health professionals (Kohn, Corrigan, & Donaldson, 2000).

A consensus report, focused singularly on nursing, was jointly issued by the Robert Wood Johnson Foundation and the IOM in October 2010. This report, which bore the title *The Future of Nursing: Leading Change, Advancing Health*, provided four key messages to guide changes and remove barriers that prevent nurses from being able to function effectively in a rapidly evolving healthcare system:

■ Nurses should be enabled to practice to the full extent of their education and training.
■ Nurses should be able to access higher levels of education and training in an improved education system that allows for academic progression.

- Nurses should be full partners in the interprofessional redesign of the U.S. healthcare system.
- Effective workforce planning and policymaking need better data collection and information infrastructures.

Eight recommendations for fundamental change are found in the report, along with related actions for Congress, state legislatures, CMS, the Office of Personnel Management, the Federal Trade Commission, and the Antitrust Division of the Department of Justice. The recommendation most relevant to regulation is the first: to remove scope-of-practice barriers. Other recommendations with implications for regulation include the call to prepare and enable nurses to lead change to advance health—that is, nurses who serve on boards and commissions serve in such roles—and the suggestion to build an infrastructure for the collection and analysis of interprofessional healthcare workforce data (IOM, 2010). Regulatory boards often survey their licensees as a part of renewal, providing excellent sources of workforce data. Some progress toward accomplishment of the *Future of Nursing* report recommendations has been made, but, importantly, barriers to expansion of APRN scopes of practice remain (IOM, 2016).

Another area ripe for regulatory reform relates to structures that encourage interprofessional collaboration. The Josiah Macy Jr. Foundation, an organization dedicated to improving the health of the public through the advancement of health professions education, has been instrumental in providing direction for regulatory reform. In 2013, this foundation held a consensus conference with health professions education leaders to discuss a vision for a joint future of healthcare practice and education. Recommendations for action in five areas were made; one of these was to "revise professional regulatory standards and practices to permit and promote innovation in interprofessional education and collaborative practice" (Josiah Macy Jr. Foundation, 2013, p. 2).

Together these reports and recommendations provide a substantive body of evidence that can be leveraged for health professions regulation reform, thereby ensuring these professions can meet the needs of 21st-century healthcare consumers. APRNs have a window of opportunity to act on these recommendations but must be open to the notion that collaboration with other health professions is essential if new regulatory models are to emerge. Regulation determines who has access to the patient, who serves as gatekeeper in a managed care environment, who is reimbursed, and who has autonomy to practice. APRNs must be visible participants in the political process that authorizes APRNs to practice to the full extent of their education in a collaborative environment as equal team members and ensures consumer choice and protection.

▶ Current Issues in Regulation and Licensure: Regulatory Responses

Changes to the Affordable Care Act

The ACA increased access for under-insured and uninsured U.S. residents, who are estimated to number more than 50 million. This law/program also had a significant impact on the estimated 6,400 shortage areas in the United States, including 66 million Americans who have limited access to primary care (ANA, 2011). The need for APRNs to work in a variety of settings, but particularly in primary care, has been enormous, but their usefulness has been dependent on lifting practice restrictions in their state of licensure.

The ACA is now in the midst of partisan controversy, and the future of its key provisions is currently uncertain. Key policy issues related to the ACA include regulation of health insurance coverage and costs, potential changes to Medicaid and Medicare, potential changes in reimbursement for prescription drugs and prescribing practices, and handling of reproductive health services (Kaiser Family Foundation, 2016). Both state and federal regulatory agencies will play a part in enacting these changes; regulations governing the health insurance marketplace (HealthCare.gov, 2010) and the Medicaid and Medicare programs (CMS, 2014) will need to reflect any changes made by the U.S. Congress. Programs that rely on state matching funds (e.g., Medicaid) will likely be forced to reevaluate their state's contribution.

Reimbursement

Significant breakthroughs have been made in reimbursement policy for APRNs, largely as a result of grassroots lobbying efforts and coalitions of APRN specialty nursing organizations. With the passage of federal legislation in 1997 allowing APRNs to bill Medicare directly for services, consumer access to care provided by APRNs has improved. Managed care markets value efficiency and provider effectiveness. Understanding the concept of market value has motivated APRNs to become more skilled in costing out their services and winning contracts in a competitive market.

Scope of Practice

The *Future of Nursing* progress report (IOM, 2016) noted that only minimal change in expansion of nurses' scopes of practice had been accomplished since 2010. APRNs continue to struggle with these issues, although progress has been made in some states as well as at the federal level. A 2014 report from the Federal Trade Commission (FTC) provided an unbiased analysis of the consequences of continuing to impose restrictions on APRNs' scopes of practice. The report noted associations between mandatory physician supervision/collaborative practice agreement regulations and restriction of independent APRN practice. The FTC (2014) projected that these environmental factors would likely lead to decreased access to healthcare services, higher costs, and reduced quality of care, leading to minimization of nursing's ability to innovate in the delivery of health care. The Department of Veterans Affairs (VA) recently finalized a regulation allowing full scope of practice for APRNs with the exception of CRNAs (Dickson, 2016).

Boundary disputes within and across the health professions create tension and are counterproductive to efforts to improve nursing's contributions to care, as those efforts rely on equitable teamwork. It is imperative for APRNs to be cognizant of reports such as that published by the FTC and to keep abreast of inroads such as those made in the VA. Compelling evidence (e.g., the FTC report) and progress in high-level government agencies (e.g., the VA) can serve as leverage when negotiating with lawmakers and other stakeholders at the state level to enact changes in scope of practice laws.

Increased Use of Unlicensed Assistive Personnel

Unlicensed assistive personnel (UAPs) are individuals who are unregulated in many states, inexpensive, and employed in acute and primary care settings. In many settings, UAPs are used appropriately. However, when employers misunderstand the UAP's role or expand job descriptions in an effort to provide more care at less cost, there is a risk that UAPs may be asked to function beyond their capacity and in a way that approaches nursing practice. Potential dangers include unsafe patient care and liability for nurses who, because of their employment situations, feel forced to delegate more nursing tasks to UAPs than safe standards of delegation would dictate.

Electronic Access to Healthcare Services

The impact of technology on the delivery of health care, including telehealth, was mentioned earlier in this chapter in the context of questions about whether the federal government has an interest in interceding in the standardization of state licensing requirements to facilitate interstate commerce. Such action would pre-empt the states' authority to license health professionals. However, the states maintain their right to protect their citizens. Today, nurses who live in one multistate-regulation state and practice telehealth in another multistate-regulation state have the benefit of multistate regulation (but must affirm licensure in the second state). Where no multistate compact exists between states, however, the nurse must generally seek licensure in the state in which the patient resides.

Interstate Mobility and Multistate Regulation

Cumbersome licensure processes across geopolitical boundaries make seamless transition difficult or impossible, particularly for APRNs. The Nurse Licensure Compact (NLC) model, adopted by the NCSBN, is nursing's mutual recognition model of multistate regulation and licensure for RNs. States adopting this model voluntarily enter into an interstate compact, which is a legal agreement between states to recognize the license of another state and to allow for practice between states. This allows the nurse to possess a "home state" license and practice in a remote state without obtaining an additional license. The compact must be passed as law by the state legislature and implemented by the BON in each state (NCSBN, 1998).

A number of states moved quickly to enter the compact when it was instituted, but many states remain independent. As of January 2017, 25 states were participating as compact states (NCSBN, 2017b).

Until 2015, there was no system for APRN participation in a nursing compact. Consequently, although the compact may apply to a nurse's RN license, it does not extend to cover advanced practice, and APRNs must apply for licensure in each state of practice. In May 2015, NCSBN approved the APRN Compact model, which would allow APRNs to hold one multistate license and extend privileges to practice in other APRN Compact states (NCSBN, 2017a). To participate in this system, state NPAs would need to be revised to include the Uniform APRN Requirements. Currently, no states have enacted APRN Compact legislation.

▶ Conclusion

The capacity to adapt is crucial in an era of rapid change. Today's politically astute nurses have many opportunities to shape public policy, by working in coalition together and with other health professionals and consumers, and to advocate for state and federal health policies and regulations that will allow the public greater access to affordable, quality health care. The window of opportunity that opened with the enactment of the comprehensive ACA will look somewhat different as we move forward. It is essential for nurses and APRNs to develop skills to capitalize on the chaos present in the healthcare and political environments and to create opportunities to advance the profession as a whole.

Familiarity with the regulatory process will give nurses and APRNs the tools needed to navigate this dynamic environment with confidence. Knowing how to monitor the status of critical issues involving scopes of practice, licensure, and reimbursement will allow APRNs to influence the outcomes of debates on those issues. Participation in specialty professional nurse organizations is especially advantageous. Participation builds a membership base, providing the foundation for strong coalition building and a power base from which to effect change in the political and regulatory arenas. Participation also gives members ready access to a network of colleagues, legislative affairs information, and professional and educational opportunities. Although supporting the profession through participation is central, it is equally important to remember that each professional nurse has the ability to make a difference.

▶ Discussion Points

1. Compare and contrast the legislative and regulatory processes.
2. Describe the major methods of credentialing. List the benefits and weaknesses of each method from the standpoint of public protection and protection of the professional scope of practice.
3. Discuss the role of state BONs in regulating professional practice.
4. Obtain a copy of a proposed or recently promulgated regulation. Using the questions in Exhibit 4-1, analyze the regulation for its impact on nursing practice.
5. Describe the federal government's role in the regulation of health professions. To what extent do you believe this role will increase or decrease over time? Explain your rationale.
6. Analyze the pros and cons of multistate regulation (choose multistate regulation of RNs, APRNs, or a combination). Based on your analysis, develop and defend a position either for or against multistate regulation.
7. Prepare written testimony for a public hearing defending or opposing the need for a second license for APRNs.
8. Contrast the BON and the national or state nurses association vis-à-vis mission, membership, authority, functions, and source of funding.
9. Identify a proposed regulation. Discuss the current phase of the process, identify methods for offering comments, and submit written comments to the administrative agency.

10. Evaluate the APRN section of the nurse practice act in your state using the *NCSBN Model Act* (NCSBN, 2012) or regulations using the *NCSBN Model Rules* (NCSBN, 2014a).

11. Identify the states that have implemented nurse-staffing ratios. List some of the obstacles one of the states has encountered in the implementation phase.

⌕ CASE STUDY 4-1: *Delegation of Medication Administration by APRNs*

The authority to administer medications in one state is restricted and specific. The NPA allows RNs to delegate medication administration only to BON-certified medication aides in nursing homes and residential care facilities. Otherwise, unlicensed persons may only assist an individual with self-administration of certain medications, may give oral medication or apply topical medication in accordance with the laws and regulations of the Department of Disabilities, and may administer prescribed medication to a student if the RN is employed by a board of education or charter school if those medication administration procedures are in accordance with the laws regulating boards of education. However, with the exception of these special instances, RNs and APRNs are not permitted to delegate medication administration to non-nurses, including medical assistants. This restriction is problematic for APRNs, particularly NPs and CNSs who function in primary care settings.

Patients in primary care settings frequently need immunizations, tuberculosis skin tests, and routine medications. Because the current law largely prohibits APRNs from delegating medication administration to unlicensed personnel, the flow of patient care must be interrupted. APRNs must perform all medication administration and associated tasks themselves, unless there is another RN who is available to administer the medication. This prohibition is a significant barrier to productivity and efficiency.

APRNs and stakeholder nurse associations approached a legislator who has been a friend to nursing and is interested in improving healthcare delivery in the state. This member of the state House of Representatives sponsored a bill to allow APRNs to delegate medication administration to a trained, unlicensed person, such as a medical assistant, so long as certain conditions are met. These conditions include (1) the APRN has assessed the patient prior to administration to determine appropriateness; (2) the APRN has determined the unlicensed person has completed the requisite education and has the knowledge, skills, and ability to administer the drug safely; and (3) delegation is in accordance with rules that are established by the BON. Additional safeguards include (1) the drug must be within the formulary established by the BON for APRNs, is not a controlled substance, and is not to be administered intravenously; (2) the employer has given the APRN access to employment records documenting the unlicensed person's education, knowledge, ability, and skills with regard to medication administration; and (3) the APRN must be physically present at the location where the drug is administered by the unlicensed person. Language in the bill clarifies that the APRN delegating authority would not affect or change the current law governing delegation authority in certain facilities, including nursing homes and residential care facilities.

This legislation received four hearings in the House Health Committee and was reported out with two sponsor amendments. One amendment added ambulatory surgical facilities to the list of sites where an APRN cannot delegate medication administration, and the other moved the rule authority language to the general rule authority of the nurse practice act. Although this second amendment is technical, it is beneficial to APRNs in that it will authorize the BON to promulgate rules without the advice and counsel of its multidisciplinary Committee on Prescriptive Governance.

One state nursing association and one APRN testified on behalf of nursing as proponents for the bill. The state medical association remained neutral throughout the process.

Discussion Points

1. Identify ways to increase the likelihood that the legislation will pass.
2. Determine a complete list of possible stakeholders. In addition to state nurses associations, which other associations or organizations might have an interest?
3. Discuss the position of neutrality on the part of the state medical association. Would you expect this? Why or why not? Could this organization's position change? Why or why not? If so, what could you do in anticipation to assure its continued neutrality or future support for the bill?
4. Although a number of state nurses' associations have an interest in this bill, only one formally provided proponent testimony for the record. In addition, one adult NP, who represented herself as a single practitioner, provided testimony. What are the implications of limited proponent testimony? What does a small turnout, or silence, say to legislators? What might be done differently, or in addition, when the bill reaches the Senate?

🔎 *CASE STUDY 4-2:* *Evidence Versus Stakeholder Interests in Rule Making*

Prelicensure nursing education in the United States is tightly regulated by BONs. Nursing education regulations include curriculum requirements and typically include provisions regarding what must be included in classroom instruction, in laboratory/simulation, and in clinical experience. "Clinical" generally refers to those faculty-supervised experiences that occur in authentic patient settings with persons who need nursing care. Some BONs specify minimum numbers of hours of clinical experience; some do not. Prelicensure nursing education rules do not directly affect APRNs; however, their indirect effect can be substantial. APRNs may serve in administrative leadership roles or oversee the care of patients in healthcare organizations where graduates of programs will hold future employment.

One BON was approached by rural-area nursing educator stakeholders, who had encountered difficulties in securing clinical experiences for students in obstetrics, newborn care, and pediatrics. The BON asked its education advisory

(continues)

🔍 *CASE STUDY 4-2:* Evidence Versus Stakeholder Interests in Rule Making *(continued)*

committee to discuss the matter. The committee made a recommendation, based on a simulation study conducted by NCSBN, that as many as 100% of clinical experiences in those areas could be replaced by high-, mid-, or low-fidelity simulation in a skills laboratory setting.

The BON heard testimony at its rules hearing from proponents, primarily representatives from the nursing education programs having difficulty finding the experiences for students. Testifying in opposition were individuals representing several nursing organizations, including the deans and directors of baccalaureate and higher-degree nursing education programs, an organization representing all chief nursing officers in the state, the state nurses association, and the state pediatric nurses association. Proponents verified difficulty in obtaining clinical experiences for students and cited their rationale for substituting simulation for authentic clinical experiences. Opponents noted the findings of the NCSBN study that indicated a maximum of 50% of clinical experiences could be replaced with simulation and spoke to qualitative differences between authentic clinical experiences and simulation. The individual representing chief nursing officers offered to work with nursing programs to facilitate procurement of clinical experiences.

Following deliberation, the BON determined to file the rule as proposed, allowing substitution of up to 100% of clinical experience in the three specialties (obstetrics, neonatal, pediatrics) with simulation.

Discussion Points

1. Which additional questions would you want answered about the methodology and detailed findings from the NCSBN simulation study?
2. Who were the stakeholders? Which specific arguments can you anticipate stakeholders on both the proponent and the opponent sides made for or against the rule change, respectively?
3. If you were a nursing leader or practicing APRN in one of the specialty areas, do you have any concerns about the proposed rule? Given your position, are there any current or future actions you might take to safeguard patients?

References

American Nurses Association. (2011). Advanced practice nursing: A new age in health care. *American Nurses Association Backgrounder*. Retrieved from http://www.nursingworld.org/functionalmenucategories/mediaresources/mediabackgrounders/aprn-a-new-age-in-health-care.pdf

APRN Joint Dialogue Group. (2008). Consensus model for APRN regulation: Licensure, accreditation, certification & education. Retrieved from http://www.aacn.nche.edu/education-resources/APRNReport.pdf

Carey, M. P. (2013, June 17). The federal rulemaking process: An overview. *Congressional Research Service Report RL32240*. Retrieved from http://www.fas.org/sgp/crs/misc/RL32240.pdf

Centers for Medicare and Medicaid Services (CMS). (2014). History. Retrieved from https://www.cms.gov/About-CMS/Agency-information/History/

Damgaard, G., & Young, L. (2017). Application of an evidence-informed health policy model for the decision to delegate insulin administration. *Journal of Nursing Regulation, 7*(4), 33–44.

Dickson, V. (2016, December 13). VA finalizes rule that expands scope of nurse practice. *Modern Healthcare.* Retrieved from http://www.modernhealthcare.com/article/20161213 /NEWS/161219974

Dower, C., & Finocchio, L. (1995). Health care workforce regulation: Making the necessary changes for a transforming health care system. *State Health Workforce Reforms, 4,* 1–2.

Federal Trade Commission (FTC). (2014). Policy perspectives: Competition and the regulation of advanced practice nurses. Retrieved from https://www.ftc.gov/system/files /documents/reports/policy-perspectives-competition-regulation-advanced-practice-nurses /140307aprnpolicypaper.pdf

Garner, B. A. (2014). *Black's law dictionary* (10th ed.). St Paul, MN: Thomas Reuters.

Gobis, L. J. (1997). Licensing and liability: Crossing the borders with telemedicine. *Caring, 16*(7), 18–24.

Hartigan, C. (2011). APRN regulation: The licensure–certification interface. *AACN Advanced Critical Care, 22*(1), 50–65.

HealthCare.gov. (2010). Need a 2017 plan? Act fast to beat the deadline. Retrieved from http:// www.healthcare.gov

Institute of Medicine (IOM). (2010). The future of nursing: Leading change, advancing health. Retrieved from https://www.nap.edu/download/12956

Institute of Medicine (IOM). (2016). Assessing progress on the Institute of Medicine report. *The Future of Nursing.* Retrieved from https://www.nap.edu/download/21838

Josiah Macy Jr. Foundation. (2013). Transforming patient care: Aligning interprofessional education with clinical practice redesign. Conference recommendations. Retrieved from http://macyfoundation.org/publications/publication/aligning-interprofessional-education

Jost, T. S. (1997). *Regulation of the health professions.* Chicago, IL: Health Administration Press.

Kaiser Family Foundation (2016, November 9). Where president-elect Donald Trump stands on six health care issues. Retrieved from http://kff.org/health-reform/issue-brief /where-president-elect-donald-trump-stands-on-six-health-care-issues/#opioid

Kohn, L. T., Corrigan, J. M., & Donaldson, M. S. (Eds.). (2000). *To err is human: Building a safer health care system.* Washington, DC: National Academies Press.

Legal Information Institute. (n.d.). Supremacy Clause. Retrieved from http://www.law.cornell .edu/wex/supremacy_clause

Loversidge, J. M. (2016a). A call for extending the utility of evidence-based practice: Adapting EBP for health policy impact. *Worldviews on Evidence-Based Nursing, 3*(6), 399–401.

Loversidge, J. M. (2016b). An evidence-informed health policy model: Adapting evidence-based practice for nursing education and regulation. *Journal of Nursing Regulation, 7*(2), 27–33.

Melnyk, B. M., & Fineout-Overholt, E. (2015). *Evidence-based practice in nursing and healthcare: A guide to best practice* (3rd ed.). Philadelphia, PA: Lippincott Williams & Wilkins.

National Council of State Boards of Nursing (NCSBN). (1993). *Regulation of advanced nursing practice position paper.* Retrieved from https://www.ncsbn.org/1993_Position_Paper_on _the_Regulation_of_Advanced_Nursing_Practice.pdf

National Council of State Boards of Nursing (NCSBN). (1998, April). *Multi state regulation task force communiqué.* Chicago, IL: Author.

National Council of State Boards of Nursing (NCSBN). (2002). Uniform advanced practice registered nurse licensure/authority to practice requirements. Retrieved from https://www .ncsbn.org/APRN_Uniform_requirements_revised_8_02.pdf

National Council of State Boards of Nursing (NCSBN). (2008). Contact a board of nursing. Retrieved from https://www.ncsbn.org/contact-bon.htm

National Council of State Boards of Nursing (NCSBN). (2012). NCSBN model act. Retrieved from https://www.ncsbn.org/14_Model_Act_0914.pdf

National Council of State Boards of Nursing (NCSBN). (2014a). NCSBN model rules. Retrieved from https://www.ncsbn.org/14_Model_Rules_0914.pdf

National Council of State Boards of Nursing (NCSBN). (2014b). Nurse practice act, rules & regulations. Retrieved from https://www.ncsbn.org/1455.htm

National Council of State Boards of Nursing (NCSBN). (2016). APRN consensus 2016. Retrieved from https://www.ncsbn.org/9314.htm

National Council of State Boards of Nursing (NCSBN). (2017a). APRN compact. Retrieved from https://www.ncsbn.org/aprn-compact.htm

National Council of State Boards of Nursing (NCSBN). (2017b). Map of NLC states. Retrieved from https://www.ncsbn.org/nurse-licensure-compact.htm

O'Sullivan, J., Chaikind, H., Tilson, S., Boulanger, J., & Morgan, P. (2004). *Overview of the Medicare Prescription Drug, Improvement and Modernization Act of 2003.* Congressional Research Service. Order Code RL31966. Washington, DC: Library of Congress.

Pew Health Professions Commission. (1994). *State strategies for health care workforce reform.* San Francisco, CA: UCSF Center for the Health Professions.

Pew Health Professions Commission. (1995). *Report of task force on health care workforce regulation* (executive summary). San Francisco, CA: UCSF Center for the Health Professions.

Phillips, S. J. (2017). 29th annual legislative update. *Nurse Practitioner, 42*(1), 18–46.

Roberts, M. J., & Clyde, A. T. (1993). *Your money or your life: The health care crisis explained.* New York, NY: Doubleday.

Russell, K. A. (2012). Nurse practice acts guide and govern nursing practice. *Journal of Nursing Regulation, 3*(3), 36–42.

Safriet, B. J. (1992). Health care dollars and regulatory sense: The role of advanced practice nursing. *Yale Journal of Regulation, 9*(2), 419–488.

U.S. Department of Health and Human Services (DHHS). (2014). The Affordable Care Act, section by section. Retrieved from http://www.hhs.gov/healthcare/rights/law/

U.S. Department of Health and Human Services (DHHS), Centers for Medicare and Medicaid Services (CMS). (2016, October). Advanced practice registered nurses, anesthesiologist assistants, and physician assistants. *Medical Learning Network.* ICN901623. Retrieved from https://www.cms.gov/Outreach-and-Education/Medicare-Learning-Network -MLN/MLNProducts/Downloads/Medicare-Information-for-APRNs-AAs-PAs-Booklet -ICN-901623.pdf

CHAPTER 5

Public Policy Design

Catherine Liao

With thanks to Patricia Smart, PhD, RN

This chapter retains several older but classic references from the previous texts because they are considered seminal works that define the topics discussed.

▶ Introduction

In today's world and political climate, it is imperative that healthcare providers, administrators, and educators be knowledgeable about and active in the policy process, particularly as it relates to their professional work. The purpose of this chapter is to examine public policy formulation processes and tools that governments use to solve large and complex societal problems (**FIGURE 5-1**).

The scope of government's involvement in social issues in the United States expanded rapidly in the 20th and 21st centuries. The development of federally funded public programs such as Medicare and Medicaid in 1965 made a major impact on how health care is delivered by providers and accessed by the public. National costs for health care began rising immediately after the advent of Medicare and swelled to $3.2 trillion—or $9,990 per person—in 2015 (CMS, 2017).

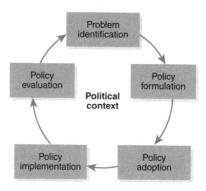

FIGURE 5-1 Stages of the policy process.

Public policy related to financing health care not only must assure access and quality but also bend this cost curve downward.

The creation of Medicare and Medicaid was preceded by efforts in the early 20th century to provide a "safety net" for more Americans in terms of ability to afford health care. The concept of a national health insurance program for Social Security beneficiaries was first proposed by the Surgeon General in 1937 (CMS, 2015). Nearly 10 years later, a federal agency was created to administer programs in health, education, and social insurance. In the two decades that followed, a social awareness of the need for a true safety net emerged. By 1965, in response to this pressure, Congress had enacted legislation creating Medicare and Medicaid as Title XVIII and Title XIX of the Social Security Act, granting hospital insurance (Part A) and medical insurance (Part B) to nearly all Americans older than age 65.

According to the Centers for Medicare and Medicaid Services (CMS), the elderly population at that time was likely to be living in poverty, and a majority of them were uninsured. In addition to extending health insurance and coverage to this population group, the law helped to desegregate hospitals, which were financially motivated to integrate given the "generous" payments offered in exchange for compliance with the Civil Rights Act of 1964. Facility costs in the form of building and renovating structures were high, and Medicare reimbursement could provide more than half of a hospital's income (Smith, 2005)—an attractive lure to hospitals.

All health insurers tend to follow and adopt whatever Medicare will reimburse, making the deliberations regarding this publicly funded program critical to the health insurance benefits available to the vast majority of the nonelderly insured population. The impact was even greater with the passage of the Patient Protection and Affordable Care Act (ACA) in 2010. With the recent election of Donald Trump as president and Republican majorities in Congress, the ACA is expected to undergo rigorous redesign or replacement.

One of the factors that most inhibits the success of public policy is the inability to predict consumer behavior and participation in a social program. The gap in matching desired behavior with appropriate government tools is discussed in this chapter.

Health care is fraught with a multitude of factors that are difficult to identify and control, and the issue of healthcare reform has polarized the country.

Policies related to access to affordable, quality health care have complicated the debate, including raising questions about the following issues:

- How to restore Medicare and Medicaid payments to hospitals that were cut to pay for the subsidies offered under the ACA to low-income individuals
- How to implement new payment models that reward quality over quantity of the healthcare service provided
- How to provide enough public funding for basic and clinical research, provider education and professional development programs, and loan forgiveness for professionals who are practicing in underserved areas

The United States has one of the most sophisticated healthcare systems in the world with respect to innovation, health information technology, and preparation of healthcare professionals. Yet in many of the health indices designed to evaluate the overall health of a country, the United States rates comparatively low. For example, the average life expectancy for females in the United States is 81.6 years, whereas in Japan, Canada, and the Netherlands—all of which are also developed countries—female life expectancy is 86.8, 84.1, and 83.6 years, respectively (World Health Organization, 2016). Infant mortality is another important measure of a nation's health. The United States ranks low among industrialized countries on this measure and also has a high rate of low and very low birth weights, a major contributor to infant mortality (Centers for Disease Control and Prevention [CDC], 2016b). The U.S. healthcare system continues to evolve and, therefore, will continue to benefit from improvements made to its performance, effectiveness, and efficiency by way of evidence-based policymaking.

Efforts have been made by previous administrations to address the issues of access, cost, and quality—often referred to as the three pillars of healthcare policy—but past policy proposals have reflected the prevailing political philosophies and ideologies popular at the time. For example, government programs in the 1960s, under Democratic administrations, reflected an ideology wherein there was less concern with outcome-based planning and more concern with access. Two decades later, under a Republican administration, regulatory efforts attempted to reduce costs through outcome-based choices, individual responsibility for cost, and smaller expansion of healthcare coverage. Policy changes designed to influence one of the three pillars (access to care, quality of care, and cost of care) inevitably affect all three; that is, none of the pillars may be altered without consequences to the other two.

Policies are usually designed to influence behavior and motivate individuals to do what they ordinarily might not do. Although many studies regarding the policy process have been conducted, few have examined the process of policy design specific to individual issues of health care. The focus of most policy studies has been on the implementation of effective programs, and data have been gathered on statistical outcomes. A policy may be more successful if its design is incorporated into all phases of the policy process. For example, in the agenda-setting phase, the problem or social issue could be stated in such a way that it will capture the attention of lawmakers and framed so that government response will be feasible and adaptable. During the implementation phase, the policy's design provides guidance and an overall picture of the plan by specifying the intended outcomes. During the evaluation phase, the program objectives are clearly identified and measurable to ensure that the proposed change produces the desired outcome.

Public policy is, by nature, complicated. The root of public problems has no simple single answer; if it did, more than likely the effort to address those problems would take the form of a guideline, recommendation, or rule implemented by the private sector. Health care is perhaps the most convoluted of public issues because it is affected by a multitude of factors, such as state, federal, and international economies; social movements; education; resources; and religion. As a result, solutions that seek to provide accessible, affordable, and quality health care without leaving a large segment of the population uninsured, driving up the costs of health care, and sacrificing quality are often complicated, fragmented, and difficult to implement across various healthcare settings and populations. The nursing profession should engage in providing stories, data, and insight to help policymakers design the most effective policies to improve access and quality and reduce costs.

▶ The Policy Design Process

Policies reflect public opinion as well as evidence-based data. The policymakers comprise a collection of stakeholders whose task is to find solutions to problems that cannot be resolved by nongovernmental or philanthropic organizations. Policies that address social problems in the United States usually are formulated by a combination of legislators and aides, the executive branch, and special-interest groups and advocates on both the federal and the state levels. Policies may subsequently be altered or struck down by the judicial branch (the courts).

Professional experts such as registered nurses are often asked to serve as panel members or consultants or to serve on committees that provide input to policymakers. Other nurse leaders also are increasingly playing leadership roles in critical policy arenas. For example, under the Obama administration, Marilyn Tavenner became the first nurse to lead the Centers for Medicare and Medicaid Services, while Lieutenant General Patricia Horoho became the first nurse appointed as the Surgeon General for the U.S. Army. State nurses associations also have increasingly taken on a leadership role in advocating directly for change, leaving the sidelines of simply monitoring policy proposals under consideration. Nurses and organizations representing nurses advocate for policies that may be seen as self-serving: Policies that include advanced practice registered nurses (APRNs) in reimbursement models, eliminate supervisory requirements, or increase scope of practice fall into this category. Labor unions representing registered nurses often advocate for policies that may improve working conditions for nurses, with staffing and safety being perennial topics of debate.

The proliferation of participants in policy formation makes systematic program design that is focused on outcomes difficult to achieve. In her classic research, Safriet (2002) reports that most social issues are not brought to the attention of policymakers until there is a crisis with multiple causative factors. The decisions that relate to or have an impact on perceived social problems often are made hastily because of lack of information, constituency impatience, and lack of expertise.

Much policy that regulates nursing practice is determined at the state level, and the policy process conducted here is no less complicated than at the federal level. In the 2016–2017 legislative session of the North Carolina General Assembly, for instance, legislation was introduced that would have made several changes to

North Carolina's Nursing Practice Act, including increasing the scope of practice for nurses in the state. Nursing advocates, including the North Carolina Nurses Association and the North Carolina Association of Nurse Anesthetists, played a significant role in designing the legislation to overhaul the existing law and expand the scope of practice of APRNs. In the most recent legislative session, advocates for change were bolstered by an economic analysis showing North Carolina could significantly reduce healthcare spending by removing physician supervision of APRNs in the state (Conover, 2015). The long-running debate over independent practice for APRNs will continue, however, as N.C. legislators declined to act again on this issue in the 2017 session.

▶ Research Informing the Policy Process

Health services research is typically defined as a multidisciplinary scientific field that examines a multitude of factors, systems, and processes in the delivery of health care. More specifically, nursing health services research can inform policymakers of clinical practice areas that involve the direct patient care experience of the nursing community (Jones & Mark, 2005). In their assessment, Jones and Mark note that nursing health services research can lead to the development of knowledge that improves access, health, and patient safety, among other things. Over the long term, they argue, such research can improve nursing care and patient outcomes—two broad policy issues that benefit in some ways from state or federal regulation.

A recent example of how clinical practice has informed policy involves safe patient handling to protect nurses from musculoskeletal disorders and injuries. The American Nurses Association (ANA, n.d.) notes how common these disorders are in nurses and endorses the call for safe patient handling and mobility (SPHM) programs and policies that protect the nursing workforce from manual lifting and repositioning of patients.

In the 114th Congress (2015-2017), the ANA advocated for the Nurse and Health Care Worker Protection Act, which was introduced to require the Occupational Safety and Health Administration to develop and implement an SPHM standard to eliminate manual lifting of patients by nurses; require employers to purchase, use, and maintain equipment; and require employers to train healthcare workers annually on proper usage of equipment. Congress did not consider the bill before it adjourned, but it is likely similar legislation will be reintroduced in the current Congress (115th), and the nursing workforce community will continue to pursue a strengthening of SPHM programs.

Schneider and Ingram (2005) suggest several issues that may affect failure to take actions needed to ameliorate social, economic, or political problems: (1) lack of incentives or capacity; (2) disagreement with the values implicit in the means or ends; and (3) the existence of high levels of uncertainty about the situation that make it unclear what people should do or how to motivate them.

Health services researchers can inform policy in a myriad of ways, ranging from identifying a problem, to weighing the risks and benefits of possible solutions, to providing estimates for how much a solution may cost government and society (Clancy, Glied, & Lurie, 2012). Such research often relies on large national data sets that offer insight into a particular problem. The Medical Expenditure

Panel Survey (MEPS), for example, consists of large-scale surveys of families and individuals, their healthcare providers, and employers across the country. According to the Agency for Healthcare Research and Quality (AHRQ; the federal agency responsible for producing evidence-based information to make health care safe, high quality, and accessible), MEPS gives researchers the most complete data on the cost and use of health care and health insurance coverage in the United States (AHRQ, 2017). Another helpful resource is the National Healthcare Quality and Disparities Reports housed on the AHRQ website and retrievable at https://www.ahrq.gov/research/findings/nhqrdr/index.html (AHRQ, 2015). These annual reports offer summarized data that can stimulate ideas for further study or research as well as cursory analyses to jumpstart projects. The reports provide reliable and updated data that can lead to meaningful policy change in improving care, lowering costs, and reducing health disparities.

▶ The Design Issue

Unclear mandates often result in a mismatch between legislative intent and bureaucratic behavior. For instance, Congress enacted the Emergency Medical Treatment and Labor Act (EMTALA) in 1986 to ensure access to emergency care for patients with unstable conditions. Although the legislation requires hospitals to provide specific emergency services to patients seeking treatment, regardless of their citizenship, legal status, or ability to pay, the federal government does not reimburse for the cost of that care. EMTALA was intended to eliminate the practice of hospitals refusing to accept or treat unstable patients without proof of insurance; patients were sometimes sent over long distances to a public or county hospital. Despite the good intentions to ensure care for those in need, an **unfunded mandate** puts pressure on hospitals, which can face high costs when they are required to provide uncompensated care.

Policy design became a focus of research studies several decades ago. Linder and Peters (1987), whose work established a classical starting point for design research, reported that poor policy design is often the reason for policy failure. Describing some programs as "crippled at birth," these scholars noted that the best bureaucracies in the world may not be able to achieve desired goals if an excessively ambitious policy is used (i.e., the problem is too complex for a single policy or agency). A recent example of complexity was the launch of the healthcare.gov website to guide Americans in obtaining health insurance under the ACA (also known as "Obamacare"). The extreme complexity of this project resulted in multiple delays and frustration with the launch. Also, if there is a misunderstanding of the nature of the problem, inappropriate policies may be formulated. Linder and Peters proposed that implementation should be examined but only as one of the conditions that must be satisfied for successful policymaking. They maintain that by shifting the focus of study to policy design, more reliable and explicit answers can be found, leading to greater chances of policy success.

The design phase remains an integral part of the policy process. An understanding of the policy tools or instruments chosen for policy design and the underlying assumptions of policymakers during the design process is critical to an understanding of the overall policy process.

▶ Policy Instruments (Government Tools)

The study of the instruments or tools by which the government achieves desired policy goals has shed light on lawmakers' intentions during policymaking and allowed researchers to infer the predictive capabilities of tools. Two scholars proposed a framework for studying policy based on policy tools. Schneider and Ingram (1990), in their classic work, offer a framework to analyze implicit or explicit behavioral theories found in laws, regulations, and programs. Their analysis uses government tools or instruments and underlying behavioral assumptions as variables that guide policy decisions and choices. Their contention is that target group compliance and utilization are important forms of political behavior that should be examined closely. When these tools are combined with process variables such as competition, partisanship, and public opinion, Schneider and Ingram argue, the tools approach moves policy beyond considering the standard analysis and improved frameworks. They note that policy tools are substitutable, and states often use a variety of tools to address a single problem.

To understand which tools are most efficient, emphasis should be placed on using them in conjunction with a particular policy design. According to Howlett, Mukherjee, and Rayner (2014), **policy tools**—that is, those methods chosen by policymakers to help solve a problem or social issue—are so critical in policy design that policy implementation cannot be achieved without them.

Howlett (2011) describes five specific policy tools used by governments in designing policy. In addition, he identifies five broad categories of tools: authority, incentives, capacity building, symbolic or hortatory, and learning. Professional nurses can use their knowledge of policy tools to make suggestions and recommendations to government leaders who are designing policies and programs.

Authority Tools

Authority tools are used most frequently by governments to guide the behavior of agents and officials at lower levels. Authority tools are statements backed by the legitimate power of government that grant permission and prohibit or require action under designated circumstances. An example of an authority tool is a law, regulation, or mandate that requires vaccination for daycare and school entry under regulated criteria.

Incentive Tools

Incentive tools assume individuals have access to the resources they desire most and will not be motivated positively to take action without encouragement or coercion. Having access to what is most desired leads to wanting to get the greatest value for each expenditure. Incentive tools rely on tangible payoffs (positive or negative) as motivating factors. Incentive policy tools manipulate tangible benefits, costs, and probabilities that policy designers assume are relevant to the situation. Incentives assume individuals have the "opportunity to make choices, recognize the opportunity, and have adequate information and decision-making skills to select from among alternatives that are in their best interests" (Schneider & Ingram, 1990, p. 516).

An example of an incentive tool is payment or reimbursement for travel costs to eligible veterans seeking health care at Veterans Affairs medical centers.

However, if the professional nurse assumes that lack of transportation is a barrier to accessing primary care (in that transportation options do not exist, regardless of cost), the outcome from an attempt to use this particular incentive may fail.

Capacity-Building Tools

Capacity-building tools provide information, training, education, and resources to enable individuals, groups, or agencies to make decisions or carry out activities. These tools assume that incentives are not an issue and that target populations will be motivated adequately. For capacity-building tools to work, populations must be aware of the risk factors inherent in the tools and the ways in which these tools can help.

Capacity-building tools focus on education and technical support. For example, information may point out the risks of drugs, and information on such risk factors may be distributed to the target population through brochures, email, online videos, or other presentations. The underlying assumption is that information regarding the importance of addiction cessation is considered valuable and users will stop using substances of abuse to protect their health. Capacity-building tools also are used to encourage people to recognize the value of health care and to sign up for healthcare insurance.

Symbolic or Hortatory Tools

Symbolic or hortatory tools assume that people are motivated from within and decide whether to take policy-related actions on the basis of their beliefs and values. An example of this type of tool is the use of lower-number legislative bills reserved by congressional leadership. Procedural rules in the U.S. House of Representatives allow certain bill numbers, such as House of Representatives (H.R.) 1, to be reserved and assigned to significant legislation. For example, Congress approved H.R. 1, legislation to create the Part D program under Medicare—the Medicare Prescription Drug, Improvement, and Modernization Act—in 2003. Some of the lowest bill numbers are also reserved for use by leadership in the U.S. Senate (Congress.gov). The way in which bill numbers are assigned indicates their legislative significance (often symbolic) and signals that certain policy changes are a high priority for the majority party.

Another hortatory tool is a federal request for proposals to research a particular topic of significant interest to the government. Universities capable of conducting such research will apply for available grant awards, both to undertake the research and to enjoy the benefits that accompany such funding.

Learning Tools

These tools are used when the basis upon which target populations might be moved to take problem-solving action is unknown or uncertain. Policies that use learning tools often are open-ended in purpose and objectives and have broad goals. A needs assessment of the target population may be conducted by a task force, which provides knowledge and insight for policymakers. For example, if a community program addressing childhood obesity is proposed, a needs assessment must be conducted beforehand to determine which information is needed before a proposal is presented to the county council.

Policy tools are important resources for the professional nurse because experience using them can enlighten policymakers and persuade them to support or oppose a policy. Policy tools are similar to educational brochures and other materials that nurses provide to patients and families so that the patient can make informed decisions. For example, one of the primary goals of nursing is to provide the patient with comprehensive information regarding whether the patient has a chronic or acute illness or has undergone a stress-causing, life-changing event. More specific educational guidelines relating to health promotion behaviors and signs and symptoms of illness can reinforce information received from the care provider. Similarly, policy briefs, talking points, and factsheets about specific health conditions often are given to policymakers to help them understand a health policy issue.

▶ Behavioral Dimensions

In addition to understanding the types and roles of tools in formulating policy, professional nurses must understand behavioral assumptions and the political context in which tools exist. The political climate in which social problems are addressed often prescribes the choice of tools to be implemented. Various tools are used when addressing social problems, and often these tools are interchanged, frequently resulting in differing outcomes when the tools are applied by different agencies, states, or countries. In the United States, for example, liberal policymakers are inclined to use capacity-building tools when developing policies for poor and minority groups, such as grants to communities for social programs, whereas conservative policymakers might use the same types of tools in developing policies applicable to businesses, such as strategic planning and business development activities.

For example, with the growing incidence and prevalence of opioid abuse across the United States, advocacy groups, healthcare providers, and federal and state government have sought to propose policy and other interventions that alleviate the epidemic's burden while maintaining access to legitimate prescription drug care (Bagalman, Sacco, Thaul, & Yeh, 2016).

🔎 CASE STUDY 5-1: *The Opioid Epidemic*

In 2013, the Trust for America's Health characterized prescription drug abuse as an epidemic, noting drug overdose deaths had doubled in 29 states since 1999 and outnumbered deaths from heroin and cocaine combined as well as deaths from motor vehicle–related accidents. According to the CDC (2016a, 2016b), more than 500,000 people died from drug overdoses between 2000 and 2015, and 91 Americans die every day from an overdose of prescription pain relievers, or opioids.

In 2014, the U.S. Department of Health and Human Services estimated that 4.3 million individuals abused opioids. The amount of prescription drugs administered and sold continues to increase significantly, despite a lack of corresponding pain reported by Americans (Chang, Daubresse, Kruszewski, & Alexander, 2014; Daubresse et al., 2013).

Public opinion also may have influenced government action in addressing the opioid epidemic. In April 2016, the Kaiser Family Foundation's Health Tracking Poll found that nearly two-thirds of Americans blame the federal and state governments for not doing enough to fight the opioid epidemic. In addition, 44% of those surveyed said they personally knew someone addicted to prescription painkillers.

At the federal level, multiple members of Congress introduced legislation to address the opioid epidemic in a variety of ways. The Comprehensive Addiction and Recovery Act (CARA, S. 524), which Congress enacted in July 2016, represented a comprehensive approach to addressing the problem, ranging from strengthening of efforts at the primary care level to improvements to criminal justice reform. Among other things, the law authorized grants to states and federally qualified health centers (FQHCs) to improve access to overdose treatment, reversal medicine access, and education programs. It also authorized grants to states to develop a treatment alternative to incarceration programs and to train first responders to administer opioid overdose treatments. Other provisions of the law support treatment and recovery organizations and provide incentives to states to address prescription opioid abuse through education, prescription drug monitoring programs, and prevention efforts.

The CARA bill was the first major federal addiction legislation in 40 years. Despite the bill being enacted following lengthy negotiations between lawmakers and the advocacy community, including physician groups and addiction advocates, the bill's passage was not heralded as a complete success. Congress authorized a number of new programs to overhaul the way in which opioid abuse is treated and prevented, but it failed to appropriate any funding for their implementation. Not until the end of 2016 did Congress include $1 billion in funding to states to combat the epidemic. Congressional Republicans, who held the majority in the 114th Congress, sought Democratic support on another comprehensive bill designed to speed up research conducted by the National Institutes of Health and drug approvals by the Food and Drug Administration. Funding of $1 billion for anti-opioid programs and interventions in this bill was included solely for the purpose of enticing Senator Democrats to support the underlying bill.

Although the federal government is working to coordinate the national response to the opioid epidemic, states have been approving legislation and promulgating rules at a more local level, particularly in harder-hit areas. Ohio and Kentucky were two of the five states with the highest rates of death due to drug overdoses in 2015, with each state seeing nearly 30 deaths for every 100,000 people, according to the CDC. In March 2017, Ohio Governor John Kasich approved regulations that limit the amount of opiates physicians and dentists can prescribe to adults and children, requiring prescribers to include a diagnosis or procedure code on every controlled substance prescription. The state made exceptions for opioids prescribed for cancer, palliative care, or hospice care. In April 2017, Kentucky Governor Matt Bevin signed into law legislation (HB 333) that limits physicians to issuing three-day painkiller prescriptions for patients with acute pain.

The North Carolina General Assembly (2017) also approved legislation that requires pharmacists to immediately enter a patient's prescription information into a database. Under the bill, physicians will review the information before prescribing, and they will be limited to giving five- to seven-day doses for the initial treatment. *Politico* also reports that multiple bills aimed at curbing opioid abuse have been introduced in the Michigan and Minnesota legislatures, including legislation that would increase the fee drug makers pay to sell opioids; limit dentists to prescribing medication in four-day increments; and require physicians to use the Prescription Drug Monitoring Program to prevent patients from "doctor shopping" for access to pain medication.

▶ Conclusion

As a component of professional nursing, active participation in the policy process is essential in the formulation of policies designed to provide quality health care at sustainable costs to all individuals. To be effective in the process, RNs and APRNs must understand how the process works and at which points the greatest impact might be made. The design phase of the policy process is the point at which the original intent of a solution to a problem is understood and the appropriate tools are employed to achieve policy success.

▶ Discussion Points

1. Using the https://www.congress.gov/ website, identify recently proposed health policy legislation.
   a. Research the background for the problem or issue being addressed by the policy.
   b. Is there an evidence base to support the proposed policy?
2. Using your understanding of the behavioral assumptions underlying the tools, predict the potential for success or failure of the policy. Identify policy variables that will affect success or failure.
3. Using the https://www.congress.gov/ website, search the 109th Congress to identify a policy (e.g., rule, regulation) that has been in use for several years yet has had little success. Identify the variables that may be inhibiting success and offer possible solutions.
4. How does the political climate affect the choice of policy tools and the behavioral assumptions made by policymakers?
5. Identify opportunities that are currently in place for RNs and APRNs to begin activity in policymaking.

References

Agency for Healthcare Research and Quality (AHRQ), U.S. Department of Health and Human Services. (2015). National healthcare quality and disparites reports. Retrieved from https://nhqrnet.ahrq.gov/inhqrdr/

Agency for Healthcare Research and Quality (AHRQ), U.S. Department of Health and Human Services. (2017, April). Medical expenditure panel survey. Retrieved from https://meps.ahrq.gov/mepsweb/

American Nurses Association (ANA). (n.d.). Safe patient handling and mobility. Retrieved from http://www.nursingworld.org/handlewithcare

Bagalman, E., Sacco, L., Thaul, S., & Yeh, B. (2016, February 23). Congressional research service: Prescription drug abuse. Retrieved from https://fas.org/sgp/crs/misc/R43559.pdf

Centers for Disease Control and Prevention (CDC). (2016a). Drug overdose death data. Retrieved from https://www.cdc.gov/drugoverdose/data/statedeaths.html

Centers for Disease Control and Prevention (CDC). (2016b). Infant mortality. Retrieved from https://www.cdc.gov/reproductivehealth/maternalinfanthealth/infantmortality.htm

Centers for Disease Control and Prevention (CDC). (2016c). Understanding the epidemic. Retrieved from https://www.cdc.gov/drugoverdose/epidemic/index.html

Centers for Medicare and Medicaid Services (CMS), U.S. Department of Health and Human Services. (2015, July). Medicare and Medicaid milestones: 1937–2015. Retrieved from https://www.cms.gov/About-CMS/Agency-Information/History/Downloads/Medicare-and-Medicaid-Milestones-1937-2015.pdf

Centers for Medicare and Medicaid Services (CMS), U.S. Department of Health and Human Services. (2017). National health expenditure data: Historical NHE, 2015. Retrieved from https://www.cms.gov/research-statistics-data-and-systems/statistics-trends-and-reports/nationalhealthexpenddata/nhe-fact-sheet.html

Chang, H., Daubresse, M., Kruszewski, S., & Alexander, G. C. (2014). Prevalence and treatment of pain in emergency departments in the United States, 2000–2010. *American Journal of Emergency Medicine, 32*(5), 421–431.

Clancy, C., Glied, S., & Lurie, N. (2012). From research to health policy impact. *Health Services Research, 47*(1 Pt 2), 337–343.

Congress.gov. (2016). S. 524—Comprehensive Addiction and Recovery Act of 2016. Retrieved from https://www.congress.gov/bill/114th-congress/senate-bill/524?q=%7B%22search%22%3A%5B%22s524%22%5D%7D&r=2

Congress.gov. (2017). Glossary. Retrieved from https://www.congress.gov/help/legislative-glossary/#glossary_reservedbillnumbers

Conover, C. J. (2015). Economic benefits of less restrictive regulation of advanced practice registered nurses in North Carolina. Center for Health Policy & Inequalities Research. Retrieved from http://chpir.org/_homepage-content/completed-projects/economic-benefits-of-less-restrictive-regulation-of-advanced-practice-registered-nurses-in-north-carolina/

Daubresse, M., Chang, H., Yu, Y., Viswanathan, S., Shah, N. D., Stafford, R. S.,... Alexander, G. C. (2013). Ambulatory diagnosis and treatment of nonmalignant pain in the United States, 2000–2010. *Medical Care, 51*(10), 870–878.

Howlett, M., Mukherjee, I., & Rayner, J. (2014). The elements of effective program design: A two-level analysis. *Politics and Governance, 2*(2), 1–12.

Howlett, M. (2011). *Designing public policies: Principles and instruments.* New York, NY: Routledge.

Jones, C. B., & Mark, B. A. (2005). The intersection of nursing and health services research: Overview of an agenda setting conference. *Nursing Outlook, 53,* 270–273.

Kaiser Family Foundation. (2016). Key facts about the uninsured population. Retrieved from http://kff.org/uninsured/fact-sheet/key-facts-about-the-uninsured-population/

Kasich, J. (2017). New limits on prescription opiates will save lives and fight addiction. Retrieved from http://fightingopiateabuse.ohio.gov/Portals/0/PDF/AcutePrescribingLimits_FINAL.pdf

Linder, S. H., & Peters, G. B. (1987). Design perspective on policy implementation: The fallacies of misplaced prescriptions. *Policy Studies Review, 6*(3), 459–475.

North Carolina General Assembly. (2017). HB 243—Strengthen Opioid Misuse Prevention (STOP) Act. Retrieved from http://www.ncleg.net/gascripts/BillLookUp/BillLookUp.pl?Session=2017&BillID=hb243&submitButton=Go

Pradhan, R., & Ehley, B. (2017). State Week: New opioid limits catch fire in hard-hit states. *Politico Pro Healthcare.* Retrieved from https://www.politicopro.com/states/new-jersey/story/2017/03/state-week-110905

Safriet, B. J. (2002). Closing the gap between can and may in health-care providers' scopes of practice: A primer for policymakers. *Yale Journal on Regulation, 19,* 301–334.

Schneider, A., & Ingram, H. (1990). Behavioral assumptions of policy tools. *Journal of Politics, 52*(2), 510–529.

Schneider, A., & Ingram, H. (2005). *Public policy and the social construct of deservedness.* New York, NY: Sage University Press.

Smith, D. B. (2005). The politics of racial disparities: Desegregating the hospitals in Jackson, Mississippi. *Milbank Quarterly, 83*(2), 247–269.

Trust for America's Health. (2013). Prescription drug abuse: Strategies to stop the epidemic. Retrieved from http://healthyamericans.org/reports/drugabuse2013/

World Health Organization. (2016). World health statistics 2016: Monitoring health for the SDGs. Retrieved from http://www.who.int/gho/publications/world_health_statistics/2016/EN_WHS2016_AnnexB.pdf?ua=1

CHAPTER 6
Policy Implementation

Leslie Sharpe

▶ Introduction

Why is understanding the process of policy implementation important for nurses? Nurses make up the largest segment of health professionals in the United States—3.6 million strong (American Nurses Association [ANA], 2017). However, Cramer (2002) noted that nurses are disproportionately underrepresented in actively shaping health policy. Senator Edward Kennedy pointed out many years ago that "nurses are America's largest group of health professionals, but they have never played their proportionate role in helping shape policy, even though that policy profoundly affects them as both health providers and consumers" (1985, p. xxi). As policy implementers, patient advocates, and healthcare consumers, nurses are overwhelmingly qualified to sit at the table as experts in health policy planning and implementation, but many lack the confidence due to the complexity of health policy implementation.

The United States is in the process of implementing healthcare policies that will transform its healthcare system, and nurses can and should play a fundamental role in this transformation. Cramer (2002) asserts that "today, more than ever, nurse participation is needed to shape health policy" (p. 98). The Institute of Medicine (IOM, 2010), in its *Future of Nursing* report, provides key messages that structured the discussion and recommendations presented in the report, including the following:

- Nurses should practice to the full extent of their education and training.
- Nurses should be full partners, with physicians and other healthcare professionals, in redesigning health care in the United States.
- Effective workforce planning and policymaking require better data collection and an improved information infrastructure.

Nurses should participate in and lead decision making and be engaged in healthcare reform–related implementation efforts. Nurses also should serve actively on advisory boards on which policy decisions are made to advance health systems and improve patient care. The implementation of health policy is complex, with a variety of actors and organizations involved in this endeavor. The power to improve the current regulatory, business, and organizational conditions does not rest solely with any one entity, however, but rather requires that all must play a role.

Implementation of health policy occurs when an individual, group, or community operationalizes a policy or program to protect and promote the health of individuals and the community. The policymaking process is cyclical, dynamic, imperfect, and often complex. The relative success or failure of a policy or program depends heavily on what happened during the implementation process—that is, how the organization carried out the instructions indicated in the policy/program. Helfrich, Weiner, McKinney, and Minasian (2007, p. 281) define **implementation** as "the transition period, following the decision to adopt an innovation, during which intended users bring the innovation into sustained use." It is difficult to discuss policy implementation in isolation, because the success of policy implementation relies heavily on the planning process as well as on feedback from the evaluation process. Without adequate planning to address potential barriers, implementation can fail miserably. The evaluation framework developed by the Centers for Disease Control and Prevention (CDC, n.d.) recommends that the implementation evaluation questions be considered as early as the planning stage. For example, are the steps of the implementation process clearly outlined? Are the necessary resources available for implementation of the policy? Formulating these questions at the beginning will facilitate a smooth planning and implementation process to enhance the likelihood of success. For the purposes of this chapter, we will focus only on the implementation of health policy.

Policies come in many forms: Some are statutory and result from legislative enactment or permanent rule; others are nonstatutory in origin, such as procedural manuals and institutional guidelines. Health policies reflect the mix of public health needs and desires of special-interest groups and often involve the choice of who will get health care and how, when, and where the health care will be delivered. Implementation is about who participates, including both actors and organizations; why and how they participate, including procedures and techniques that reflect command, control, and incentives; and with what effect, meaning the extent to which the program goals were supported—the output and the measurable change (the outcome). The implementation of healthcare laws and policies can change the physical environment in which people live and work, affect behavior, affect human biology, and influence the availability and accessibility of health services (Longest, 2010).

▶ Federal and State Policymaking and Implementation 101

Formulation of health policy on the federal and state levels can originate in any of the three branches of government—legislative (senate or house), executive (president or governor), or judiciary (Gostin, 1995). The preferences and influence of interest groups, political bargaining, and individual and organizational biases play a significant role in the policymaking process, especially during implementation. Ideology often poses the biggest barrier to unbiased formulation and implementation of health policy that truly protects and promotes the health of the population. Some policies, once implemented, may have unintended negative consequences and may need the advocacy of nurses or other groups to step in and campaign for change.

The executive branch has substantial power in the policymaking arena through executive orders, rule making, and guidance in interpretation of laws. The executive branch also has access to vast amounts of information, data, research, and recommendations from experts to guide the formulation of health policy. Whether the members of this branch choose to listen to the recommendations of experts or follow guidelines is an entirely different matter. For example, President Ronald Reagan never implemented the recommendations from the President's Commission on AIDS (Black AIDS Institute, n.d.; Presidential Commission on the Human Immunodeficiency Virus Epidemic, 1988).

Much of U.S. health policy formulation and implementation is initiated in the legislature. In a democratic society, the legislative branch is considered to be diverse, independent, impartial, and accountable to the public. Like the executive branch, the legislature has access to extensive information collection capabilities from objective resources to gather and analyze scientific data in the creation of sound policy. However, politics can still get in the way. The legislature may be dominated by one political party and ideological beliefs, such that policymaking may lack impartiality, implementation of existing policy may be blocked, and current health policy may be repealed. Moreover, legislators' decisions may be influenced by large professional organizations or special-interest groups, which may make large financial contributions to their election campaigns.

In terms of health policy on the federal level, it is important to recognize that not all health programs are assigned to the U.S. Department of Health and Human Services (DHHS) for implementation. Six major government healthcare programs provide services to about one-third of Americans: Medicare, Medicaid, the Children's Health Insurance Program (CHIP), TriCare, the Veterans Health Administration (VHA), and the Indian Health Service (IHS) program (IOM Committee on Enhancing Federal Healthcare Quality Programs, 2002). Congress can order pilot programs, demonstrations, or full implementation in any of these six programs. For example, the decision may be made to assign implementation to the Department of Defense (DOD) or the Department of Veterans Affairs (VA); if implementation is successful at this level, the hope is that the broader health community will be more willing to adopt these programs. Examples of program implementation that relate to health but are carried out by other agencies include TriCare, which is administered by the Office of the Assistant Secretary of Defense (IOM Committee, 2002), and the Supplemental Nutrition Assistance Program (SNAP—formerly known as the food stamp program), which is administered by the U.S. Department of Agriculture (Center for the Study of the Presidency and Congress Health and Medicine Program, 2012). These decisions may be very political in nature, but they are often quite strategic when positioning programs for success with implementation.

The final branch of government that affects the implementation of health policy is the judicial branch. The court system is often called on to intervene when a policy may intrude on basic human rights or when the programs or policies are not implemented according to the original intent. Challengers to implementation may have to turn to the judiciary system for resolution of their protests. While many may perceive that the court system is impartial, it is important to remember that judges in the higher courts are appointed by political figures, have no accountability to the public, hold long-term appointments, have minimal experience in scientific thinking, and rarely have any expertise in health issues. Despite these concerns, the judiciary system has contributed to health policy in the areas of reproductive rights, the right to die, and mental health.

▶ Implementation Research

The body of evidence from implementation research in health care is growing, including research that provides information about factors influencing nursing's implementation of evidence into practice. Organizations that want to make evidence-based practice (EBP) and best practice guidelines the norm in their operations need to be aware of complex and varied challenges for successful implementation. Helfrich and colleagues' (2007) conceptual framework on complex innovation implementation (adapted from Klein and Sorra, 1996) illustrates the determinants of complex innovation implementation in large organizations; healthcare organizations can improve their chances of success by using this framework. This framework can also be useful when evaluating unsuccessful policy implementation to determine whether the failure is due to poor implementation or flaws in the innovation or policy.

Conceptual Framework

Helfrich and colleagues (2007) adapted Klein and Sorra's (1996) framework for innovation implementation in the manufacturing setting to the healthcare setting. Helfrich et al. found that several factors were essential to ensure effective implementation of complex innovations. Management support that clearly emphasizes the rationale and priority for the innovation as well as allocation of adequate financial resources to support the new innovation or policy are necessary antecedents to successful implementation. The **implementation climate**—that is, the targeted users' "shared summary perceptions of the extent to which their use of a specific innovation is rewarded, supported, and expected within their organization" (Klein & Sorra, 1996, p. 1060)—is a critical factor in determining the effectiveness of the implementation. Helfrich and colleagues expanded Klein and Sorra's framework by exploring the relationship between the **innovation–values fit** (the perception that the innovation or policy is consistent with the mission and values of the organization) and the use of champions and their impact on implementation climate. They found that the implementation climate was enhanced if the innovations–values fit was strong and champions were used to promote the innovation. According to their research, a stronger implementation climate is more likely to contribute to higher **implementation effectiveness**.

Successful policy implementation on the organizational level depends on the fit between the organization and the objectives of the policies it must implement. "Fit is determined by whether (1) the organization is sympathetic to the policy's goals and objectives and (2) the organization has the necessary resources—authority, money, personnel, status or prestige, information and expertise, technology, and physical facilities and equipment to implement the policy effectively" (Longest, 2010, p. 135). When policy implementation is examined or evaluated, one question that begs discussion is the notion of what is considered acceptable compliance. Is 100% compliance realistic? If not, which measures need to be taken to get closer to an acceptable compliance rate? Who determines what is acceptable (and based on which data)? Does the policy need to be reexamined? What are the implementers doing and reporting? Is this a policy, person, or systems problem? Do the measures of success need to be reconsidered or redefined?

🔎 CASE STUDY 6-1: Training For New Computer Systems Enhances Implementation

Many health systems have been upgrading to new computer systems. If you have ever experienced this kind of change, you know that it is quite a complex process with many opportunities to derail the project.

Several years ago, a local health system implemented a computer upgrade to a new electronic medical record (EMR) system. Management and administration had been preparing for this upgrade for several years. The administration allocated the necessary resources to make the implementation a success not only financially but also in terms of increasing information technology (IT) staff and training of "superusers"

(continues)

$\mathcal{P}$ CASE STUDY 6-1: Training For New Computer Systems Enhances Implementation *(continued)*

or champions. These "superusers" were from within the organization and from every level of the organization and were given extensive training well ahead of other users.

In preparation for this change, management spent time and resources educating those working within the organization about the importance of this upgrade in achieving the mission of the organization by increasing connectivity with other health systems, maximizing reimbursement, and achieving meaningful use compliance (innovations–values fit). This pre-education enhanced the implementation climate by helping the intended users understand that the transition to an upgraded EMR was an organizational priority, thereby enhancing the implementation effectiveness. Over several months, the targeted users (nursing staff, providers, managers, front desk workers, and coding and billing personnel) were trained in preparation for the change. Target dates for the change were set, and clinic schedules were reduced to allow time for using the new system (another example of management support).

Although it was a bumpy ride, the upgrade to the new computer system, as well as the implementation effectiveness, was very successful. Others may argue that the **innovation effectiveness** (the benefit of the new computer system to the organization and ease of use) is not quite so apparent.

Discussion Points

1. Who are the champions in your organization? What qualifies them to be champions, or which qualities do they possess?
2. When your organization has implemented a major change, did it have the benefit of a strong implementation climate? Which steps did the organization take to ensure successful implementation effectiveness? What could it have changed to improve the climate and effectiveness?
3. How did your organization determine the success of the implementation of the new policy or innovation? Which measures were evaluated? Should the organization have reexamined the implementation or made the decision to change course? Why or why not?

The work of Ploeg, Davies, Edwards, Gifford, and Miller (2007) offers additional insight into the perceptions of administrators, staff, and project leaders about factors influencing implementation of nursing best practice guidelines at the individual, organizational, and environmental levels. The factors that facilitate implementation include learning about the guideline through group interactions, positive staff attitudes/beliefs, the presence of champions, support from leadership at all levels of the organization, and interprofessional teamwork and collaboration. In addition, financial support from professional associations and partnerships across agencies and sectors is important. Making changes in an incremental manner (adding to current knowledge and practice) rather than as radical breaks (totally new concepts) facilitates implementation as well (Ploeg et al., 2007).

Barriers to implementation may include negative staff attitudes and beliefs as well as limited integration of the guideline recommendations into the organizational structure and processes. The most common examples of such barriers are inadequate staffing for implementation activities such as educational sessions and lack of the recommendations' integration into the organization's policy, procedures, and documents. Time and resource constraints for implementers may include a heavy workload, being short-staffed, and feeling rushed due to the short timeline imposed by the funder. Consideration needs to be given regarding which other organizational changes might be occurring at the broader system level at the time of implementation. For example, nurses have described the difficulty of adding a practice guideline change when they were already dealing with multiple stressors in the work environment, such as short-staffing or structural renovations on a unit (Ploeg et al., 2007).

The majority of problems that interfere with policy implementation are "people problems," referring to those individuals who interact with the recipients of the policy or program. Personal attitudes and perceptions come into play during policy implementation. Nurses are often implementers and directly encounter many of the dilemmas that can occur when interacting with clients. Implementers must practice coping strategies such as negotiation and may find themselves in unforeseen circumstances or being confronted with rules that are often vague but with which they are compelled to comply. Implementers see themselves as required to interpret the policy involved in a creative but justifiable way. Sometimes they may be working with scarce resources. How often have you heard someone say, or even thought to yourself, "If they would just come down here and see how it is in the real world, they wouldn't make policies that are impossible to carry out!" When faced with these kinds of pressures, implementers may decide to alter the policy/procedure based on their perception of shortcomings in the policy. These perceptions of policy shortcomings may reflect the implementer's desire to enhance his or her professionalism, strengthen leadership, and perhaps restructure the organization (Hill & Hupe, 2002). In essence, public employees or frontline workers, often referred to as "street-level bureaucrats," function as policy decision makers because they wield considerable discretion in the day-to-day implementation of public programs or policies as they interact with the recipients of those policies (Tummers & Bekkers, 2014).

Implementing policies in ways that please everyone involved is incredibly difficult. When the results of a policy are determined to be disappointing or even worse, administrators are often quick to blame the implementers. When policymakers find out that the policy they wrote yields disappointing results, they may be inclined to take additional measures in hopes of ensuring tighter control. Both policymakers and administrators may add more (internal) rules and regulations.

The following list summarizes the key elements to be considered when making policy and examining policy implementation. Think about a policy or program you have been involved in. Did it turn out the way you thought it would or should? Were there gaps in the implementation process that affected the outcomes? Take a look at the following list and see if you identify with any of these reasons for implementation success or failure (Mazmanian & Sabatier, 1983, cited in Hill & Hupe, 2002):

1. Policy needs to be relevant, feasible, and based on sound theory with an appropriate rationale that will correctly identify the design conditions and the desired effect on the target groups.
2. Policy objectives need to be clear and consistent or, at a minimum, identify criteria for resolving goal conflicts.

3. Policy should provide the persons in charge of implementation with sufficient jurisdiction and leverage points over the target groups to help reach the desired goals.
4. Policy must maximize the likelihood that the implementing officials and target groups will have sufficient resources to comply with the policy.
5. Policy needs to be examined periodically to ensure it has ongoing support from outside and within the agency/organization and that conditions have not changed over time in a way that might affect implementation.

Policy implementation is a complex process and one in which it is almost impossible to separate policies from politics. Many political barriers arise that could potentially impede successful implementation. It is easy to understand why the U.S. public feels frustrated with government; this frustration reflects the perceived failure of government to turn promise into performance. Looking back at the list of key elements for successful implementation, think about what happens when a policy lacks clarity, such as the travel ban executive order issued by President Trump in 2017 (Perez, Brown, & Liptak, 2017). When the ban was implemented, few people within the Trump administration, much less airport officials trying to implement the policy, were clear on which countries were included in the ban, resulting in widespread confusion for travelers and airport customs officials.

The following case study illustrates how citizens negatively affected by a policy can provide feedback and advocate for change through political activism.

⌕ *CASE STUDY 6-2:* When Policy Implementation Is Rejected by Citizens: Reinstatement of the Medical Expenses Deduction on North Carolina State Income Taxes

In 2013, the North Carolina General Assembly overhauled the state's tax code, which had been in effect since the 1930s. The proposed plan eliminated several deductions from individuals' state income taxes. The initial proposal eliminated deductions for mortgage and property taxes, contributions to nonprofit organizations, medical expenses, long-term care insurance, government and private retirement income, and contributions to the NC 529 college savings plans. In an effort to offset the elimination of these deductions, the proposal increased the standard deduction for single people from $3,000 to $7,500 and for married couples filing jointly from $6,000 to $15,000. Lobbyists for realtors and nonprofit organizations were successful in persuading the legislature to keep their deductions, although mortgage and property tax deductions were limited to $20,000. Senior citizens did not have anyone lobbying on their behalf, and most of the eliminated deductions affected them.

The N.C. General Assembly's fiscal research staff forecasted that taxpayers across all categories would see some slight reduction in their tax burden. However, they also acknowledged that those 65 and older might pay more because several of the categories affected them. In contrast, the N.C. Budget and Tax Center said those taxpayers making less than $84,000 would end up paying more in taxes. The majority of citizens 65 and older are in that category.

The legislation took effect in 2014. It turned out that almost all senior citizens suffered sticker shock when they filed their 2014 state income taxes. On average, their income tax increased by $1,800. That summer, the North Carolina Continuing Care Residents Association (NorCCRA) created a legislative committee and organized a letter-writing campaign to members of the House Appropriations Committee. Because nothing could happen in the 2014 short legislative session to remedy the perceived problems, the campaign was essentially an educational piece letting legislators know that residents would be back in the 2015 session seeking to reinstate the medical expenses deduction.

Sindy Barker, chair of the newly formed statewide Legislative Committee, had retired in 2006 after spending 19 years lobbying the N.C. General Assembly on behalf of the North Carolina Nurses Association. Her knowledge of how to successfully lobby for nursing issues enabled the NorCCRA Legislative Committee to develop a systematic plan for approaching members of the 2015 General Assembly.

Questions were raised as to whether an organization that had never lobbied before could pull together a successful lobbying effort, especially when there did not appear to be much support for its issue among members of the General Assembly. In fact, when HB46, Senior Tax Deduction for Medical Expenses, was introduced, the Fiscal Research Division said the state would lose $37.9 million in revenues from this deduction in 2015 alone. That forecast escalated to $44.1 million by fiscal year 2019–2020. Moreover, this loss to state revenues assumed that the deduction was reinstated only for citizens age 65 and older.

Members of the General Assembly did understand that a high percentage of senior citizens vote, and that retired individuals also have more time to make contact with their legislators. Over the course of several months, the 20,000 residents living in continuing care retirement communities (CCRCs) in North Carolina were asked to write 650 individual letters or emails to the following legislators:

- The 15 members of the House Committee on Aging, explaining the bill and then thanking them for a favorable report
- The 74 members of the Republican Caucus
- The 42 members of the House Committee on Finance
- The 81 members of the House Appropriations Committee
- All 120 members of the House, thanking them for including the medical expense deduction in the budget
- The 50 members of the Senate, asking them to include the medical expense deduction in their version of the budget
- The 83 members of the Budget Conference Committee, asking them to support the House version of the deduction with no cap
- The 170 members of the General Assembly, thanking them for reinstating the medical deduction in the final budget

One CCRC held a letter-writing party and sent 1,761 letters in one day. Several simply put out petitions for their residents to sign and then forwarded those letters to the appropriate legislators. The typical petition contained upward of 150 signatures. Members of the General Assembly soon realized this was an issue dear to the heart of many of their regular voters.

Ms. Barker, the Legislative Committee chair, brought her husband in a wheelchair to the General Assembly when she appeared before committees, and he became the face of what "high medical expenses" look like. The issue made the

(continues)

🔍 *CASE STUDY 6-2:* When Policy Implementation Is Rejected by Citizens: Reinstatement of the Medical Expenses Deduction on North Carolina State Income Taxes *(continued)*

front page of several major state newspapers and was featured in online stories and local newscasts.

By the end of March 2015, NorCCRA had been joined in its campaign by AARP, N.C. Retired Government Employees, and organizations that represent children and adults with chronic diseases and disabilities. This coalition meant more letters, emails, and phone calls to legislators. In one week in April, they achieved more than 7,000 contacts, or approximately 40 contacts per legislator.

When the reinstatement of the medical expenses deduction was included in the House budget toward the end of May, the policy advocates were halfway home. It was not a very smooth ride, but by the middle of September, the medical expenses deduction was reinstated in the final budget passed by the General Assembly.

The reinstatement of medical expenses deduction took effect for 2015 taxes, so 2014 was the only year with the higher increase. NorCCRA conducted another survey in 2016 following income tax filing in the spring. The senior citizens' average tax bill was $1,400 less than it had been in the previous year. The other deductions that were eliminated in 2013 remain in place, but the one that clearly had the biggest impact was the medical expenses deduction. Members of the General Assembly again received thank-you letters from NorCCRA, letting them know what a difference their legislation had made.

Discussion Points

1. How can legislation with such negative consequences for a large group of citizens be prevented or stopped?
2. Using the models you have studied in this text, where did the N.C. General Assembly "go wrong" with the policy aimed at gaining more revenue from taxpayers?
3. Once the original policy to eliminate specific tax deductions was passed by the legislature, which steps in the implementation process might have prevented the backlash by citizens?
4. Why might forecasts regarding the impact of a policy be incorrect and lead to unintended consequences?
5. Were the consequences of the original legislation intended or unintended? Why or why not?

Successful implementation depends heavily on the manipulation of many variables. These variables include private agencies and groups that are often contractors for carrying out policies; the target groups themselves; public attitudes; resources; the commitment and leadership of officials; and the socioeconomic, cultural, and political conditions in the environment in which policies are supposed to operate (Palumbo, Calista, & Policy Studies Organization, 1990).

The presumption that regulations and policies are enacted according to their original intent turns out to be fallacious in many cases. The conscious or unconscious refusal to follow the policy directives can result in noncompliance, making the actual implementation process far from what the policymakers originally envisioned.

Bardach (1977), in his classic study of implementation, describes political factors and maneuvers that can impede implementation of policies and result in poor performance, escalating costs, and delays. Types of maneuvers that may derail policy implementation include **diversion of resources, deflection of goals**, and **dissipation of energies**.

Diversion of resources manifests itself in several ways. Organizations and individuals who receive government money tend to provide less in the way of exchange for services for that money. Playing the budget game is another diversion. Persons responsible for the budget do what they can to win favor in the eyes of those who have power over their funding. Incentives shaped for implementers by those who control their budgets influence what the implementers do with respect to executing policy mandates.

During the implementation phase, goals often undergo some change resulting in the second type of maneuver—deflection of goals. The change in the goals can be the result of multiple factors: (1) perception that the original goals were too ambiguous or too specific; (2) goals that were based on a weak consensus; (3) goals that were not thought out sufficiently; (4) an organization that realizes the program will impose a heavy workload; (5) a program that takes the organization into controversy; or (6) required tasks that are too difficult for the workers to perform. An agency may try to shift implementation of certain unattractive elements to different agencies. If no one wants the responsibility of taking charge of those elements, consumers get the runaround and each agency involved can claim it is not their problem (Bardach, 1977).

The third maneuver—dissipation of energy—wastes a great deal of the implementers' time. Dissipation of energy occurs when implementers avoid responsibility, defend themselves against others, and set themselves up for advantageous situations. Some may use their power to slow or stall the progress of the program until their own terms are met. This action can lead to delay, withdrawal of financial and political support, or total collapse of a program.

▶ Conclusion

Policy implementation is the stage of the policy process immediately after passage of the law. The relationships between rule making and operational activities involved with implementation are cyclical. The series of decisions and actions that occur during implementation will impact the extent to which the program goals are supported and the measurable change that occurs. In this stage, the content of the policy, and its impact on those affected, may be modified substantially or even negated. In analyzing this stage in the policymaking process, one needs to examine how, when, and where particular policies have been implemented.

Problems with policy implementation are widespread. During the implementation process, the political forces of individuals, groups, organizations, and sometimes governmental bodies are at work. These various forces may be trying to change the policy to meet their own needs and control a part of the implementation process. When the implementers are not working in concert to meet the intended legislative goals, the recipients lose. Remember, the entire nursing community and other health professionals can affect implementation in both positive and negative ways.

⌕ CASE STUDY 6-3: Using the ICD-10 Codes

The Department of Health and Human Services (DHHS) mandated that all healthcare organizations and hospitals transition from coding based on the International Classification of Diseases, 9th revision (ICD-9) to the International Classification of Diseases, 10th revision (ICD-10) by October 1, 2015 (CDC, 2015). ICD-9 codes had been the standard classification of diseases since the 1970s (Athenahealth, 2016). These codes are used in healthcare settings such as hospitals and outpatient clinics and serve many purposes. The ICD-10 codes enhance the quality of data used to aid in determination of reimbursement for services rendered, assist with the tracking of public health conditions, aid in clinical decision making, facilitate identification of fraud and abuse, improve the ability to gather data for epidemiological research, and measure outcomes of patient care (CDC, 2015). The new codes were much more specific, with the number of diagnosis codes skyrocketing from 14,025 codes to 69,823.

While the implementation of ICD-10 had been anticipated for several years, many issues still arose when the actual implementation occurred in 2015 (Weiner, 2015). First, the Centers for Medicare and Medicaid Services promised a "grace period" in which it would accept codes in the correct "family" of codes, even if they were not to the highest level of specificity (Girgis, 2015; McCarthy, 2015). Unfortunately, other insurers expected correct coding from day one, contributing to increased work from providers and coders to make sure the coding was correct. Insurance companies were not fully prepared to answer questions related to the coding issues; some websites were not available for a few days, and sometimes billers spent hours on hold with these companies. Finally, while many facilities had put time and money into the information technology side of the equation, professionally trained coders were in short supply. Delays in submitting correct coding can significantly affect timely and accurate reimbursement, so effective implementation is crucial in this situation.

▶ Discussion Points

Evaluate the feasibility of implementing an evidence-based practice, best practice guideline, meaningful use measures, or federal mandate in your work site.

1. Identify how the proposed innovation/policy will result in improved care or contribute to the sustainability of the organization.

2. List the resources, including interprofessional teams, personnel, and economic resources, you will need for implementation. Which is the best department or agency to implement your program, innovation, or policy? Who are the necessary team members/champions to facilitate successful implementation?

3. Using the Helfrich et al. (2007) conceptual framework of complex inno-
    vation implementation, think about barriers that might potentially derail
    the implementation. Which recommendations would you suggest to im-
    prove the likelihood of success with the implementation of your EBP or
    policy? How can you improve the implementation climate to enhance the
    probability of successful implementation? Who are the champions in your
    organization? Which qualities are important for a champion to possess?

References

American Nurses Association (ANA). 2017. Advocacy: Becoming more effective. Retrieved from
   http://www.nursingworld.org/MainMenuCategories/Policy-Advocacy/AdvocacyResources
   Tools

Athenahealth. (2016). What is ICD-10? Retrieved from http://www.athenahealth.com/knowledge
   -hub/icd-10/what-is-icd-10

Bardach, E. (1977). *The implementation game: What happens after a bill becomes a law.*
   Cambridge, MA: MIT Press.

Black AIDS Institute. (n.d.). 30-Year AIDS report card: Which presidents make the grade.
   Retrieved from https://www.blackaids.org/index.php?option=com_content&view=article
   &id=859:30-year-aids-report-card-which-presidents-make-the-grade&catid=87:news-2011
   &Itemid=55

Center for the Study of the Presidency and Congress Health and Medicine Program. (2012).
   SNAP to health: A fresh approach to Strengthening the Supplemental Nutrition Assistance
   Program. Retrieved from https://www.snaptohealth.org/policy-recommendations

Centers for Disease Control and Prevention (CDC). (2015). International Classification of
   Diseases, (ICD-10-CM/PCS) transition—background. Retrieved from https://www.cdc
   .gov/nchs/icd/icd10cm_pcs_background.htm

Centers for Disease Control and Prevention (CDC). (n.d.). Step by step: Evaluating violence
   and injury prevention policies: Brief 4: Evaluating policy implementation. Retrieved from
   https://www.cdc.gov/injury/pdfs/policy/Brief%204-a.pdf

Cramer, M. (2002). Factors influencing organized political participation in nursing. *Policy,
   Politics, & Nursing Practice, 3*(2), 97–107.

Girgis, L. (2015). 6 glaring and disruptive ICD-10 glitches. *Healthcare IT News.* Retrieved from
   http://www.healthcareitnews.com/news/6-glaring-disruptive-icd-10-glitches

Gostin, L. (1995). The formulation of health policy by the three branches of government. In
   R. E. Bulger, E. M. Bobby, & H. V. Fineberg (Eds.), *Society's choices: Social and ethical decision
   making in biomedicine* (pp. 335–357). Washington, DC: National Academy of Sciences.
   Retrieved from https://www.nap.edu/read/4771/chapter/17

Helfrich, C. D., Weiner, B. J., McKinney, M. M., & Minasian, L. (2007). Determinants of
   implementation effectiveness: Adapting a framework for complex innovations. *Medical
   Care Research and Review, 64*(3), 279–303.

Hill, M. J., & Hupe, P. L. (2002). *Implementing public policy: Governance in theory and in practice.*
   Thousand Oaks, CA: Sage.

Institute of Medicine (IOM). (2010). The future of nursing: Leading change, advancing health.
   Retrieved from http://www.nationalacademies.org/hmd/Reports/2010/The-Future-of
   -Nursing-Leading-Change-Advancing-Health.aspx

Institute of Medicine (IOM) Committee on Enhancing Federal Healthcare Quality Programs.
   (2002). J. Corrigan, J. Eden, & B. Smith (Eds.), *Leadership by example: Coordinating
   government roles in improving health care quality.* Washington DC: National Academy of
   Sciences. Retrieved from http://www.nap.edu/catalog/10537.html

Kennedy, E. M. (1985). Foreword. In J. J. Mason & S. W. Talbot, *Political action handbook for
   nurses* (p. xxi). Menlo Park, CA: Addison-Wesley.

Klein, K., & Sorra, J. (1996). The challenge of innovation implementation. *Academy of Management
   Review, 21*(4), 1055–1080.

Longest, B. (2010). *Health policy making in the United States* (5th ed.). Chicago, IL: Health Administration Press.

Mazmanian, D. A., & Sabatier, P. A. (1983). *Implementation and public policy*. Dallas, TX: Scott, Foresman.

McCarthy, K. (2015). 5 early problems encountered with ICD-10. Retrieved from http://www.nuemd.com/news/2015/10/09/5-early-problems-encountered-with-icd-10

Palumbo, D. J., Calista, D. J., & Policy Studies Organization. (1990). *Implementation and the policy process: Opening up the black box*. New York, NY: Greenwood Press.

Perez, E., Brown, P., & Liptak, K. (2017). Inside the confusion of the Trump executive order and travel ban. Retrieved from http://www.cnn.com/2017/01/28/politics/donald-trump-travel-ban/

Ploeg, J., Davies, B., Edwards, N., Gifford, W., & Miller, P. E. (2007). Factors influencing best-practice guideline implementation: Lessons learned from administrators, nursing staff, and project leaders. *Worldviews on Evidence-Based Nursing, 4*(4), 210–219.

Presidential Commission on the Human Immunodeficiency Virus Epidemic. (1988). Presidential Commission on the Human Immunodeficiency Virus Epidemic report. Retrieved from https://eric.ed.gov/?id=ED299531

Tummers, L., & Bekkers, V. (2014). Policy implementation, street level bureaucracy, and the importance of discretion. *Public Management Review, 16*(4), 527–547.

Weiner, L. (2015). ICD-10: Post-implementation challenges. Retrieved from http://www.health leadersmedia.com/technology/icd-10-post-implementation-challenges

CHAPTER 7

Health Policy and Social Program Evaluation

Anne Derouin

What cruel mistakes are sometimes made by benevolent men and women in matters of business about which they can know nothing and think they know a great deal.

—**Florence Nightingale**, *Notes on Nursing*

Informed consent: The process by which the treating healthcare provider discloses appropriate information to a competent patient so that the patient may make a voluntary choice to accept or refuse treatment.

Policy: A law, regulation, procedure, administrative action, incentive, or voluntary practice of governments or other institutions that generally operates at the systems level, aiming to improve the health and safety of a population.

Policy evaluation: An activity that uses principles and methods to examine the content, implementation, or impact to understand the merit, worth, and utility of a policy.

Program evaluation design: A subset of policy design, which is often left up to the responsible agency; the method selected to collect unbiased data for analysis to determine the extent to which a social program is meeting its designated goals, objectives, and outcomes and to assess the program's merit and worth. Evaluation methods may be qualitative or quantitative.

Program/outcomes evaluation: Analysis of social programs using a set of guidelines to gain an understanding of how well the policy, program, or intervention is meeting the objectives and goals set forth in the policy's design.

Theory: An idea used to design a program and its interventions and to explain and predict broad phenomena observed after data analysis.

Triple aim: A framework developed by the Institute for Healthcare Improvement that asserts health system performance will be optimized through healthcare designs that simultaneously pursue three dimensions: improving the patient experience of care (including quality and satisfaction), improving the health of populations, and reducing the per capita cost of health care.

Unintended consequences: Outcomes of evaluation that are not the ones foreseen by a purposeful action or a program or policy. These effects can be viewed as either positive ("luck" or a "windfall") or negative ("drawback" or "backfire").

▶ Introduction

This chapter highlights the process of evaluation—the critical step in all **policy** and programming that ultimately provides an informed means of feedback, improvement, and justification of resources. The primary discussion here relates to the Patient Protection and Affordable Care Act of 2010 (ACA), which has been the overarching health policy law of the United States since 2011.

We also discuss the relationship between **policy evaluation** and the healthcare quality movement in the United States, which has emerged in the recent reform era as governmental agencies required programs to plan, perform, and report performances. Evaluation has become increasingly valuable as federal, state, and local policymakers recognize that nearly every decision they make and every program they propose ultimately affects the health status of the population (Rigby & Hatch, 2016). The **health-in-all policies** approach applies to programs such as urban development, education, and transportation that are being planned, as their effects are ultimately linked to population health outcomes. Evaluation of these policies and their economic impact requires reliable and relevant policy and program evaluation data. It is critical that professional nurses are familiar with evaluation principles and can apply aspects of evaluation throughout all phases of healthcare program planning, implementation, and outcome assessment.

▶ Nurses' Role in Policy/Program Evaluation

Professional nurses, regardless of their practice setting, expertise, and level of education, are typically well versed in evaluating and analyzing the effectiveness of their assessment, planning, and implementation efforts; the foundational **theory** of the nursing process includes the critical step of evaluation. The same principles that nurses use to assess the impact and effectiveness of clinical interventions, procedures, or clinical practices can be applied to **program/outcomes evaluation** or policy evaluation. Assessing impact, effectiveness, and value in improving the health, social, and economic conditions of various stakeholders and determining the need for enhancement or improvement are essential aspects of quality healthcare policy and programming (Centers for Disease Control and Prevention [CDC], 2011; Her Majesty's Treasury, 2011). Like the nursing process, which is intended to ensure safe and effective patient care, create and facilitate excellent health professional academic and training programs, and ensure reliable research data and dissemination, qualitative and quantitative program evaluations are integral to effective policy and programming.

Two emerging themes of healthcare policy planning and evaluation over the past decade were accelerated and brought into the light by the passage of the ACA in 2010: (1) promotion and demonstration of leadership among all professional nurses and (2) an overarching goal to meet the quadruple aim. The term *quadruple aim* was coined in 2014 to highlight the four main aims of healthcare reform efforts (and evaluation thereof) that were the focus of the ACA: improved quality of patient care, reduced healthcare costs, improved population health status, and job satisfaction among healthcare workers (Bodenheimer & Sinsky, 2014). Prior to this time, evaluation of the healthcare reform policy had been termed the **triple aim**; this evaluation focused only on quality, cost savings, and effectiveness of patient care evaluations. The triple aim was expanded to the quadruple aim owing to the emerging shortage of healthcare providers, especially physicians and nurses, along with evaluation data that demonstrated dissatisfied healthcare providers had a negative impact on the triple aim goals. Along the way, the value of reliable data became clear to policymakers, healthcare providers, and the public: Rational changes cannot be made to policies and programs without such data because evaluation often is the "missing link" in the policy process. See the chapter entitled *The Impact of EHRs, Big Data, and Evidence-Informed Practice* for further discussion of big data.

Concurrently, a call for enhanced nursing leadership was highlighted in the Institute of Medicine's (IOM, 2010) landmark report, *The Future of Nursing*. The report noted that nurses were vital to the redesign of healthcare systems, needed to be viewed as partners of physicians and other healthcare providers, and needed to be "at the table" to ensure effective planning, implementation, and ongoing evaluation of healthcare policies. The IOM report prompted the proliferation of leadership training and interprofessional learning opportunities for nurses in the United States, which in turn contributed to the advancement of nurses in roles of advocacy, quality improvement, healthcare research, and innovative healthcare programming and policy planning.

As members of the largest segment of the healthcare workforce, which is currently in the midst of an evolution (or revolution), nurses have an important role in policy and program evaluation. The American Nurses Association (ANA) is the largest professional U.S. nursing organization responsible for professional advocacy and offers a *Code of Ethics*, stating that professional nurses are "responsible for . . . shaping and reshaping health care in our nation, specifically in areas of health care policy and legislation that affect accessibility, quality, and the cost of health care" (Fowler, 2010). Evaluation is a critical aspect of the efforts to reshape the U.S. healthcare system, helping all stakeholders understand the true impact of each step of the gradual process of change and helping direct and define the aims and goals for the future. Evaluation is also a critical aspect of the nursing profession, serving as the key to improving quality, safety, efficiency of clinical practice as well as assessing the impact of emerging innovations and science (Polit & Beck, 2012).

Processes of Evaluation

The process of evaluating policy and programs may be instituted informally or formally. In small clinical settings such as private practices and in rural health centers with limited resources, internal policies and programming occasionally will be evaluated informally through word of mouth, in a "water-cooler discussion" among a small group, by sharing opinions and experiences through social media, or during in-person team meetings or debriefings. As one might imagine, informal evaluation may actually be gossip: The data can be skewed, disjointed, and inaccurate, making any improvement processes ineffective. In contrast, a formal evaluation process, termed **program evaluation design**, relies on standardized strategic evaluation processes that ensure all stakeholders are involved in planning and evaluation after implementation of policy or programming. Andersen, Fagerhaug, and Beltz (2009) note that formal evaluation is the appropriate stage after policy implementation to assess effectiveness in terms of accomplishing goals and objectives. The researchers suggest policy evaluation plans should be designed to discover the short-term and long-term expected outcomes of implementation, include an explanation of how the data relative to healthcare policy will be collected, and outline a clear plan for how the results will be used.

Evaluation processes may also be considered formative or summative in nature. Formative evaluations assist program developers and stakeholders in understanding the progress throughout the development of a program, addressing concerns or **unintended consequences** and providing opportunities for improvements or enhancements in the program or policy. Summative evaluation occurs at the end point of a program (summing up the data) and seeks to determine the extent to which goals were achieved. Both types of evaluation are critical in assessing healthcare policies and invaluable for nurses to utilize and understand the policies' implications.

Evaluation of federal healthcare policies and programs was first mandated through the National Performance Review and the Government Performance and Results Act of 1993 (GPRA), updated in 2010, to focus on accountability, performance measurement, and results (Office of Management and Budget [OMB], 2011). States, because of funding matches provided by the federal government, also require that programs be evaluated.

Program evaluation follows a standard set of guidelines or a framework, with the aim being to provide information that assists others in making accurate and well-informed judgments about a program, service, policy, organization, or

TABLE 7-1 Policy and Program Evaluation Benefits

Assess effectiveness (short/long-term performance measurements)	Assess achievement of goals/aims (accountability measures)	Assess efficiency (cost–benefit relationship)	Determine impact (unintended consequences)	Establish future improvements and goals

practice (CDC, 2011). Evaluation is used to examine programs, gain an understanding of the achievement of predetermined goals and objectives, and assist in determining how human services policies and programs are solving the social problems they were designed to alleviate (Sonpal-Valias, 2009; Westat, 2010). **TABLE 7-1** highlights the overarching benefits of evaluation.

To promote a national standardized framework for evaluation of healthcare policies, the CDC (2014) designed a theoretic model, or "map," for evaluating healthcare policies and program effectiveness. Illustrated in **FIGURE 7-1**, the five-step framework guides nurses, healthcare team members, economists, politicians, scientists, and administrators in strategically planning processes for collecting and utilizing evaluation data throughout the entire policy or program development process in an effort to ensure new policies are feasible, useful, accurate, and effective.

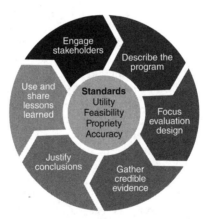

FIGURE 7-1 CDC framework for evaluation in public health.
Reproduced from Centers for Disease Control and Prevention. (2017). A framework for program evaluation. Retrieved from https://www.cdc.gov/eval/framework/

The CDC framework also offers practical guidelines for planning, implementing, and disseminating evaluation results. It highlights the value of evaluation in the context of the entire policy process as a means to promote effective changes and improvements to health care and society. Within the framework, three main types of evaluation can be systematically performed: policy content (clearly articulated goals, implementation and evaluation plans of the policy), the implementation of the policy (Was the policy implemented as planned?), and the outcome of the policy (Did the policy produce the intended outcomes or impact?).

Steps in the Evaluation Framework

The first step in the program/policy evaluation process begins as the program or policy is being planned. This step engages key stakeholders in discussions to determine their interest and degree of buy-in on the development of the proposed policy. It also seeks to establish goals, preliminary objectives, and timelines.

Step 2 is the development of a formalized process that involves identifying the person(s) responsible for each part of the process, choosing which qualitative and quantitative data will be collected (and by whom), and selecting a timeline. In Step 3, data are gathered using the determined format and analyzed to reach a conclusion. In Step 4, the evaluator tries to understand the extent of the success of the policy or programs in attaining the objectives and goals.

Step 5 involves formally sharing the data conclusions and lessons with stakeholders in the **evaluation report**, a formalized document that highlights the evaluation methods and results. The dissemination of this report is the last step in the CDC framework, and it leads to planning for the next consequential cycle of policy/program evaluation. Typically, a report of the results provides data measurements, discusses the "lessons learned" through the implementation phase of the project, and highlights objectives of the healthcare policy or program that were achieved (if the policy reached its outcomes) and next steps for improvement and sustainability.

The CDC framework for evaluation in public health is an example of a process evaluation cycle that can be continually repeated to analyze outcomes, assess program/policy effectiveness, and plan for improvements and adaptations, similar to the nurse process. At the federal level, oversight and evaluation of policies through this process occurs in the executive agencies and in the General Accounting Office, which has mandated reporting guidelines.

The process evaluation framework may be used to evaluate apparent problems or unintended effects of a policy or program. When evaluating an untoward effect, such as an unplanned budget deficit, the evaluation cycle may be called a rapid cycle quality improvement (RCQI) evaluation. Rather than occurring at planned intervals of evaluation, such as an annual report, the RCQI would be implemented expediently at the time of a problem's discovery to address an immediate concern. The RCQI does not replace the standard outcome evaluation (summative evaluation) but rather would be completed in addition to the standard cycle to address a specific concern (formative evaluation).

Another example of using both evaluation cycles would be the planned monthly, mid-year, and end-of-fiscal-year outcome evaluations undertaken by accredited healthcare facilities, which must comply with standards and criteria to maintain their funding and status (summative). If the **agency** noted a shortfall in its financial budget due to high patient readmission rates, it could also perform a RCQI to determine the patient population being readmitted and the factors associated with the problem, using the results to strategically plan to decrease the readmission rates (formative).

The formal evaluations of accredited agencies help assure the public of the agency's reliability and trustworthiness. RCQI program evaluation helps discover causes of problems and aims to address any "unexpected effects that resulted from politics surrounding a policy or the development and implementation of a policy" (Porche, 2012, p. 3).

A more complex formal evaluation process is called *policy analysis*. This process, which is commonly used by legislatures to create federal and state policies and laws, focuses on the political costs and benefits of healthcare policy reform (Harrington & Estes, 2004). Policymakers formulate their decisions (and legislative votes) for reforms based on factors such as the following:

- The proposed technical merits, costs, and benefits of the policy or program
- The potential effects of the reform policy on the political relationships among the bureaucracy, government groups (political parties), and their beneficiaries, including the potential impact on governmental stability
- The perceived severity of the problem and whether the government is in a crisis
- Pressure or support from national and international healthcare agencies and political activities or interest groups

Before federal healthcare policies or programs are proposed and approved, and funds are appropriated for their enactment, each of these factors is carefully considered by the policymakers. Results of the analysis are used to determine the extent of support for a proposed healthcare policy or program. The details of the analysis provide specific examples of the degree to which a program or policy has met its goals and objectives and, in some cases, whether the desired change has occurred. The complexity of policy analysis at the federal level often impacts state and local policies and programs, making evaluation methods and the results of healthcare reform programs difficult to interpret.

Implications of Evaluation for Healthcare Reform

Although formative and summative evaluations have provided valuable data for planning and implementing healthcare reform policies in the United States, both informal and formal evaluation processes have had a profound effect on the healthcare policy landscape over the past several years. Informal evaluation of the ACA began long before the policy became law in the United States; the nation was awash with a wide variety of opinions of and misconceptions about the ACA (also known as "Obamacare") and its probability of effectiveness and success, risks to the national landscape, costs, and various implications for the nation's citizens, economy, health, and national and state infrastructure. Both the federal and the state policy analyses included cost-benefit analysis; healthcare insurance coverage rates for children, elderly, disabled, and formerly uninsured Americans; costs of annual insurance coverage and tax benefits or penalties; and the impact on Medicare, Medicaid, and private healthcare insurance rates and costs. Monitoring health status on a national scale, within each state, and most recently at the county level was also an important aspect of evaluating effects of legislation.

As the ACA was implemented, policy analysis also included implications for national and state employment rates, risks to small-business owners, lack of medical providers to meet healthcare demands of the population, and financial impacts on state hospital and public health departments. These analyses incorporated the expertise of financial and policy stakeholders, healthcare providers, and the general public. Professional nurses were urged to engage in the evaluation process, advocate for cost transparency, campaign for patient education regarding enrollment in subsidized health insurance plans, and assist with the dissemination of accurate evaluation results. Many professional nursing organizations—such as the American Nurses Association (ANA), the National League of Nursing (NLN), the American Association of Colleges of Nurses (AACN), and the American Association of Nurse Practitioners (AANP)— provided formative data to lawmakers throughout the evaluation processes of the ACA. These groups were asked to assist with data collection and eventual dissemination of summative evaluation data through their professional communication networks, to patients, to interprofessional team members, and to other stakeholders.

Dissemination of the initial outcome analysis of the impact of the ACA began in 2014. For many reasons, including the complexity of the results, the overall impact of the policy initially proved difficult for many to clearly understand. Informal evaluation of the ACA's impact was evident in political debates, news reports, and social media. The effectiveness, value, and unintended consequences of the many aspects of the ACA vary depending on personal ideology, information sources, and geographic location.

At the time of this writing, the future of the ACA was the subject of contentious debates in Congress, where the final "repeal, replace, repair, or improve" decisions were still unknown. It is clear that informal evaluation and RCQI will continue throughout the process, but ongoing cycles of formal evaluation with summative reports have become paramount to healthcare and social policy and programming.

▶ Challenges to Effective Policy and Program Evaluation

Most challenges in program evaluation can be addressed with appropriate planning, the use of effective evaluation design, and the use of reliable or consistent indicators that can be measured using standardized methods of data collection, analysis, and reporting. Having a skilled and knowledgeable point person (a champion), a skilled analyst who is responsible for completing the evaluation, and adequate resources is key to a successful evaluation.

Conditions of program or policy evaluation that may be beyond the control of the evaluators include the rapid (or delayed) pace of policy changes, executive-branch pressure for expedient production of evaluation results, and public scrutiny of the results. Some stakeholders may be dissatisfied with the data collection or analysis methods, believe results are politically tainted, or request further data collection, analysis, or explanation of the findings. Other external factors influencing evaluation results include economic conditions of the affected communities or systems, public awareness of the policy or program, social media, and political campaigns. Policy evaluation results may be difficult to interpret when similar communities or contexts for making comparisons cannot be readily identified. As new innovations or policies are implemented and evaluated, there may be a lack of appropriate comparative data results, making it difficult to clearly understand their impact. **EXHIBIT 7-1** summarizes the challenges that policy evaluators may face.

In some situations, evaluation results can polarize communities and lead to a new focus of social or health policies that were unexpected and must be addressed

EXHIBIT 7-1 Challenges to Health Policy Evaluation

- Lack of resources to complete evaluation
- Lack of a champion
- Lack of stakeholder collaboration/buy-in
- Lack of comparative results
- Rapid pace of policy/program evolution
- Demands for early (preliminary) results
- Request for further evaluation and details
- Social media, public opinion, and campaigning

by governmental and healthcare professionals. For example, the water quality policy evaluation reports in Flint, Michigan, in 2014 showed significant health risks due to contamination of the city's water supply over a two-year period. In a policy decision to save money during the ongoing economic depression, city officials decided to change the city water source to the Flint River, which had been previously deemed unhealthy. Ongoing public health concerns by public health officials and residents living in Flint, media attention, and analysis of the water (led by a local pediatrician and research team) eventually spurred city government action. This is a recent example of the power of the national media spotlight and highlights the importance of considering a health-in-all-policy approach. The evaluation of Flint's water after the city switched its water source to the Flint River revealed that the number of children with elevated lead levels in their blood had nearly doubled. In neighborhoods with the most severe contamination problems, lead levels in children had tripled. (See the timeline here: https://www.nytimes.com/interactive/2016/01/21/us/flint-lead-water-timeline.html.)

When implementing policies or programs designed to improve the health of populations and communities, professional nurses must adopt strategies to minimize the evaluation challenges. Resources are available to guide effective evaluation and offer solutions to common challenges. When reading evaluation results and reports, carefully consider the following questions:

- Were data strategically collected, analyzed, and disseminated by a reliable research team, and is the report unbiased and complete?
- Does the evaluation answer the question, "Is this program or policy achieving the objectives and goals for which is was designed?"

Ethical Considerations

Ethical issues represent another set of challenges relevant to policy and program evaluation. The Flint water crisis is an example of an ethical dilemma that faced researchers, advocates, and policymakers when significant concerns among many stakeholders were ignored and principles of ethical conduct were violated.

To avoid conflicts and dilemmas, many professional organizations—including the American Psychological Association (2010), the American Counseling Association (2014), and the American Evaluation Association (2011)—have published ethical guidelines for evaluation. The CDC (2011) also offers guidelines to program and policy evaluators that include a brief review of ethical principles and questions that professional nurses can ask themselves when faced with an ethical challenge. The fact that these principles are specifically addressed by so many professional groups highlights both the risks and the impact of ethics related to healthcare programming and policy. The overarching themes of each guideline include the key principles of ethics: (1) Healthcare policy and programming should help people while avoiding harm, and (2) application and evaluation of programs should be fair and respectful.

These themes of beneficence, safety (nonmaleficence), autonomy, and justice resonate with nurses who are guided by the ANA Code of Ethics (ANA, 2015). Although all the included provisions are helpful in guiding the practice of professional nursing, three of the nine provisions in the Code of Ethics directly relate to the ethical principles of policy and program evaluation (**TABLE 7-2**).

The Health Insurance Portability and Accountability Act of 1996 (HIPAA) mandated privacy standards that protect participants' medical information, thereby addressing a key area of ethical concern. Most large agencies, universities, and clinical settings have established institutional review boards (IRBs) to guide safe and ethically sound evaluations. In such an evaluation, only pertinent patient information is collected during the evaluation phase, and all data are kept in a secure and private location. Evaluation data are analyzed by evaluation team members only; no outlying data or personal information is shared outside of the study team. After analysis and dissemination of results, all data are disposed of in a secure and permanent manner in accordance with federal policies governing human subject studies (**FIGURE 7-2**).

Avoiding ethical conflicts that threaten the safe implementation of programs or policies is a paramount concern, highlighting the importance of planning and thoughtful preparation for evaluation throughout all phases of a project. Conflicts and unintended ethical issues can be avoided through clear delineation of roles (who is responsible for communicating) and clear evaluation objectives (what will be communicated) related to program/policy evaluation. Disseminating results described using culturally appropriate, nonbiased jargon or terminology eliminates an ethical conflict by communicating effectively so that data can be readily interpreted by interdisciplinary professionals, patients, families, or populations.

Communication Strategies That Reduce Conflicts

Due to the complex nature of the U.S. federal, state, and local political environments, the expanse of social programs, and the ongoing quality-focused healthcare delivery revolution, difficult ethical conflicts are bound to occur. Social programs tend to engage stakeholders who range from savvy political and social leaders to healthcare workers, staff, and program recipients—and each of these parties requires an understanding of how a given program or policy is applicable to them.

Clarke (1999) suggested five strategies related to communication that can reduce conflict and ethical risks during program evaluation:

1. Identify specific cultural, political, and social environmental factors to address critical aspects of program evaluation.
2. Identify stakeholders and ensure objectives and goals of the project are established and communicated routinely and consistently to all.
3. Recognize the potential for conflicts among stakeholders and diplomatically address any contentious issues promptly.

TABLE 7-2 ANA Code of Ethics: Provisions and Applications to Policy and Program Evaluation

Code of Ethics Provision	Application to Policy and Program Evaluation
Provision 1: Respect for human dignity	▪ Risks of implementing evaluation methods can include disruption to patients' lives (sacrificing time to answer questions, travel time, lost wages), emotional distress, safety concerns, and social harm. ▪ Rules for **informed consent** are followed. Participants are clearly and sufficiently informed that an evaluation is taking place; know who will access data; know how data will be stored, shared, and safeguarded; know what the evaluation data will be used for; know whether the results will be accessible to them for review; and are offered the option to refuse.
Provision 3: Promote and advocate for and protect the rights, health, and safety of patients, individuals, family units, systems, or a community	▪ Identifies standardized nursing policies requiring ongoing evaluation. ▪ Addresses protection of patients, including sharing data inappropriately, suggesting positive or negative program outcomes without evidence, offering opinions rather than analysis and facts, negating or promoting program outcomes prior to analyzing evaluation results, and failing to protect the identity of all stakeholders.
Provision 7: Advancement of the profession through research, scholarly inquiry, professional standards development, and the generation of nursing and health policy	▪ A nurse may be both healthcare provider and program administrator and face an ethical conflict if also serving as the evaluator. ▪ A policy or program requiring intense personal investment to develop has the risk of evaluation and dissemination of results being skewed, enhanced, or altered. ▪ Establish clear, but separate, roles for the social program administrator and the evaluator. ▪ Establish clear evaluation protocols to determine which objective (rather than subjective) data will be collected. ▪ Complete a standardized evaluation analysis to avoid conflicts.

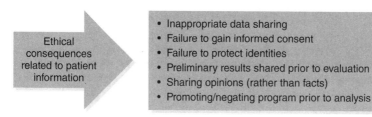

FIGURE 7-2 Ethical consequences.

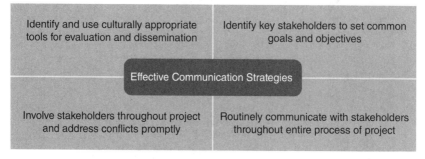

FIGURE 7-3 Effective program development communication.

4. Involve multiple stakeholders throughout the project planning, design, implementation, and dissemination of results.
5. Routinely communicate the progress of the project as it evolves through the implementation and evaluation cycles.

These strategies will be familiar to professional nurses, who typically engage in similar communication approaches when collaborating in patient care settings and with intraprofessional and interprofessional team members in clinical or academic environments. These strategies, in combination with the use of healthcare program and policy evaluation theories and the application of professional ethical guidelines, have helped elevate the value and impact of improvement efforts and outcome reporting while also diminishing ethical dilemmas. **FIGURE 7-3** summarizes effective strategies for communicating evaluation results.

▶ Conclusion

Evaluation is an invaluable component of all policy and social programs resulting from the policy process. Evaluation provides data, commentary, and critical evidence for ongoing improvement, enhancement, and effectiveness of programs. It helps policymakers, administrators, clinicians, financial stakeholders, and the general public understand what works and what needs to change to improve the health and well-being of individuals, populations, and communities. Participation of nurses in all aspects of healthcare policy and programming evaluation (planning, implementing, collecting data, and disseminating results) is vital. Given that nurses represent the largest segment of the healthcare workforce and have critical insights into the application of policies and programs, the voice and wisdom of professional nurses must be considered during all stages of evaluation. The importance of the engagement of nurses in policy and programming cannot be overemphasized in the era of healthcare reform.

When they embrace the health-in-all-policies mentality, professional nurses utilize their critical thinking and expert communications skills to consider the benefits of all programs and public policies, much in the same way they might consider the effectiveness of a nursing intervention for a patient receiving care, the implementation of a new clinic policy, or an innovative community health program. As our understanding of the breadth and impact of social determinants on the well-being of people grows, it is becoming evident that *all* social and economic policies ultimately impact population health and should be carefully considered by nurses. Evaluation, therefore, is a critical part of the ongoing cycle of health improvement and quality programming.

Program evaluation may create anxiety and a sense of vulnerability among government officials, health economists, lawmakers, bureaucrats, and other stakeholders (including nurses), but careful evaluation planning, methods of analysis, and dissemination of evaluation results can prevent conflicts, circumvent ethical dilemmas, and avoid unintended negative consequences. An example of unintended consequences can be seen in *Education Week* commentary "Good Intentions, Bad Intentions" by Robert Sternberg (2004), which addresses the many negative implications that resulted from the No Child Left Behind Act (NCLB) (PL107-110). NCLB was intended to improve the academic standards and performance of U.S. primary school students but did not effectively use stakeholder buy-in and effective evaluation planning strategies throughout the policy's implementation process. Unintended consequences of NCLB included educator dissatisfaction; claims of students, teachers, and schools cheating on tests; students dropping out of school prior to graduation; and inappropriate assessments of disabled and non-English-speaking students. Many of these consequences might have been avoided if the program developers had paid careful attention to evaluation principles and strategies.

Evaluation efforts that are carefully outlined and planned for during the early stages of the program implementation cycle can help ensure the data collected later will provide evidence that shows whether the policy or program met its intended goals and outcomes. This cycle, known as quality improvement, can be applied in either rapid/short or extended time periods across the life of programs, in healthcare innovations, and in policies to evaluate effectiveness and opportunities for improvement or enhancement.

The use of evaluation as a tool to ensure reliability and effectiveness should be perceived as an opportunity rather than as a daunting or fearsome challenge. Standardized frameworks, theories, and tools are readily available to guide effective quantitative and qualitative program evaluation methods and to ensure that reported data can be trusted as reliable and meaningful for all stakeholders. Evaluation is an essential step in policy and program development and offers lawmakers, administrators, and program planners a compass for direction in the journey toward a future characterized by improved efficiency, effectiveness, and quality of health outcomes in the United States.

Nurses historically have been under-utilized in policy planning and evaluation efforts but are increasingly being recognized as valuable members of policy and healthcare teams. Nurses are poised to participate in national, state, and local policy planning and ongoing evaluation as healthcare reform and social programming continue in the post-ACA era. As service leaders, the largest segment of the healthcare workforce, and the "hub" of all healthcare delivery systems, professional nurses are urged to use their voices, expertise, and collective power to influence all levels of healthcare systems and to support a future of positive (and measurable!) change.

▶ Discussion Points

1. List three advantages of using a theoretical framework or model to evaluate policy and social or healthcare programs.
2. Describe the impact of policy, policy evaluation, and social program evaluation on professional nursing practice.
3. What does health-in-all-policies imply? What are the implications of health-in-all-policies for professional nurses?
4. Describe common challenges to policy and program reporting and strategies to diminish the effects of these challenges.
5. Analyze potential ethical conflicts in policy and program evaluation and reporting. How can these conflicts be avoided or addressed?
6. Describe specific ways in which professional nurses can become engaged in evaluation of program and policy evaluation efforts.
7. Describe useful resources available to professional nurses who are planning a healthcare program or innovation.

🔎 CASE STUDY 7-1: Evaluating Clinical Services

A school-based health clinic (SBHC), located in an isolated region of the county, has been serving high school students from the school and surrounding community for more than 15 years through financial support from the state and a regional healthcare system. The advanced practice registered nurse (APRN) working in the clinic has provided services to more than 5,000 clients in the past years and has partnered with a number of education and health professionals to promote the benefits of the SBHC. Due to budget constraints related to the ACA, the state no longer intends to fund the SBHCs in the coming year. The APRN has been asked to address both the health system and the administrative teams to discuss closure of the clinic.

Discussion Points
1. Where should the APRN begin?
2. Which evaluation methods and data should the APRN be prepared to share with the administrative team at the health system and with policymakers?
3. Who are the stakeholders in this evaluation process, and how should they be engaged?
4. Describe some ethical considerations and role conflicts the APRN may face.
5. Which communication strategies might the APRN utilize to ensure that an effective message is shared with the stakeholders?
6. Describe possible unintended consequences (positive and negative) of the evaluation effort.
7. How can RNs and APRNs use similar evaluation data to influence the state policymakers to reinstitute funding for school clinics?

🔎 *CASE STUDY 7-2: Walk-In Versus Scheduled Appointments*

A state-funded teen clinic located in an urban setting has routinely used appointment-only visits to schedule adolescents for well-health and acute visits, including contraception counseling and treatment and screening for sexually transmitted infections. The clinic, led by an APRN, serves as a teaching site for graduate nursing and medical students and receives reimbursement for precepting students from the local professional schools. Recently, the medical school threatened to withdraw its learners from the clinic because of low patient volume, which has limited the learning experiences of the students. This threat prompted the clinic administrators to evaluate clinic usage. The analysis found that more than half of the appointments scheduled resulted in "no shows." The administrators have decided to change the clinic to a walk-in only scheduling format and have suggested using social media to promote availability.

Discussion Points

1. As the APRN working in the teen clinic, do you agree with this decision? Why or why not?
2. Describe the next steps for evaluating this proposal.
3. Which evaluation data would be important for this clinic to collect?
4. Who are the stakeholders in this scenario, and who would be essential in the evaluation process?
5. Suggest how the planned scheduling changes might be evaluated and the results disseminated.
6. Discuss ethical considerations anticipated when changing the clinics' scheduling format and the use of social media to promote enrollment.
7. Who would be most appropriate to evaluate the clinic policy, and who would pay for the evaluation?

References

American Counseling Association. (2014). *ACA code of ethics.* Alexandria, VA: Author. Retrieved from http://www.counseling.org/Resources/aca-code-of-ethics.pdf

American Evaluation Association. (2011). American Evaluation Association statement on cultural competence in evaluation. Fairhaven, MA. Retrieved from http://www.eval.org/p/cm/Id/fid=92

American Nurses Association (ANA). (2015). *Code of ethics for nurses with interpretive statements.* Washington, DC: Author. Retrieved from http://www.nursingworld.org/MainMenuCategories/EthicsStandards/CodeofEthicsforNurses/The-New-Code-of-Ethics-for-Nurses-Part-II.pdf

American Psychology Association. (2010). *Ethical principles of psychology and code of conduct.* Washington, DC: Author. Retrieved from http://www.apa.org/ethics/code/index.aspx

Andersen, B., Fagerhaug, T., & Beltz, M. (2009). *Root cause analysis and improvement in the healthcare sector: A step-by-step guide.* Milwaukee, WI: ASQ Quality Press.

Bodenheimer, T., & Sinsky, C. (2014). From triple to quadruple aim: Care of patient requires care of the providers. *Annals of Family Medicine, 12*(6), 573–476.

Centers for Disease Control and Prevention (CDC). (2011). Introduction to program evaluation for public health programs: A self-study guide. Retrieved from http://www.cdc.gov/eval/guide/CDCEvalManual.pdf

Centers for Disease Control and Prevention (CDC). (2014). Evaluation. Retrieved from https://www.cdc.gov/workplacehealthpromotion/model/evaluation/index.html

Centers for Disease Control and Prevention (CDC). (2017). A framework for program evaluation. Retrieved from https://www.cdc.gov/eval/framework/

Clarke, A. (1999). *Evaluation research: An introduction to principles, methods and practice.* London, UK: Sage.

Fowler, M. (Ed). (2010). *Guide to the Code of Ethics for Nurses.* Silver Spring, MD: American Nurses Association.

Harrington, C., & Estes, C. L. (2004). *Health policy: Crisis and reform in the U.S. health care delivery system.* Burlington, MA: Jones and Bartlett.

Her Majesty's Treasury. (2011). The magenta book: Guidance for evaluation. Retrieved from https://www.gov.uk/government/publications/the-magenta-book

Institute of Medicine (IOM). (2010). Future of nursing 2010 report. Retrieved from https://campaignforaction.org/resource/future-nursing-iom-report/

Office of Management and Budget. (2011). Government Performance and Results Act (GPRA) related materials. Retrieved from http://www.whitehouse.gov/omb/management.grpa/index-grpa

PL107-110 No Child Left Behind Act of 2001. https://www.congress.gov/bill/107th-congress/house-bill/1

Polit, D., & Beck, C. (2012). *Nursing research: Generating and assessing evidence for nursing practice.* Philadelphia, PA: Wolters Kluwer/Lippincott Williams & Wilkins.

Porche, D. (2012). *Health policy: Application for nurses and other healthcare professionals.* Burlington, MA: Jones and Bartlett.

Rigby, E., & Hatch, M. (2016). Incorporating economic policies into a health-in-all-policies agenda. *Health Affairs, 35*(11), 2044–2052.

Sonpal-Valias, N. (2009). Outcome evaluation: Definition and overview. Retrieved from http://www.acds.ca/images/webpages/evaluation/MTD_Module_1_Outcome_Evaluation_Definition_and_Overview.pdf

Sternberg, R. (2004). Good intentions bad intentions: A dozen reasons why the No Child Left Behind Act is failing our schools. *Education Week.* Retrieved from http://www.edweek.org/ew/articles/2004/10/27/09sternberg.h24.html

Westat, J. F. (2010). *The 2010 user-friendly handbook for project evaluation.* National Science Foundation Directorate for Education & Human Resources, Division of Research, Evaluation, and Communication. Arlington, VA: National Science Foundation.

Online Resources

AcademyHealth (http://www.academyhealth.org): Provides links to health services researchers in health policy and practice and fosters networking among a diverse membership.

Agency for Healthcare Research and Quality (http://www.ahrq.gov): Provides links to multiple resources. The mission of this agency is to improve the quality, safety, efficiency, and effectiveness of health care for all Americans.

American Evaluation Association (http://gsociology.icaap.org/methods/): Free resources for program evaluation and social research methods.

ANA Code of Ethics (http://nursingworld.org/DocumentVault/Ethics-1/Code-of-Ethics-for-Nurses.html): The American Nurses Association's code of ethics for nursing practice, including interpretative statements.

Centers for Disease Control and Prevention, Program Performance and Evaluation Office (http://www.cdc.gov/eval/resources/index.htm): Provides links to multiple resources for information or assistance in conducting an evaluation project.

Education Week (http://www.edweek.org/ew/index.html?intc=main-topnav): An online weekly resource that provides commentary on evaluation results and unintended consequences related to federal policy. This resource may be useful to view when considering health-in-all-policies for children, education, and communities.

Free Management Library (http://www.managementhelp.org): Developed by Authenticity Consulting. Provides extensive online resources for program evaluation and personal, professional, and organization development, including many detailed guidelines, worksheets, and more.

National Registry of Evidence-Based Programs and Practices (https://www.healthdata.gov /dataset/national-registry-evidence-based-programs-and-practices-nrepp): Focuses on mental health, but the module to develop and evaluate a program is well organized, concise, and easy to read.

National Science Foundation (http://www.nsf.gov/): An independent government agency responsible for advancing science and engineering. In this role, the NSF has developed multiple tools to use in the evaluation of programs that are applicable to a variety of programs.

United Nations World Food Programme (http://www.wfp.org/): Focuses on the United Nations' food program. The site presents links to 14 modules providing step-by-step advice on monitoring and evaluation guidelines. A useful resource to review.

CHAPTER 8

The Impact of EHRs, Big Data, and Evidence-Informed Practice

Toni Hebda

Discovery informatics: A specialty that focuses on scientific models and theories to create computer discovery of new learning with big data rather than through reliance upon human cognition.

Knowledge society: A state in which new meanings can be created from data, allowing for improvement of the human condition.

Meaningful Use: A Medicare and Medicaid incentive program that established requirements for electronic capture and submission of patient information to the Centers for Medicare and Medicaid Services.

Meta-analysis: A systematic review that summarizes the results of prior eligible studies to answer a specific research question.

Nurse informaticist: A specialist who uses nursing and other sciences to manage and communicate data, information, knowledge, and wisdom to support nurses, healthcare professionals, consumers, and other stakeholders in their decision making.

Personalized medicine: Treatment customized for the individual on the basis of his or her genetic make-up.

Population health: Initiatives that support care and reimbursement models that reward positive health outcomes.

Predictive analytics: A facet of data mining that uses extracted data to forecast trends.

▶ Introduction

As a society, we are situated at a virtual junction. Technological advances now allow us to collect, store, and manipulate huge pools of data, which can reveal previously unknown patterns to inform us, guide our decisions, and improve outcomes (Boulton, 2014). Businesses leverage technology daily to collect information on shopper preferences with each use of a preferred shopper's card, completion of a survey, or product registration; the information is then used to improve services, target specific populations, and improve efficiencies. The healthcare delivery system in the United States has begun to embrace the same types of tools used by business and industry in an attempt to achieve some of the same types of benefits (Spencer, 2016). Electronic health records (EHRs) from one organization, or from many organizations, with data in those records collected through **Meaningful Use**, represent one source of data.

Collectively, the enormity of the available data sets dwarfs the results from a single study or even a **meta-analysis**. This capability to collect large data sets (i.e., **big data**), and to manipulate and analyze those data to discover new knowledge, is exciting and consistent with our transformation from an information society to a **knowledge society** (Mehmood, Rehman, & Haider Rizvi, 2014; Ricaurte, 2016). A knowledge society exists when there is the ability to create new meanings from data, allowing for improvement of the human condition. The theoretical underpinnings for a knowledge society are attributed to the writings of Peter Drucker, a sage known for his work in management theory and knowledge work, including his classic 1985 work, *Innovation and Entrepreneurship: Practice and Principles* (Karpov, 2016; Turriago-Hoyos, Thoene, & Arjoon, 2016).

The transition to a knowledge society holds great potential to improve health care but also requires the development of new skills and responsibilities to realize those advances. Education in research methods is integral to socialization of all young people for life in a knowledge society (Karpov, 2016). As Brennan and Bakken (2015) noted, in the healthcare realm, nurses must play a pivotal role in developing and using the tools and methods associated with big data and the subsequent knowledge generated so as to influence health policies that consider healthcare consumer needs and provide for the best use of resources. This role is consistent with the American Nurses Association's Social Policy Statement. Nurse involvement is imperative to ensure that discoveries are useful for nursing.

In an effort to prepare nurses for this role, this chapter addresses the following aims:

- Provide an overview of electronic resources and their relationship to health care.
- Define and discuss big data, its significance for health care and nursing, and its uses and issues.
- Review the relationship between evidence-informed practice and big data.
- Outline initiatives that support big data.
- Examine the relationship among big data, policy, and health care.
- Discuss implications for registered nurses (RNs), advanced practice registered nurses (APRNs), and other healthcare professionals.

▶ Electronic Resources: Their Relationship to Health Care

Healthcare professionals and consumers alike have ready access to a wide variety of electronic resources that serve to expedite access to information and services. **TABLE 8-1** provides an overview of the types of available resources, while **TABLE 8-2** lists some of the many services that are available online. A critical consideration for both healthcare professionals and consumers is whether sources provide truly reliable and valid information. Government, academic, and professional organization websites are considered to be good sources, although they are not entirely free of bias. Scrutinizing a website for the sponsoring organization's mission statement, funding sources, and background information on who sits on the board of directors can sometimes reveal political bias (for more information on how to discern bias in a source, refer to the chapter entitled *An Insider's Guide to Engaging in Policy Activities*). Information with no clear authorship, date of publication or review, or evidence of subject-matter expertise for posted content should be avoided.

The process of making text, audio, and images available electronically for ease of access, processing, storage, and transmittal via computer technology is known as **digitization**. Nearly all the world's stored data have been converted to a digital format (McNeely & Hahm, 2014). In addition to increased availability and access, digitization affords new opportunities to examine collected data and is fundamental to the big data phenomena.

TABLE 8-1 Types of Electronic Resources with Some Exemplars

Type	Exemplar
Websites	Professional organizations American Nurses Association American Association of Nurse Practitioners American Medical Association American Association of Medical Colleges American Association of Colleges of Nursing
Social media	Social networking: Facebook, Google+, LinkedIn Photo sharing: Pinterest, Snapchat, Flickr, Instagram Video sharing: YouTube, Vimeo, Yahoo video, Shutterfly video Microblogging: Twitter, tumblr Blogging: WordPress, Blogger Crowdsourcing: Ishahidi, CrowdFunding Live streaming: Facebook Live, Blab, Periscope, YouTube Live
Search engines (in order of volume of users)	Google Bing Yahoo Baidu Ask AOL Search Wolfram Alpha (for computational searches) DuckDuckGo (does not retain your search histories) DogPile (uses other search engines to compile results) Others
Electronic databases	Literature PubMed/Medline CINAHL Ovid Specialty databases ClinicalTrials.gov TOXNET National Cancer Database U.S. National Library of Medicine: electronic databases and directories by alphabetical listing
Information systems	Electronic health records (vendors): Epic, Cerner, Allscripts, NextGen, Athena Health Clinical support systems Administrative systems

TABLE 8-2 Types of Services Available Electronically	
Information	Professional Political/policy Opinions Consumer health advice Comparing providers, facilities
Networking/ communication	Job searches Webinars/conferencing Document sharing Real-time patient communication (Twitter, texting) Language translation
Education	Online degrees Continuing education Libraries Personalized learning assessments
Provision of services	Manage appointments and schedules Professional license application, renewal, and verification Patient registration and history Reminders to patients Communicate with healthcare providers
Marketing	Branding Advertising Price comparisons
Maintain or view records	Access patient portal: ask questions, renew medications

▶ Big Data

The term *big data* originally referred to very large data sets (Spencer, 2016). It includes data of different types, levels of complexity, formats (structured and unstructured), and processed and unprocessed items from several sources that can be analyzed to reveal patterns, trends, and associations (Jukić, Sharma, Nestorov, & Jukić, 2015; Manerikar, 2016). The healthcare industry defines big data by its size, the ability to make sense of the data, its complexity, and the degree to which the data flow into the organization (Spencer, 2016). Big data is beyond human capability to comprehend or manage without the aid of computers (Brennan & Bakken, 2015). In many cases, it endeavors to encompass entire, complex processes (Gharabaghi & Anderson-Nathe, 2014). Healthcare professionals and health services researchers manipulate and analyze big data to provide policymakers and thought leaders with vital information.

Background

Data, information, and knowledge are valuable assets. Examination of big data internally enables an organization to identify effective processes, eliminate wasteful processes, improve products, improve customer experience, and establish a competitive advantage (Spencer, 2016). In the healthcare arena, big data provides a tool to benchmark performance against other organizations, improve patient outcomes, reform healthcare delivery, and lead to significant cost savings. In this way, big data complements traditional sources of data, such as the data obtained from the trending of vital signs for a single patient or the findings of a study; the latter data are sometimes referred to as small data because they can be analyzed by a single person (Brennan & Bakken, 2015; Sacristán & Dilla, 2015).

The ability to use big data as a tool requires an understanding of what it is, what its background and sources are, which surrounding issues are relevant, and how it can be applied to healthcare delivery and policy. Nurse informaticists, health services researchers, and **data scientists** have special expertise in these areas and can facilitate the collection, analysis, and application of knowledge gleaned from big data. A **nurse informaticist** is a specialist who integrates nursing and other sciences to "identify, define, manage, and communicate data, information, knowledge, and wisdom" (American Nurses Association [ANA], 2015, pp. 2-3) to support nurses and healthcare professionals, consumers, and other stakeholders in their decision making.

Significance for Healthcare Delivery and Policy

As Americans struggle to reform the U.S. healthcare delivery system and improve patient outcomes, scarce resources and increased demands for accountability call for informed decision making, which in turn requires data; increasingly, these data equate to big data (Gharabaghi & Anderson-Nathe, 2014; McNeely & Hahm, 2014). Big data has the potential to create approximately $300 billion annually in value in the healthcare realm (Roski, 2014). Much of that value would likely come from lower costs associated with the more effective outcomes obtained with **personalized medicine**. Additional value would come from data generated by individual healthcare consumers to tailor diagnostic and treatment decisions, educational messages to foster desired health practices, and improved **population health** analysis. Big data also supports tools for improved fraud detection and prevention.

Big Data Sources

By definition, big data is derived from multiple data sources. The list of sources discussed in this chapter is not comprehensive but does serve to acquaint the reader with a few reputable big data sources relevant to health care. Exemplars of both traditional and emerging data sources are discussed, followed by a discussion of issues related to big data.

Traditional data sets are collected with an express purpose or objectives in mind. This purpose provides direction for which data are collected, its format, and methods to safeguard integrity and security. The structure in traditional data sets is at odds with the definition for big data, but the potential of these sources to contribute to new knowledge is rich. Electronic health records and databases are two examples of traditional sources of big data.

Electronic health records (EHRs) represent one of the best sources of big data in health care today. Individual organizations commonly use data found in EHRs to track metrics such as patient outcomes, length of stay, number of sentinel incidents, and costs to support research. EHRs may offer users the opportunity to customize views of patient data for individuals or groups, access **clinical decision support** using evidence-based practice guidelines and literature, provide treatment reminders, use lockout features and alarms, and integrate the EHR with monitoring devices and other clinical systems. Integration with monitoring devices and point-of-care devices, such as glucometers or urine output, provides additional data streams for EHRs while eliminating the need to manually enter measurements such as vital signs, thereby simultaneously streamlining workflow and improving data quality. Data may also be transmitted in a real-time manner from EHRs directly into databases, also saving time and money. This approach has been demonstrated successfully on a limited basis to collect data on patients who have undergone thoracic surgery and bariatric procedures (Salati et al., 2014; Wood et al., 2012). Currently, the realization of large-scale data collection on a real-time basis for research purposes requires resolution of issues that include, but are not limited to, interoperability across different vendor platforms (Coorevits et al., 2013). Today's EHRs are composed of a mix of different data types that include text and images.

A **database** is a collection of information organized and used to provide ease of access, management, and updates to its contents. EHRs fit this basic definition because of their reliance upon database technology to house information, but EHRs' emphasis on their content rather than overall functionality leads most individuals to consider databases to be a separate entity from EHRs. A staggering amount of health-related information now exists in different databases across various settings. One example that is familiar to U.S. healthcare providers and consumers is the Hospital Consumer Assessment of Healthcare Providers and Systems (HCAHPS) survey. HCAHPS collects data on hospitalized patients' perspectives on their care experience (Centers for Medicare and Medicaid Services [CMS], n.d.). It has created a national standard that enables comparison across all participating hospitals. HCAHPS scores provide financial incentives in the form of increased or decreased Medicare reimbursement for hospitals to improve the quality of care provided; results are available to the public. Notably, hospital reimbursement from the Centers for Medicare and Medicaid Services is determined by HCAHPS ranking (Keith, Doucette, Zimbro, & Woolwine, 2015).

Other databases collect information about specific diseases, encounter information, and clinical data. Disease registries enable tracking of clinical care and outcomes for specific patient populations, such as those impacted by cancer, heart disease, trauma, infectious diseases, diabetes, or asthma. Input is accepted from multiple sources. The underlying intention in creating such a registry is to minimize fragmentation of care, identify at-risk populations, and improve care through evidence-based practices (Davis, 2016). Chronic disease registries also support evaluation of providers to ensure that they use current evidence; however, this evaluation may not include data that reflect patient choice and provider judgment.

The Healthcare Cost and Utilization Project (HCUP) maintains encounter-level information on inpatient hospital stays, emergency department visits, and ambulatory surgery in U.S. hospitals. The HCUP databases are created by the U.S. Department of Health and Human Services' Agency for Healthcare Research and Quality (AHRQ) through a federal–state–industry partnership. An excellent resource of databases and repositories is Health Services Research Information Central, which can be accessed through the HCUP website (https://www.hcup-us.ahrq.gov/databases.jsp).

The National Patient-Centered Clinical Research Network (PCORnet) supports a repository of clinical data gathered in a variety of healthcare settings, including hospitals, physician offices, and community clinics, for the purpose of conducting **comparative effectiveness research**. PCORnet collects and stores data in standardized, interoperable formats to facilitate secure sharing designed to ensure confidentiality of the data (Patient-Centered Outcomes Research Institute, 2017). *Interoperable* refers to the exchange of data and information while retaining their meaning.

Although global digitization makes it easier to create, post, and transmit information for healthcare professionals and the public, there is no mechanism in place to uniformly ensure the accuracy of information available on the Internet. Healthcare professionals recognize the potential to study data gleaned from a variety of electronic resources, including Internet searches, social media, crowdsourcing, mobile applications (apps), and body sensors; these data may serve as a valuable source of research and knowledge and learning through big data exploration.

The Internet facilitates the creation, collection, sharing, and use of information, but it can also be used to collect research information and big data. In excess of 2 billion people are connected to the Internet, with projections estimating there will be 50 billion connected devices by 2020 (Khan et al., 2014). Internet searches to find health information to aid healthcare decision making are one common use of this resource by healthcare consumers. Researchers continue to work to determine how consumers choose these websites, how many searches are performed, and which websites are visited (Song, Song, An, Hayman, & Woo, 2014; Zhang, Sun, & Kim, 2017).

Social media data have been mined to detect early signs of disease outbreaks, recruit subjects, provide interventions, and monitor population health and behavior (Kuehn, 2015; Sinnenberg et al., 2017). One specific social networking site that has been explored is Twitter, where users interact via messages limited to 140 characters. **EXHIBIT 8-1** describes features of Twitter that make it an effective source of data for disease detection and management.

In excess of 6,000 mobile apps now exist to track activity, food intake, and calories (Peek, 2015). Real-time data streams from fitness tracking apps and sensors, particularly when combined with Twitter data, might be mined to provide early warnings of emergency situations, adverse drug reactions or drug misuse,

---

EXHIBIT 8-1 Advantages of Twitter for Disease Detection and Management

- Real-time nature
- Used across the globe
- High volume of messages
- Ability to search messages for content, frequency of discussion, or response by topic
- Analysis of content as a means to predict demand for services or patient outcomes

and the development of chronic disease issues. These kinds of apps may allow public health officials, healthcare delivery systems, and individual nurses to better prepare for these events, assuming that someone is analyzing data for trends and that agency policy supports this approach (Kuehn, 2015).

Crowdsourcing is a process in which a task or problem is posed and solutions solicited, resulting in the formation of an unofficial group of individuals who are geographically dispersed and who offer their help. The PatientsLikeMe platform is a healthcare-related example, which allows patients and their families to share medical data and experiences to help others learn. This platform compiles data to answer frequently asked questions (Chiauzzi & Lowe, 2016). It can also provide insights for healthcare professionals into the patient experience. As with other forms of social media, there is no assurance of the accuracy of all posted information. Along with its potential benefits, this form of publicly available medical data presents concerns related to privacy and the possibility of discrimination, erroneous research findings, and even litigation (Hoffman, 2015).

Issues

Issues associated with big data include, but are not limited to, data quality, different data types and formats that complicate the ability to exchange data, **data governance**, barriers to sharing data, understanding results, available tools and human resources, uneven production of learning, and possible misinterpretation or misuse. Quality data are accurate, complete, consistent, clear, precise, and useful (Otto, 2015). Poor data quality can occur when, for example, fields are left blank, a wrong choice is entered, or a typing or spelling error is made. Organizations can improve poor quality data through machine methods (computer applications or software) that scrub or clean data, but correct entry from the beginning is always the best option (Vaziri, Mohsenzadeh, & Habibi, 2016). Poor-quality data negatively impacts decision making, raises information management costs, and compromises big data findings (Clarke, 2016).

At present, there is a lack of standardization in methods to share big data, along with a mix of raw and processed types and of structured and unstructured data (Copping & Li, 2016; Spencer, 2016). Structured data are typically organized into a repository or database for effective processing. Unstructured data may exhibit internal organization but do not reside in databases. Examples of unstructured data include documents, emails, and multimedia resources. The lack of data standardization can lead to lost opportunities for learning when it impacts the type and amount of data analyzed (Auffray et al., 2016).

Data governance refers to the policies, standards, processes, and controls applied to the organization's data to ensure that it is available when, where, and to whom it is needed; is usable; and is appropriately secured (Dutta, 2016). At present, the growth in new information is outpacing the ability to develop policies and technology, thereby exposing organizations to legal, financial, and organizational risks (Marbury, 2014). Data governance needs to reflect knowledgeable and appropriate use of data both within and beyond the walls of any one organization (Roski, 2014).

Big data benefits cannot be realized unless the vast amounts of diverse data are amassed and analyzed. This outcome will require sharing of data. Barriers to sharing include concerns by healthcare delivery systems that divulging information to competitors may negatively impact market share (Bordone, 2013; Roski, 2014) and an inconsistent slate of state and federal privacy laws (Habte, 2015).

There are also concerns about the ethics of the process of collecting and storing data that may be about or from vulnerable populations in the event that those data may prove useful at a future date (Gharabaghi & Anderson-Nathe, 2014).

Conventional strategies do not support big data analysis. A knowledge strategy and infrastructure, expertise, and tools are required to discover new learning and knowledge in big data (Dulin, Lovin, & Wright, 2016; Kabir & Carayannis, 2013). The late arrival of healthcare organizations to the big data phenomenon and the shortage of skilled personnel capable of dealing with this resource have placed this industry at a disadvantage for turning data first into knowledge and then into actionable results (Copping & Li, 2016; Spencer, 2016; Steinwachs, 2015). Adding to the chaos is the fact that many critics believe that the adoption of EHRs may not yield the consistent results desired by health policymakers.

The Relationship Between Evidence-Informed Practice and Big Data

The terms *evidence-informed practice (EIP)* and *evidence-based practice (EBP)* are sometimes used interchangeably but actually refer to different concepts (Melnyk & Newhouse, 2014). EBP is an approach that takes the best evidence, evidence-based theories, clinician expertise, and patient preferences and values to make decisions about patient care using a five-step process. EIP requires practitioners to be familiar with the levels of research evidence and clinical insights and to use them creatively without introducing nonscientific bias or the need to go through the five-step process of EBP (Nevo & Slonim-Nevo, 2011). EIP extends beyond evidence to incorporate other factors that influence the nurse's care decisions—namely, context and patient values (Florczak, 2017).

The demand for the best evidence leads healthcare professionals to consider options that include combining data from separate studies for a greater impact of research findings as well as analyzing big data. Combining data from separate studies requires common data elements (Cohen, Thompson, Yates, Zimmerman, & Pullen, 2015). Increasingly, big data is seen as a form of evidence either on its own or as a supplement to clinical trials and is being used to inform policy and practice decisions (de Lusignan, Crawford, & Munro, 2015; Kennedy, 2016). A learning health system captures and delivers the best available evidence to guide and support decision making (Steinwachs, 2015).

Laying the Groundwork for Big Data

Effective big data use requires a combination of policy, legislation, and a knowledge strategy, infrastructure, and skills. Health policies need clear objectives if they are to be effective (Heitmueller et al., 2014). The following questions, among others, should be considered when formulating policies for big data use:

- Which aspects of big data are relevant for health care?
- What is the intent of the policy/data use?
- Which barriers exist to achieving the objectives of the policy?
- What are the incentives to share information?

Examination of these questions will determine whether data are classified as personal, proprietary, or government-held, leading to strategies for how to link or share the appropriate types of data. Intent speaks to the ways that the data may be used. In health care, improvement of patient outcomes and reform of payments to providers constitute examples of intent. Barriers include concerns over how data will be used, privacy, loss of competitive advantage, technology issues, and user fatigue with technology, among others. Incentives revolve around building a case for data sharing as well as providing financial incentives for this practice.

The paradox is that while health policy helps to establish a framework for big data, big data also serves to inform policy. Legislation establishes requirements and incentives so that policies can be carried out. Some important exemplars of U.S. legislation and initiatives that helped to provide a framework for use of big data in the healthcare realm appear in **TABLE 8-3**. As big data use increases, legislation and professional practices will need to keep pace to ensure that data are always used appropriately and mistakes are avoided (Williamson, 2014).

TABLE 8-3 Important Legislation and Initiatives for Big Data in Health Care

Public Laws, Executive Orders, and Initiatives	Year Enacted	Major Content Related to Data
Health Insurance Portability and Accountability Act	1996	Impacts healthcare data availability. Assures a bridge for health insurance coverage for persons who have a change in employment. Requires national electronic standards for claim submission. Provisions protect the privacy of personal health information.
Medicare Improvements for Patients and Providers Act	2008	Provides financial incentives for electronic prescribing (e-prescribing), which creates digital data for analysis.
American Recovery and Reinvestment Act	2009	Economic stimulus package. Allocated funds to create jobs, boost economic growth, and increase accountability and transparency in government spending. Funded comparative effectiveness research. Created a nationwide health information network. Provided financial incentives for hospitals and physicians who adopted and began using EHRs. Strengthened HIPAA privacy and security requirements. Included Title VIII Health Information Technology for Economic and Clinical Health Act.

(continues)

TABLE 8-3 Important Legislation and Initiatives for Big Data in Health Care   *(continued)*

Public Laws, Executive Orders, and Initiatives	Year Enacted	Major Content Related to Data

Health Information Technology for Economic and Clinical Health Act	2009	Offers financial incentives to providers participating in Medicare and Medicaid for adoption of certified EHRs; ushered in widespread adoption of EHRs in the United States.
		    Goals included improvements in care and reduced disparities.
		    Increased digital data for big data purposes.

Patient Protection and Affordable Care Act	2010	With its amendment, the Health Care and Education Reconciliation Act is known as Obamacare.
		    Provides incentives for reporting provider performance; established public reporting of quality and cost metrics.
		    Increases hospital data collection and analysis.
		    Increases the ability to share data across settings.

Genetic Information Nondiscrimination Act	2008	Protects individuals from discrimination by insurers and employers based on the results of genetic information and test results, encouraging data collection and use.
Medicare Access and CHIP Reauthorization Act of 2015	2015	Reforms Medicare payments to physicians, other providers, and suppliers to reflect a value-based payment model, effective 2019. Monitors program effectiveness and reports on Medicare-eligible provider performance.
Executive order 13642: Making Open and Machine Readable the New Default for Government Information	2013	Federal government requirement to make information easy to find, access, and use. Adds to the amount of digital data available for exploration and to support decision making.
Precision Medicine Initiative	2015	Research initiative that considers individual differences in genetic makeup, environments, and lifestyles. Seeks to improve treatments for cancer, expand research, create new public–private partnerships, and infrastructure needed to expand cancer genomics.

▶ Implications for RNs, APRNs, and Other Healthcare Professionals

More than at any previous point in history, RNs, APRNs, and other healthcare professionals now have the power of knowledge gleaned from large pools of information within reach primarily through EHRs and various databases and increasingly via additional data streams from mobile technology, wearable sensors, social medial, and tracking apps. The ability to harness and use this knowledge requires awareness of the potential of big data as a new form of evidence, a plan for how it may be used, skills to understand the significance of findings, and the ability to apply the evidence and learning in practice settings. Working to obtain this level of awareness and learning will necessitate the combination of personal and professional strategies, professional accountability, and advocacy.

Nurses have experience in the traditional uses of EHRs, claims data, and public health data, and this experience provides good foundational skills to use big data. RNs, APRNs, and other healthcare professionals need to consider which data and information they would like to be able to retrieve from EHRs as evidence to better support their work and patient outcomes. As an example, it would be logical for patients rated as being at a high risk of falling to require more staff attention, but the current fall risk assessments may not provide the real-time aggregate information on increased acuity levels that is needed for safe staffing on a unit-by-unit basis or throughout the organization. This type of information would support safe staffing levels, enhance patient safety, and demonstrate the need for increased staffing (and costs) when greater numbers of at-risk patients are receiving care. APRNs concerned about the possibility of position cuts could request data that would demonstrate a link between level of staff preparation and patient outcomes. There are an infinite number of ways to apply big data from EHRs, public databases, and other data streams so as to further contribute to learning, patient safety, patient satisfaction, and lower costs.

Understanding Big Data

Nurses in practice settings need to have a grasp of big data within the context of evidence-informed practice (Brennan & Bakken, 2015). Although the concept of evidence gleaned from big data is not difficult to understand, the ability to discern patterns in big data requires expertise provided through **data science**. There is a shortage of data scientists in all fields at present, with this shortage being especially pronounced in health care. There is also a lag in the inclusion of data science into course content in formal academic programs. As with other emerging areas of competencies, all healthcare professionals must make an effort to keep abreast of ongoing developments in this area. Brennan and Bakken (2015) listed the training, roles, and activities for nurses at different levels of practice relative to data science.

Data science is "the systematic study of digital data" (National Consortium for Data Science, 2017, Para. 2). This emerging discipline incorporates techniques and theories from many areas, including **predictive analytics**, a facet of data mining that uses extracted data to forecast trends. Brennan and Bakken (2015) espoused the hope that data science will support the complex inquiries needed by nurses to understand health within day-to-day life to deliver contextually relevant interventions. Data science differs from traditional nursing inquiry, which is guided by theory that determines the data selected for analysis. Data science can also benefit from nurses' expertise in the following areas:

- Data types and sets (e.g., the Nursing Minimum Data Set)
- Defining and providing context for data sets
- Use of theories to organize variables
- Creation of interventions that can help healthcare consumers interpret the results of big data analysis
- A patient-centered approach

Another emerging specialty, known as **discovery informatics**, focuses on scientific models and theories to create computer-based discovery of new learning in big data—something that in the past has been dependent upon human cognition—with the goal of accelerating discovery and learning (Honavar, 2014).

As nurses at all levels are exposed to data science content, both baccalaureate-level and advanced practice nurses will become able to evaluate and use findings generated through data science methods; in addition, the doctoral-prepared nurse could lead research supported by data science methods (Brennan & Bakken, 2015). Nurses, however, must do even more. As knowledge workers, nurses must be involved in knowledge management (Soares, Jacobs, Bolis, Brunoro, & Sznelwar, 2012). Starting at the point of data entry, all nurses have an obligation to ensure data quality. Input of accurate data and clear, unambiguous entries provide a solid foundation for usable data later. A concrete example in which information quality is critical is family history documentation that, when well done, can predict health risks and contribute to a personalized treatment approach (Hickey, Katapodi, Coleman, Reuter-Rice, & Starkweather, 2017), Nurses can provide feedback on electronic systems design and adoption of data standards to ensure that important information is collected, available in a usable format, and available for reuse later.

Nurses should craft and implement data policies and integrate findings from big data at the point of care. The doctoral-prepared nurse should use data science methods to research nursing phenomena (Brennan & Bakken, 2015). Advanced practice registered nurses have an obligation to shape health policy to support big data and to use big data findings to influence policy and resource allocation (Kostas-Polston, Thanavaro, Arvidson, & Taub, 2015). The ANA's *Social Policy Statement* provides a moral compass on the use of big data and data science.

🔎 CASE STUDY 8-1: *Research Evidence Versus Big Data*

Your hospital's evidence-based practice council has looked at levels of traditional research and ways to incorporate evidence into care, with an emphasis on building evidence into clinical pathways used to guide care and documentation. As the APRN leading the council, you believe that the members now demonstrate a good grasp of different levels of research findings and are making excellent progress with their work to integrate evidence into practice. Your chief nursing officer, however, states that this is not enough: He expects to see the integration of findings from big data at the point of care. Council members have expressed great anxiety relative to the push to use big data findings, protesting that they have limited knowledge about big data, let alone how to make the best use of its related findings.

Discussion Points

1. As the APRN leading the council, do you agree with this decision by the chief nursing officer? Defend your position.
2. Write a one-page explanation for the council outlining the differences between data and big data.
3. Compare the use of research outcomes for a specific patient problem and the use of big data in addressing population-based health problems.
4. Which resources (e.g., people, technology) would your hospital need to use big data appropriately?
5. Describe how population-based data (e.g., pre/post-intervention data) can be used to create community-level health policy.
6. Which implications does the integration of big data findings at your facility and elsewhere have for healthcare policy development at the local, state, and national levels?

🔍 *CASE STUDY 8-2:* Implications of Using Various Data Sources

The technology committee at your medical center has been asked to look at current applications within the facility that generate data streams to determine which applications should feed into patient records. Some devices, such as glucometers and other point-of-care testing devices, automatically feed results into the patient's electronic health record. Other devices that track fitness, for example, are heavily used outside of the medical center but have not been linked with health records. As the APRN representative on the committee, you have been asked to provide your expert opinion on the integration of these additional data streams.

Discussion Points

1. Which types of body sensors, tracking devices, and applications would provide valuable information to nurses and other healthcare professionals when providing care to a patient? Discuss the pros and cons of the value of each item vis-à-vis EHRs.
2. What relationships do you see between these types of data streams and the ability to inform and shape healthcare policy in your medical center?

(continues)

🔍 *CASE STUDY 8-2:* Implications of Using Various Data Sources *(continued)*

3. Describe the relationship between the policy at your organization and the inclusion of additional data streams into electronic health records. How do individual hospitals stream their EHR data into big data sets? How does national healthcare policy support, or not support, the inclusion of additional data streams into electronic health records? Into big data findings?
4. Discuss how nurse-sensitive data can be used to create health policy at the state or national level.
5. Describe ethical and security issues involved in including patients' personal information in EHRs.
6. Create a framework or model that illustrates how the integration of multiple data streams collected from point-of-service devices can be used to inform healthcare policy.

🔍 *CASE STUDY 8-3:* Magnet Status and Big Data

Your 600-bed medical center is a Magnet facility and was one of the first healthcare delivery systems in the nation to attain Magnet recognition. Maintaining Magnet recognition is a goal for the organization that requires planning and resources. You recently joined a committee that is responsible for overseeing the process to apply for Magnet recognition.

Discussion Points

1. How can aggregate data collected from this facility be used to demonstrate the value of nursing (e.g., a correlation between nurse credentials and patient outcomes)?
2. Analyze how data obtained from all Magnet facilities in the United States can be used to influence national healthcare policy relative to the following issues:
   a. The value of nursing care
   b. Allocation of resources for specific populations
   c. Funding for further education for nurses

References

American Nurses Association (ANA). (2015). *Nursing informatics: Scope and standards of practice* (2nd ed.). Silver Spring, MD: Author.

Auffray, C., Balling, R., Barroso, I., Bencze, L., Benson, M., Bergeron, J., . . . Guo, Y. (2016). Making sense of big data in health research: Towards an EU action plan. *Genome Medicine, 8*, 1–13.

Bordone, A. (2013). Ensuring big data makes a measurable difference. *Policy & Practice, 71*(3), 32, 38.

Boulton, G. (2014). The open data imperative. *Insights: The UKSG Journal, 27*(2), 133–138.

Brennan, P. F., & Bakken, S. (2015). Nursing needs big data and big data needs nursing. *Journal of Nursing Scholarship, 47*(5), 477.

Centers for Medicare and Medicaid Services (CMS). (n.d.). The HCAHPS survey: Frequently asked questions. Retrieved from https://www.cms.gov/medicare/quality-initiatives-patient -assessment-instruments/hospitalqualityinits/downloads/hospitalhcahpsfactsheet201007.pdf

Chiauzzi, E., & Lowe, M. (2016). PatientsLikeMe: Crowdsourced patient health data as a clinical tool in psychiatry. *Psychiatric Times, 33*(9), 1.

Clarke, R. (2016). Big data, big risks. *Information Systems Journal, 26*(1), 77–90.

Cohen, M. Z., Thompson, C. B., Yates, B., Zimmerman, L., & Pullen, C. H. (2015). Implementing common data elements across studies to advance research. *Nursing Outlook, 63*(2), 181–188.

Coorevits, P., Sundgren, M., Klein, G. O., Bahr, A., Claerhout, B., Daniel, C., . . . Kalra, D. (2013). Electronic health records: New opportunities for clinical research. *Journal of Internal Medicine, 274*(6), 547–560.

Copping, R., & Li, M. (2016). The promise and challenge of big data for pharma. *Harvard Business Review Digital Articles*, 2–4.

Davis, S. P. (2016). Electronic disease registries: A new tool to manage chronic diseases. *Nursing Informatics Today, 31*(2), 4–9.

de Lusignan, S., Crawford, L., & Munro, N. (2015). Creating and using real-world evidence to answer questions about clinical effectiveness. *Journal of Innovation in Health Informatics, 22*(3), 368–373.

Drucker, P. (1985). *Innovation and entrepreneurship: Practice and principles.* Boston, MA: Butterworth Heinemann.

Dulin, M. F., Lovin, C. A., & Wright, J. A. (2016). Bringing big data to the forefront of healthcare delivery: The experience of Carolinas healthcare system. *Frontiers of Health Services Management, 32*(4), 3–14.

Dutta, A. (2016). Ensuring the quality of data in motion: The missing link in data governance. *Computer Weekly*, 1.

Florczak, K. L. (2017). Evidence or clinicians or the person. *Nursing Science Quarterly, 30*(1), 17–20.

Gharabaghi, K., & Anderson-Nathe, B. (2014). Big data for child and youth services? *Child & Youth Services, 35*(3), 193–195.

Habte, M. L. (2015). Federal and state privacy laws: Strategies for analysis of big data in healthcare. *Healthcare Informatics, 32*(1), 35–36.

Heitmueller, A., Henderson, S., Warburton, W., Elmagarmid, A., Pentland, A., & Darzi, A. (2014). Developing public policy to advance the use of big data in health care. *Health Affairs, 33*(9), 1523–1530.

Hickey, K. T., Katapodi, M. C., Coleman, B., Reuter-Rice, K., & Starkweather, A. R. (2017). Improving utilization of the family history in the electronic health record. *Journal of Nursing Scholarship, 49*(1), 80–86.

Hoffman, S. (2015). Citizen science: The law and ethics of public access to medical big data. *Berkeley Technology Law Journal, 30*(3), 1741–1806.

Honavar, V. G. (2014). The promise and potential of big data: A case for discovery informatics. *Review of Policy Research, 31*(4), 326–330.

Jukić, N., Sharma, A., Nestorov, S., & Jukić, B. (2015). Augmenting data warehouses with big data. *Information Systems Management, 32*(3), 200–209.

Kabir, N., & Carayannis, E. (2013). Big data, tacit knowledge and organizational competitiveness. *Proceedings of the International Conference on Intellectual Capital, Knowledge Management & Organizational Learning*, p. 220.

Karpov, A. O. (2016). Socialization for the knowledge society. *International Journal of Environmental & Science Education, 11*(10), 3487–3496.

Keith, J. L., Doucette, J. N., Zimbro, K., & Woolwine, D. (2015). Making an impact: Can a training program for leaders improve HCAHPS scores? *Nursing Management, 46*(3), 20–27.

Kennedy, M. A. (2016). Adaptive practice: Next generation evidence-based practice in digital environments. *Studies in Health Technology and Informatics, 225*, 417–421.

Khan, N., Yaqoob, I., Hashem, I. T., Inayat, Z., Ali, W. M., Alam, M., . . . Gani, A. (2014). Big data: Survey, technologies, opportunities, and challenges. *Scientific World Journal, 2014*, 712826.

Kostas-Polston, E. A., Thanavaro, J., Arvidson, C., & Taub, L. M. (2015). Advanced practice nursing: Shaping health through policy. *Journal of the American Association of Nurse Practitioners, 27*(1), 11–20.

Kuehn, B. M. (2015). Twitter streams fuel big data approaches to health forecasting. *Journal of the American Medical Association, 314*(19), 2010–2012.

Manerikar, S. (2016). Big data. *Aweshkar Research Journal, 21*(2), 95.

Marbury, R. (2014). Managing information in the age of digital chaos. *Public Manager, 43*(3), 60–61.

McNeely, C. L., & Hahm, J. (2014). The big (data) gang: Policy, prospects, and challenges: Big (data) bang. *Review of Policy Research, 31*(4), 304–310.

Mehmood, B., Rehman, H., & Haider Rizvi, S. H. (2014). From information society to knowledge society: The Asian perspective. *Pakistan Journal of Information Management & Libraries, 15*, 37–46.

Melnyk, B. M., & Newhouse, R. (2014). Evidence-based practice versus evidence-informed practice: A debate that could stall forward momentum in improving healthcare quality, safety, patient outcomes, and costs. *Worldviews on Evidence-Based Nursing, 11*(6), 347–349.

National Consortium for Data Science. (2017). About the National Consortium for Data Science. Retrieved from http://datascienceconsortium.org/about/

Nevo, I., & Slonim-Nevo, V. (2011). The myth of evidence-based practice: Towards evidence-informed practice. *British Journal of Social Work, 41*(6), 1176–1197.

Otto, B. (2015). Quality and value of the data resource in large enterprises. *Information Systems Management, 32*(3), 234–251.

Patient-Centered Outcomes Research Institute. (2017). PCORnet: The National Patient-Centered Clinical Research Network. Retrieved from http://www.pcori.org/research-results/pcornet-national-patient-centered-clinical-research-network

Peek, H. (2015). Harnessing social media and mobile apps for mental health. *Psychiatric Times, 32*(3), 1–4.

Ricaurte, P. (2016). Pedagogies for the open knowledge society. *International Journal of Educational Technology in Higher Education, 13*(1), 1–10.

Roski, J. (2014). Creating value in health care through big data: Opportunities and policy implications. *Medical Benefits, 31*(15), 5–6.

Sacristán, J. A., & Dilla, T. (2015). No big data without small data: Learning health care systems begin and end with the individual patient. *Journal of Evaluation in Clinical Practice, 21*(6), 1014–1017.

Salati, M., Pompili, C., Refai, M., Xiumè, F., Sabbatini, A., & Brunelli, A. (2014). Real-time database drawn from an electronic health record for a thoracic surgery unit: High-quality clinical data saving time and human resources. *European Journal of Cardio-Thoracic Surgery, 45*(6), 1017–1019.

Sinnenberg, L., Buttenheim, A. M., Padrez, K., Mancheno, C., Ungar, L., & Merchant, R. M. (2017). Twitter as a tool for health research: A systematic review. *American Journal of Public Health, 107*(1), e1–e8.

Soares, M. M., Jacobs, K., Bolis, I., Brunoro, C., & Sznelwar, L. I. (2012). The worker's role in knowledge management and sustainability policies. *Work, 41*, 2713–2720.

Song, T. M., Song, J., An, J., Hayman, L. L., & Woo, J. (2014). Psychological and social factors affecting Internet searches on suicide in Korea: A big data analysis of Google search trends. *Yonsei Medical Journal, 55*(1), 254–263.

Spencer, G. A. (2016). Big data: More than just big and more than just data. *Frontiers of Health Services Management, 32*(4), 27–33.

Steinwachs, D. (2015). Transforming public health systems: Using data to drive organizational capacity for quality improvement and efficiency. *Frontiers in Public Health Services & Systems Research, 4*(2), 1–12.

Turriago-Hoyos, A., Thoene, U., & Arjoon, S. (2016, January–March). Knowledge workers and virtues in Peter Drucker's management theory. *Sage Open*, 1–9.

Vaziri, R., Mohsenzadeh, M., & Habibi, J. (2016). TBDQ: A pragmatic task-based method to data quality assessment and improvement. *PloS One, 11*(5), 1–30.

Williamson, A. (2014). Big data and the implications for government. *Legal Information Management, 14*(4), 253–257.

Wood, G. C., Xin, C., Manney, C., Strodel, W., Petrick, A., Gabrielsen, J., . . . Gerhard, G. S. (2012). An electronic health record-enabled obesity database. *BMC Medical Informatics & Decision Making, 12*(1), 45–52.

Zhang, Y., Sun, Y., & Kim, Y. (2017). The influence of individual differences on consumers' selection of online sources for health information. *Computers in Human Behavior, 67*, 303–312.

CHAPTER 9

Interprofessional Practice

J. D. Polk and Patrick H. DeLeon

▶ Introduction

The United States entered the 21st century with a fragmented "sick care" delivery system rather than a well-designed system for maintaining health and wellness. Despite well-intended laws, rules, and regulations, the country faced ongoing issues with access to care, quality and safety of care, and costs of care spiraling upward faster than the economy at large was growing. Paul Starr's seminal works, *The Social Transformation of American Medicine* (1982) and *Remedy and Reaction: The Peculiar American Struggle Over Health Reform* (2011), chronicle the incentives, traditions, culture of thought, laws, and policies that led to the fragmentation of care we continue to experience today. Nongovernmental organizations, thought leaders, health services researchers, and policymakers recognize the importance of an "all hands on deck" approach to reforming the health system. One approach calls for greater collaboration in education, practice, and research among health professionals.

This chapter provides examples from the perspectives of two distinguished thought leaders regarding interprofessional collaboration to achieve reform in the healthcare delivery system. The editors hope that the examples shared by these professionals will inspire all who read this text and who work as healthcare professionals to seek collaboration with their colleagues to transform the healthcare system in the United States.

If the U.S. healthcare system is to be transformed, not just reorganized, all of us must set aside old biases and habits so that educators, researchers, organizations, government, and health systems can move forward together in conceiving, writing, implementing, and evaluating public policy. The patient will be the ultimate benefactor.

References

Starr, P. (1982). *The social transformation of American medicine.* New York, NY: Basic Books.

Starr, P. (2011). *Remedy and reaction: The peculiar American struggle over health reform.* New Haven, CT: Yale University Press.

***

THE EVOLVING INTERPROFESSIONAL UNIVERSE

J. D. Polk

KEY TERM

Crowdsourcing: Convening professionals from many disciplines to focus on a problem by means of innovative tactics.

▶ What Is Interprofessional Collaboration?

By the time you read this chapter, the definition of interprofessional education (IPE) will have evolved. In the early days of IPE, the purpose was to show that healthcare providers other than the physician were just as important to the outcomes of the patient. Many would say that IPE was focused on teaching physicians that they were no longer in charge. This concept has since evolved into something that looks more at all the healthcare providers working as a team toward the end goal of better health outcomes for the patient (Aston et al., 2012).

Even this definition of IPE is too narrow, however. Technology, connectedness, and the changing landscape of medicine necessitate that healthcare policy take into account care by many different levels of practitioners, patient self-care, and multiple entry points of the patient into a virtual healthcare system. Technology drives the access to and usability of information in relation to patient outcomes to such a degree that IPE and the collaboration of many partners has no bounds and will continue to evolve and expand. For example, at the National Aeronautics and Space Administration (NASA), the astronaut patients may perform tests on themselves, such as an exam with an ophthalmoscope. Exam results are then transferred by satellite to the flight surgeon console. Biomedical engineers, ultrasound technicians, and nurses may interact with those data and the evaluation process. A second opinion may be obtained by sending the data across to a tertiary care center. For a cosmonaut, the data would be sent to Russia for Russian medical experts to evaluate. The astronaut is traveling at 17,500 miles per hour and is 230 nautical miles above the Earth. The data have passed through two satellites and crossed numerous countries. Interprofessional collaboration for that one exam required the astronaut patient, engineers, satellite experts, biomedical engineer, nurses, ultrasound technicians, flight surgeons, and ophthalmologists to all collaborate across numerous boundaries. NASA's health policy must take into account the technology, the international politics, and the patient.

▶ Core Attributes of Interprofessional Education

The need for and value of interprofessional education are not new concepts; IPE has been around for several decades. The World Health Organization put forward the idea of including IPE in medical education around the world in 1978, knowing that not all communities have physicians or access to quality medical care, and that the care and outcome of the patient depend on many caregivers, especially in developing countries.

The Institute of Medicine (now the National Academy of Medicine) soon followed with recommendations on incorporating IPE into medical education in its 2000 report, *To Err Is Human: Building a Safer Health System*, and in its 2003 report, *Health Professions Education: A Bridge to Quality*. Much of the current IPE movement has centered on increasing quality through teaming. Despite the United States being at the top of the scale in terms of healthcare spending, U.S. patient care outcomes are still woefully behind those in many other countries that do a better job in regard to that team-based approach.

The core attributes that constitute interprofessional education vary depending on the institution and authorship. Many of the publications from the Health Resources and Services Administration (HRSA) and the National Academy of Medicine (NAM) have focused on the need to have physician assistants, nurses, and advanced practice registered nurses fill the void that has arisen due to a physician shortage in primary care, on acceptance of nonphysician providers, and on the perceived inflection point that the Patient Protection and Affordable Care Act (ACA) requires more primary care providers. But even that goal is too narrow and not quite holistic enough. Indeed, all the various incarnations and articles describing an attribute or core educational component can be boiled down to one succinct statement and goal: to teach all healthcare providers to partner and utilize any and all resources available, both medical and nonmedical, to bring about a sustained positive outcome for the patient.

Health policy can be used as an instrument to incentivize collaboration and teamwork where none previously existed. For example, after a medical error occurs, a hospital or health system could have a policy that an interdisciplinary investigative team will be used to assess where issues occurred and make recommendations for correction or improvement. Such a team would take a holistic approach, looking at all facets and disciplines that interacted with the patient.

One of the highest-risk areas in patient care is the hand-off of the patient from one caregiver or discipline to another. Typically, nursing staff hand off patients to nursing staff, physicians hand off patients to physicians, and therapists hand off patients to therapists during a shift change or after a procedure to the recovery team. As an alternative to this series of hand-offs, a hospital or health system could implement a policy whereby there was also an interdisciplinary team hand-off. Gordon and Findley (2011) discovered there is a paucity of studies related to hand-offs completed in an interdisciplinary manner, and education focusing on hand-offs is severely lacking. This is one area in which IPE training and health policy can make a difference not just in improving outcomes but also in decreasing risk. Case Studies 9-1 and 9-2 exemplify this holistic concept and illustrate why we need to broaden our vision of IPE.

🔎 CASE STUDY 9-1: Implications of the Effects of Weightlessness in Space on Health Policy

A retired 62-year-old astronaut has just fractured his hip after taking a fall while playing tennis. The astronaut is currently being worked up in the emergency department, and the orthopedic surgeon is on his way. A NASA flight surgeon calls the attending physician in the emergency department and advises her that, although the patient is retired from NASA, the fracture may be related to the astronaut's spaceflight experience and bone density loss as a result of spending six months on the International Space Station, thus making this injury potentially work related. He also advises that the surgical procedure, rehabilitation, and forward plan may need to be revised secondary to this occupational exposure. With regard to the surgical procedure, although most young patients with hip fractures have uncemented prosthetics, this patient may need a cemented prosthetic due to loss of trabecular bone as a result of the microgravity of spaceflight. The emergency physician has asked you as the nurse manager in the emergency department to coordinate the interactions and inputs of all the caregivers at the hospital, the patient and family, and NASA.

Discussion Points

1. Assess all the potential policy implications for this collaborative team. How will the team share information from a government healthcare entity (NASA) and the hospital? Whose policies regarding electronic health records, the Health Information Portability and Accountability Act, and information sharing will take precedence? How will the team members impart the knowledge of the physiological changes from spaceflight to the surgery, nursing, and physical therapy staff so they can devise the proper plans? How can this scenario be made into an interprofessional plan?
2. Discuss the implications of this patient's injury potentially being related to a work experience in the remote past. Are there health policy or payment implications? If so, who else should be included in an expanded team (e.g., social worker, government relations personnel)?
3. NASA is governed by specific legislation related to health policy concerning the care of astronauts. Who should be liaisons with NASA, and how should communication be coordinated with the care providers, risk management, and administration at your facility?

🔎 CASE STUDY 9-2: Reframing Treatment Options Within a Policy Context

Continuing with the scenario described in Case Study 9-1, a partnership and intercollaborative agreement must be forged between NASA, the healthcare providers and their individual specialty groups, and the hospital. NASA would have the responsibility of educating the providers about the implications of specific changes related to the care of astronaut patients, such as the potential need for a cemented hip. Signed agreements, to include the patient's informed consent, would need to be written in regard to records transfer and private information conveyance, as well as payment method.

Discussion Points

1. Which kinds of operational policies might a hospital need for such specialized cases?
2. Which types of partnerships with government and perhaps private entities (commercial spaceflight organizations) might enable members to collaborate and exchange information quickly?
3. How should NASA work with policymakers to obtain specific legislation regarding astronaut health care? Why might this issue be important to NASA before the agency embarks on further long-distance human exploration journeys?
4. If you were a NASA healthcare provider, what research could you bring to or interpret for a policymaker that would help the policymaker sell the idea to his or her colleagues?
5. Would it be better for NASA to brief all the different practitioners independently or together? What are the advantages of an interprofessional educational briefing in this case?

IPE is about more than having the pharmacist, nutritional counselor, physician assistant, nurse practitioner, and physician work as a team. It is about utilizing every potential resource to bring about positive change in healthcare outcomes (U.S. Department of Health and Human Services, 2014).

▶ The "Team 4" Concept

NASA is known for being innovative and collaborative but also pretty smart. Its employees are, after all, rocket scientists! In addition, the agency has developed a concept that aligns very well with IPE.

Many readers will have seen or recall the movie *Apollo 13*, starring Tom Hanks (Howard, 1995). In one scene in the movie, the scientists at the NASA Space Center need to build a carbon dioxide scrubber, or at least alter the interface for it, so as to lower the carbon dioxide (CO_2) level in the vehicle. The engineer on the ground puts all the equipment that is currently on board the spacecraft on the table and states, "We need to make this fit into this . . . using only these" (Howard, 1995). You might think that scene was a Hollywood invention meant to dramatize the movie; in reality, it is what actually occurred. Beyond that example, NASA has developed a concept of teamwork that can serve as a potential example for IPE. Typically, for any space mission, there are three shifts or teams in the flight control room. In addition, NASA has a "Team 4": a group of people from nearly every discipline who get together to solve a problem that develops during a mission. The members of Team 4 are not just engineers; instead, the team is collaborative, cross-cultural, and cross-disciplinary.

For example, on one mission, one of the lights on the side of an astronaut's helmet had a fractured bracket. The light would not stay on the side of the helmet. The light was essential for conducting "space walks." The ground team got together to figure out which method they could use to affix the light to the helmet. Whatever solution they used had to withstand the vast 200°F temperature variations between light and dark in space, as well as the vacuum of space. The team developed a unique solution to this problem: It recommended that the astronauts use dental cement, like that typically used in the emergency department after a tooth fracture. The medical kit on board the spacecraft contained this cement just in case an astronaut suffered a tooth fracture in orbit. The cement withstands hot and cold temperatures and is not bothered by the vacuum of space. The cement was used to adhere the light bracket to the helmet, and it worked perfectly (Simpson, 2007).

In another example, the thermal blanket that protects the space shuttle from extreme heat had become torn on entry. It was feared that this tear would allow superhot gases to encroach on the vehicle during reentry, with catastrophic consequences. The Team 4 solution was less about engineering than it was about simple patient care. Specifically, the astronauts were coached to perform a two-layer closure using skin staples and sutures to repair the blanket on the exterior of the space lab, not unlike a surgeon would close a wound.

The ideas and "solvers" for solutions sometimes come from unlikely sources, and NASA's Team 4 concept recognizes this reality. No idea is dismissed out of hand, and very often the solution comes from an unlikely source. Indeed, in the two examples cited here, the ideas came from the medical community and medical kits, not from engineering.

NASA also uses collaborative approaches when crafting health policy to incentivize IPE and holistic approaches. For example, a healthcare policy created the Johnson Space Center's Human System Risk Board and defined its function. This interdisciplinary board is made up of researchers, biomedical engineers, scientists, flight surgeons, and healthcare providers, and its primary function is identifying, quantifying, and prioritizing human-centered risk in spaceflight. Each discipline brings its individual expertise to the table, and every contribution from each discipline is weighed in a holistic manner to assess and manage risks related to the human system in the endeavor of spaceflight.

An astronaut on a spacewalk. Note the light affixed to the helmet by dental cement.

Photo courtesy of NASA.

What can we learn from NASA about teaming? In health care, we tend to think of IPE as the physician, pharmacist, nurse, nurse practitioner, and physician assistant all getting along and working cohesively. NASA, however, would say we were still thinking much too narrowly.

The business of innovation has taken a cue from NASA. InnoCentive (n.d.) is a private company that focuses on **crowdsourcing** problems and challenges for customers using a worldwide network of solvers from many different walks of life, professions, and specialties in a host of countries (Allio, 2004). Rather than sending out a chemistry problem to only chemists, the problem or challenge is crowdsourced to a host of many different solvers. Sometimes—in fact, often—the answer comes from outside the specialty that would normally be looking at the problem. For example, an engineer who specializes in fluid mechanics might look at a problem much differently than the typical chemist would. He or she might offer a solution upon seeing similarities in the fluid mechanics world or work that the chemist would not have imagined. In 2007, InnoCentive helped the Oil Spill Recovery Institute post three challenges that all dealt with oil spill recovery issues. Who solved the first of the three challenges? The source of the solution was not someone from the oil industry but rather someone from the concrete industry, who looked at the problem in a whole new light.

🔍 CASE STUDY 9-3: *Innovation and IPE in a Chilean Mine*

The Chilean government took IPE to a whole new level after the collapse of one of its gold and copper mines trapped 33 miners 2,400 feet below ground in solid rock. The miners were trapped after 600,000 tons of rock collapsed in the 100-year-old mine in Copiapo, Chile. After 17 days of using a small drill to poke a hole into the caverns to see if the miners were alive or if they had perished, the miners were found alive. The movie *The 33* (2015), starring Antonio Banderas, captures the many problems encountered by rescuers.

The Chilean government did something that most governments would never think of doing: it crowdsourced solutions and collaborated with multiple countries, industries, and teams to achieve the desired outcome. Government officials threw off the cloak of bureaucracy, streamlined and flattened the leadership chain, and began an odyssey of interprofessional collaboration that was unmatched and never seen before in this type of problem and rescue. They invited NASA to participate and advise them, because the space program is well versed in the challenges of keeping people alive in enclosed spaces for prolonged periods of time and is also known for its great engineering prowess. The government invited the Chilean Navy, miners and drillers from every specialty, and members of a host of medical professions (including this author) to help them problem-solve the issues and complex problems related to feeding the miners, treating them for their ailments, drilling to rescue them, developing new drilling techniques, developing a rescue capsule, and inventing never-before-seen or -used procedures toward the successful rescue.

(continues)

🔍 *CASE STUDY 9-3:* *Innovation and IPE in a Chilean Mine* *(continued)*

Until their rescue, no miners had ever survived a collapse of this magnitude, so deep within the Earth, for so long a period. Multinational, multidisciplinary teams would bounce ideas off one another, and the Chilean leadership would implement those ideas that they felt were the most promising. What was the result of their interprofessional collaboration? All 33 miners were rescued 69 days into their ordeal as the world watched.

Dr. J. D. Polk (center) at a team meeting among engineers, miners, physicians, and drilling experts from three different countries, the Chilean Navy, and NASA.

Photo courtesy of J. D. Polk.

Discussion Points

1. Which resources would you need when team members speak various languages?
2. What are the implications of a team composed of people from different cultures who are addressing a crisis such as the one described in this case study?
3. Which health resources would you assemble in anticipation of bringing the miners to the surface or of resolving the crisis at hand?
4. What are the health policy implications of having many different practitioners from many different countries giving medical advice?
5. Which health policy considerations and actions do you think the country of Chile had to take into consideration, especially considering the international and interprofessional aspects of the situation?

▶ The Future of IPE and Interprofessional Collaboration

Prior to 1967, there were no physician assistants, and prior to 1965, there were no nurse practitioners. The healthcare field has grown in leaps and bounds since those years, and the need for multiple layers of care and multiple team members to care for the many facets of a patient's needs to guarantee a positive outcome has long been recognized. Clearly, though, the ability to create positive patient outcomes in the future may rely on more than the current subset of medical practitioners. It will require integration with public health, with industry, and with the private sector and will touch almost everything and everyone with whom the patient interacts on some level. Technology will radically change how health care is delivered, especially in regard to where patients get their information (Interprofessional Education Collaborative Expert Panel, 2011).

Today, most patients have surfed the web thoroughly before presenting to their caregiver's office. Imagine a vending machine in the future that recognizes that the customer has diabetes based on a bracelet worn, or some other method, and suggests healthy choices tailored to the customer. Imagine point-of-care testing at home to test for a *Streptococcus* infection. Technology will change how the patient interacts with the healthcare provider. It may also serve to connect and allow many disciplines to collaborate and crowdsource what is best for the patient. A nurse practitioner in a rural area can get a virtual consultation from a specialist in a major city without much difficulty, and the idea of the patient always having to go to a tertiary care center to get specialized care will become a thing of the past.

References

Allio, R. J. (2004). CEO interview: The InnoCentive model of open innovation. *Strategy and Leadership, 32*(4), 4–9.

Aston, S. J., Rheault, W., Arenson, C., Tappert, S. K., Stoecker, J., Orzoff, J., . . . Mackintosh, S. (2012). Interprofessional education: A review and analysis of programs from three academic health centers. *Academic Medicine, 87*(7), 949–955.

Gordon, M., & Findley, R. (2011). Educational interventions to improve handover in healthcare: A systematic review. *Medical Education, 45*(11), 1081–1089.

Howard, R. (1995). *Apollo 13* [Motion picture]. United States: Imagine Entertainment, distributed by Universal Pictures.

InnoCentive. (n.d.). *About us*. Retrieved from https://www.innocentive.com/about-innocentive

Institute of Medicine. (2000). *To err is human: Building a safer health system*. Washington, DC: National Academy Press.

Institute of Medicine. (2003). *Health professions education: A bridge to quality*. Washington, DC: National Academy of Sciences.

Interprofessional Education Collaborative Expert Panel. (2011). *Core competencies for interprofessional collaborative practice: Report of an expert panel*. Washington, DC: Author.

Simpson, C. (2007). Atlantis completes spectacular mission. *Spaceflight, 49*(8), 293.

U.S. Department of Health and Human Services, Agency for Healthcare Research and Quality. (2014). *TeamSTEPPS®: National implementation*. Retrieved from http://teamstepps.ahrq.gov

World Health Organization. (1978). *Alma-Ata 1978: Primary health care, report of the International Conference on Primary Health Care. 6–12 September 1978; Alma-Ata, USSR.* Geneva, Switzerland: Author.

***

INTERPROFESSIONAL COLLABORATION TO INFLUENCE POLICY

Patrick H. DeLeon

The views expressed are those of the author and do not reflect the official policy or position of the Uniformed Services University of the Health Sciences, the Department of Defense, or the United States Government.

I want to acknowledge the assistance of 1st Lt. Rachael Antone, BSN, a graduate student in nursing at the Uniformed Services University of the Health Sciences.

KEY TERM

Societal need: A gap or lack in a service in a population that creates a hardship for that population.

▶ Bipartisan–Bicameral Action

When observing the creation of far-reaching and exciting programmatic initiatives (whether they are administratively or legislatively accomplished) at the state or federal level, those interested in the public policy (i.e., political) process should strive to recognize the ongoing interaction of certain underlying principles that are essential for lasting success. Perhaps the most important principle is addressing a substantive **societal need** in a manner in which other equally competent concerned individuals had previously not contemplated. Over the years, we have learned that this kind of effort requires vision, persistence, and presence. It is often necessary to remind oneself that seeking perfection can be the enemy of the possible. Substantive change always takes time—and frequently longer than one would initially expect.

In 1984, President Ronald Reagan signed into law the Preventive Health Amendments of 1984 (P.L. 98-555), which established a new program entitled the Emergency Medical Services for Children (ESMC) initiative. Funding was authorized at $2 million for fiscal year 1985 and for each of the two succeeding fiscal years. From the beginning, this was to be a pilot (or demonstration) project that would *not* be expansive in nature. The legislation's prime sponsors were U.S. Senators Daniel K. Inouye (Democrat–Hawaii) and Orrin G. Hatch (Republican–Utah). At the time, Senator Hatch was chairman of what today is the Senate Health, Education, Labor, and Pensions (HELP) Committee (i.e., the authorization committee).

At the 10th anniversary of this legislation, Dr. C. Everett Koop opined:

I am pleased to remember that in 1984, while I was U.S. Surgeon General, the United States Congress passed legislation to improve emergency medical services for children (EMSC). It received my full support and that of many of my colleagues, because critically ill and injured children were not receiving the same high quality of emergency health care we provided for adults. But this is not unusual; throughout history children have not been our first priority. The 1984 EMSC legislation, cosponsored by Senators Inouye and Hatch, was a step toward reversing this trend. This year, 1995, represents a milestone. It has been 10 years since the first four state grants were funded. Since then, 36 more states, the District of Columbia, and Puerto Rico have received grants. I believe it is one of the most effective investments we have ever made. These grant monies have reached across the nation, and have begun the building of an infrastructure for integrating children into the Emergency Medical Services (EMS) systems of 40 states.... [I]n 1984 there was virtually no pediatric emergency interest. (Feely & Athey, 1995, p. ix)

EMSC addressed a real and substantive societal need. Nearly a decade after its creation, the Institute of Medicine (IOM) still reported:

Each year, injury alone claims more lives of children between the ages of 1 and 19 than do all forms of illness.... Overall, some 21,000 children and young people under the age of 20 died from injuries in 1988.... When prevention fails, families should have access to timely care by trained personnel within a well-organized emergency medical services (EMS) system.... For too many children and their families, however, these resources have not been available when they were needed. Although EMS systems and hospital EDs are widely assumed to be equally capable of caring for children and adults, this is not true. In many EMS systems, children's needs have been overlooked.... Care for seriously ill and injured children cannot presume that they are simply "little adults."... Attempts to ensure that children receive adequate emergency medical care are a recent development in the field of EMS. (IOM, 1993, pp. 1–3, 22)

The leadership of the EMSC program emphasized a data-driven and evidence-based orientation for improving the quality of care available to injured children and their families. Their approach envisioned encouraging EMSC to become an integrated component of the nation's overall emergency medical system (EMS). Ultimately, they succeeded in building the necessary capacity (including clinical training, treatment guidelines, and data collection ability) in all states, the District of Columbia, and the territories and freely associated states. Pediatric EMS was no longer an afterthought. Along with an impressive local hands-on orientation, there evolved a visionary national perspective. Although support for the adult EMS system (especially under the prevailing block-grant approach) was in a constant state of ebb and flow, a steady (and increasing) funding for EMSC actually provided a base for both the pediatric and the adult federal emergency medical efforts for a number of years, especially for the expansion of regionalized (multistate, tribal-state) systems of care.

The needs of rural America were especially acute, as was the catalytic impact of having identified advocates at all levels of policy development. Developing a regionalized system of pediatric care, as well as exploring necessary changes in the prehospital and emergency department settings, became a national priority. Systemic efforts were made to target federal research support for investigators who focused on high-volume child-specific injuries (e.g., those most likely to be incurred while playing sports, such as head trauma), unusual adverse drug reactions, issues relevant to school personnel responsibilities when natural disasters occur (e.g., training for school nurses and teachers' aides), and dealing with families' emotional trauma of experiencing the death of a loved one. From a historical perspective, one must appreciate that previous experience would strongly suggest that each of these issues, no matter how remarkable in retrospect the research findings might appear, would undoubtedly have remained a low priority for funding without the continued voice of EMSC advocates.

In many ways, the longevity of the EMSC program is particularly impressive and reflects the ongoing collaboration between congressional and administration staff, regardless of their political affiliation. Both Republicans and Democrats agreed that the core issue was child health. Senator Inouye, who was one of the program's prime sponsors while serving on the Senate Appropriations Committee, died in 2012; Senator Hatch still serves in the U.S. Senate. These two leaders worked "across the aisle" for a common purpose.

From the beginning, those administering the program within the Department of Health and Human Services (DHHS) possessed the vision to appreciate that for EMSC to be sustained in the long run, they would have to effectively engage a wide range of potential stakeholders, including the DHHS's budget personnel. To simply proclaim that this particular discretionary program might be "good for children" or was of "special interest to Congress" would simply not be sufficient, given the perennial budgetary constraints and competing domestic priorities and the ongoing leadership changes within presidential administrations. Program administrators seized upon this unique opportunity to undertake an exciting voyage through unchartered waters—they embraced the opportunity to work with multiple agencies and bipartisan legislators.

From the very beginning, a conscious effort was made to reach out to all professional disciplines and organizations that were involved in caring for injured children, as well as to other potentially relevant federal and state agencies. This group of stakeholders included, at a minimum, organizations representing nursing, psychology, social work, emergency physicians, surgeons, emergency medical technicians, state health departments, children's hospitals, and, most fortuitously in the long run, the American Academy of Pediatrics (AAP). EMSC was envisioned as becoming part of the national EMS system—as a distinct but complementary unit. Notwithstanding concerns regularly expressed by association lobbyists that the funding level was insufficient given the considerable needs of the nation's children, those involved at the staff level continued to focus on supporting innovative and strategic programmatic initiatives rather than funding clinical care per se. Staff did not allow seeking the perfect to become the enemy of the possible. Instead, they constantly kept their focus on the bigger picture. At its current (perhaps to some, modest) level of funding, EMSC persists in its underlying mission of serving as a catalyst for fostering innovative programmatic and clinical change that continues to improve the quality of care provided for injured children and their families.

In developing administrative support, the EMSC programmatic staff were especially creative in collaborating with the Federal Interagency Committee on EMS, a legislated federal entity with a composite of key agencies that intersect with the EMS system. Primary partners soon became the Department of Transportation's National Highway Safety Administration, as well as DHHS's Agency for Health Care Research and Quality and the Department of Defense's Uniformed Services University of the Health Sciences. In essence, DHHS staff cast a wide net of potentially interested partners rather than settle for a more comfortable smaller group of like-minded colleagues; the latter is all too frequently the case in jury-rigged systems. Importantly, staff did not consider the health of children as exclusively the purview of any one discipline (e.g., medicine) or organization (e.g., children's hospitals). Ensuring quality health care for injured children could reasonably be considered a priority of a wide range of health disciplines.

By ensuring the continued presence of EMSC spokespersons at a range of professional meetings every year, the Health Resources and Services Administration (HRSA) effectively reminded all potential stakeholders of the importance of their ongoing commitment to this important initiative. In retrospect, involvement with AAP turned out to be particularly beneficial, as that organization, more than any other, continued to make EMSC one of its top legislative priorities over the years—in contrast to several other organizations that had initially been expected to be extremely supportive given their public rhetoric. AAP followed through each year. EMSC initially received $2,000,000 in funding; by comparison, the fiscal year 2017 DHHS budget recommended $20,162,000 for this program, thereby maintaining a consistent level of funding over the past five years, regardless of which political party controlled the Congress. The interaction of multiple agencies, legislators, and healthcare professionals who served as consultants is a shining example of a powerful, positive response to a broad societal need.

▶ Personal Reflections

During its three-plus decades of existence, EMSC has faced several significant challenges. Some years, DHHS leadership declined to include the program within their budget request—thereby sending a message to the Congress that other funded programs were now meeting this need and indicating that EMSC was a lower priority. One year, when additional funding was initially included within a "must pass" antidrug bill, a major national newspaper published an editorial expressing outrage over this non-drug-related proposed federal expenditure. From time to time, proponents of other (allegedly similar) programs attempted to incorporate the successful EMSC budget within their own areas of personal priority (e.g., poison control centers, children's hospitals, and a broader trauma initiative), attempting once again to combine children's health needs with adult care. Staff from one national organization were convinced that EMSC would result in a separate, parallel, and competing system that might result in the loss of block-grant funding.

Each of these perhaps well-meaning efforts was turned back primarily because concerned child-focused congressional and administration staff were engaged.

That is, staff members from both areas were persistent and present throughout the related negotiations and strenuously objected to diluting the unique child focus of EMSC. Fortunately for EMSC, Senator Brian Schatz (Democrat-Hawaii) was elected to replace Senator Inouye after the latter's death, and a University of Hawaii-trained pediatrician on his staff has assumed the role of specifically advocating for the program, thereby providing the necessary continuation of congressional support. Owing to both her personal and professional background, this pediatrician-staffer appreciates the critical importance of EMSC's unique focus on children.

As is often the case, there is a personal "behind the scenes" story for EMSC. Over the decades, key HRSA staff were individuals who thought of the needs of children before those of their particular professional disciplines. One might say that they made "children" the noun and not the adjective while truly appreciating children's unique needs. Each of the two congressional staff members who were most engaged in shepherding this initiative through the legislative process experienced a need to rely upon their local emergency room personnel for the care of their young children. One, who was at the time a professor of medicine, reported receiving outstanding care. The other described quite a different story. His family was informed that their young daughter would be dead by morning or brain damaged for life. There was absolutely no attention paid by the emergency department personnel to the emotional/psychological aspects of being an impacted family. Fortunately, both children survived their trauma with no long-term adverse consequences. However, these dramatically different experiences led to numerous informal discussions among many stakeholders about how to ensure that all Americans, regardless of their geographical location and social status, would be able to receive the quality of emergency care that they expected for their children.

There was no immediate solution to ensuring care for all American children. Involved HRSA staff agreed that only those with the best of intentions were involved in providing necessary clinical care. Therefore, the staff felt that a demonstration approach might be the most productive answer in the long run. Staff hoped that from these pilot experiences and public hearings, future legislative direction might evolve. DHHS was not initially supportive of the proposed child-oriented demonstration. As the likelihood of enactment of the project became clearer, the discussion broadened into whether the Centers for Disease Control and Prevention (CDC) or HRSA would be the appropriate venue for implementation. Since the underlying objectives were to improve the quality of care provided (i.e., improve provider competency in the unique needs of children) and to explore potential system innovations (e.g., develop the capacity for approaching ambulances and helicopters to alert the designated emergency room personnel as to which types of equipment and medications should be readily available), HRSA was chosen.

At the 10th anniversary celebration of EMSC held in the U.S. Senate, it was emotionally gratifying to listen to the grandparents of the survivors of the tragic Oklahoma City bombing (which occurred at the Alfred P. Murrah Federal Building on April 19, 1995) describe how just the previous week the EMSC program had trained their city's first responders on how best to treat their injured loved ones. In a similar vein, it was heartwarming to see both members of the North Dakota Senate delegation (Senators Dorgan and Conrad) laud the EMSC program after the Wakefield family who had suffered an extraordinarily horrible automobile accident in the ice and snows of North Dakota's winter; they were close family members of long-time public servant Mary Wakefield, PhD, RN, the former administrator of HRSA and deputy secretary of DHHS under President Obama. The spirit of EMSC definitely lives on.

⌕ CASE STUDY 9-4: Collaboration Among Healthcare Professionals to Influence Health Policy

Rachael Antone, 1st Lt., USAF, NC, BSN, Family Nurse Practitioner student, Uniformed Services University of the Health Sciences, Bethesda, Maryland

Within a patient care setting, it is common to see nurses, physicians, pharmacists, physical therapists, and nutritionists working in silos. From the patient's standpoint, there are multiple people coming into the room throughout the hospital stay, and often they give differing, sometimes conflicting, information and guidance. This type of disjointed interaction is known as fragmentation of care.

Having a medical team that cares for a panel of patients allows for greater collaboration among healthcare professionals and better patient outcomes as evidenced and informed by the patient-centered medical home model, the Wagner chronic care model, and the creation of rules for accountable care organizations. Legislation such as the ACA defined and facilitated intercollegial teams by rewarding high-quality outcomes of care with higher reimbursement.

Discussion Questions

1. Why might it be difficult to get health professionals to reach consensus on a policy agenda?
2. Using www.Congress.gov, enter the search term (including the quotation marks) "patient-centered medical home" and perform a search of *All Legislation*. Scroll to see how many bills have been introduced related to this subject since the 110th Congress (2007–2008). Can you find any evidence in literature searches of a consensus in Congress regarding how to reduce fragmentation of care, improve communications, and improve quality of care?
3. What prompted the current emphasis on intercollegial teams?
4. To what extent do you think the force of law can change the silo practices of nurses, physicians, pharmacists, and other healthcare providers? Identify other approaches that might be successful in changing the silo practice of healthcare professionals.
5. Other than healthcare professionals, who (individuals and organizations) are stakeholders involved in reducing fragmented care? (Hint: Follow the money.) Which collaborations have the American Medical Association, American Academy of Family Physicians, American Association of Nurse Practitioners, American Academy of Nursing, and American Nurses Association already created regarding patient-centered care? To what extent are the Association of American Medicine Colleges and the American Association of Colleges of Nursing influential in this regard? Give examples.

🔍 *CASE STUDY 9-5:* Interprofessional Collaboration on Health Policy Related to Critical Congenital Heart Defects

Donna Ryan, DNP, RN, CNE, Assistant Professor, Elmira College (New York)

It was 7:00 a.m. when Christine began to breastfeed her seemingly healthy 5-day-old baby. Zach was vaginally delivered after a normal pregnancy and routine labor. Despite Christine's exhaustion as a first-time mother, everything was going fine so far. Christine looked up at her husband, Jeff, who was just out of the shower and getting ready for work. She then looked back down at Zach to find him a sickly blue-gray color: Zach had stopped breathing. Christine screamed to Jeff, and he called 911. The parents were not trained to perform infant cardiopulmonary resuscitation (CPR) and as they anxiously waited for the ambulance to arrive, they decided to rush Zach to the hospital themselves. Despite attempts to revive Zach in the emergency department of their local hospital, he was pronounced dead a few hours later. The couple's baby was dead, and they did not know why: There had been no warning signs of the heart defect that took Zach's life. A week later, Christine and Jeff were told that Zach was born with a critical congenital heart defect (CCHD). They later learned that screening for CCHD with commonly available pulse oximetry might have prevented Zach's death (Save Babies Through Screening Foundation, 2012).

Congenital heart disease (CHD) is the most common birth defect among the major anomalies involving the structure of the heart or the blood flow of the heart (Hom & Martin, 2016). Approximately 8 to 12 of every 1,000 newborns have a form of CHD (Frank, Bradshaw, Beekman, Mahle, & Martin, 2013). A prenatal diagnosis of CHD is made in only 50% of infants with this type of disease (Koppel et al., 2003; Mahle et al., 2009; Thangaratinam, Daniels, Ewer, Zamora, & Khan, 2007). Some forms of CHD cause no, or very few, problems in the health, growth, and development of the infant (CDC, 2015). CHD accounts for 24% of all infant deaths due to birth defects in the United States (CDC, 2014).

Approximately one in four babies with a heart defect has CCHD (Oster et al., 2013). CCHD is a form of CHD that is usually associated with hypoxia in the newborn period and requires intervention during the first months of life (CDC, 2015; Martin & Bradshaw, 2012). Approximately 30% to 50% of infants with CCHD may leave the hospital undiagnosed (Kumar, 2016). The consequences of delaying treatment until the infant becomes critically ill are often a higher mortality rate, a much longer stay in the intensive care unit, and a higher incidence of serious complications such as neurological impairment (Mahle et al., 2009).

Interprofessional stakeholders generally agree that sufficient evidence exists to support CCHD screening by pulse oximetry after 24 hours of age and before discharge of a newborn. Screening to promote early detection of CCHD has been endorsed by the Health and Human Services Secretary's Advisory Committee on Heritable Disorders in Newborns and Children (SACHDNC), the American Heart Association, the American Academy of Pediatrics, the American College of Cardiology Foundation (Mahle, Martin, Beekman, & Morrow, 2012), and the March of Dimes. Nurses are well positioned to play a leadership role in ensuring all newborns are screened for critical congenital heart disease.

Since newborn screening for CCHD was added to the U.S. Recommended Uniform Screening Panel in 2011, most states have passed legislation that promotes routine newborn screening for CCHD (AAP, 2015; Mahle et al., 2012; Oster et al., 2016). CCHD screening with pulse oximetry is simple and inexpensive—comparable to the cost of a diaper change. According to Ewer (2016), such screening increases the overall detection rate for CCHD to more than 90%. Ailes, Gilboa, Honein, and Oster (2015, p. 1000) estimate that approximately 875 infants with CCHD might be detected, and approximately 880 missed, annually through universal CCHD screening in the United States.

Once parents understood that in some cases, their newborn infants might not have died if they had received CCHD screening prior to discharge, they became instrumental in raising awareness of this screening and its significance in preventing undiagnosed CCHD through social media. Many parents shared their personal tragedies and advocated to state legislators to pass mandatory screening bills throughout the United States. After hearing these heart-wrenching stories from parents, policymakers were more supportive in exploring legislation.

One example of interprofessional collaboration to achieve legislation occurred in North Carolina in October 2012. Dr. Alex Kemper—a Duke pediatrician, co-editor of *Journal of Pediatrics*, and member of the SACHDNC—spoke to the Perinatal Health Committee, which is a subcommittee of the Child Fatality Task Force and the North Carolina Healthcare Senate Standing Committee (SACHDNC, 2012). Dr. Kemper, along with several parents of children with CCHD, discussed how CCHD screening by pulse oximetry could save the lives of newborns across North Carolina. They explained that this screening is a painless, noninvasive test that increases the ability to identify newborns with CCHD before they clinically decompensate.

In North Carolina, a wide range of stakeholders, including families of children with CCHD, pediatricians, neonatologists, nurse practitioners, nurse–midwives, and representatives from the N.C. Hospital Association, the N.C. Chapter of the American Heart Association, the N.C. Chapter of the March of Dimes, the Perinatal Quality Collaborative of North Carolina, the N.C. Board of Nursing, the N.C. Academy of Family Physicians, and the N.C. Academy of Physician Assistants, engaged in the development of the guidelines for CCHD screening (Perinatal Quality Collaborative of North Carolina [PQCNC], n.d., para 2). The North Carolina state legislature passed Session Law 2013-15 on July 25, 2014 (PQCNC, n.d.); it required all newborns born in hospitals, birthing centers, and homes to be screened for CCHD by 24–48 hours of age. PQCNC developed a database to handle the reporting requirements for CCHD and provides resources on this issue, including provider continuing education webinars and educational materials for parents.

Discussion Points

1. Argue the advantages and disadvantages of approaching congressional legislators versus state legislators to get this issue on the agenda.
2. Identify at least four people or organizations that would have a stake in this issue. Which information could you provide to persuade them to join you in your plan to seek a legislative solution? Do not limit yourself to research.
3. Which government agencies might have an interest in this issue? How could you find a legislator who has had personal experience with this issue who could become a policy entrepreneur/champion?
4. Suppose that one person/organization agrees to join you but has a different (albeit related) focus. Which tactics can you construct that could end with a win–win outcome? Which options do you have if the other's goal becomes a barrier to your goal?

(continues)

🔎 *CASE STUDY 9-5:* Interprofessional Collaboration on Health Policy Related to Critical Congenital Heart Defects *(continued)*

5. Develop potential language for a bill. What are three policy tools that could be used to encourage compliance with the law if passed?
6. Who might oppose this law? Develop responses to address the opposition.
7. Determine criteria for evaluating the effectiveness and efficiency of the policy/program. Develop a tool to measure the outcomes. Who will use the tool? At which point(s) should the policy/program be evaluated?

References

Ailes, E. C., Gilboa, S. M., Honein, M. A., & Oster, M. E. (2015). *Pediatrics, 135*(6), 100–1008.

American Academy of Pediatrics (AAP). (2015). American Academy of Pediatrics newborn screening for CCHD 2015 state actions. Retrieved from https://www.cdc.gov/ncbddd /heartdefects/documents/2015-critical-chd-newborn-screening-by-state.pdf

Centers for Disease Control and Prevention (CDC). (2014). Newborn screening for critical congenital heart disease. Retrieved from https://www.cdc.gov/ncbddd/heartdefects /documents/newborn-screening-for-cchd.pdf

Centers for Disease Control and Prevention (CDC). (2015). Congenital heart defects. Retrieved from https://www.cdc.gov/ncbddd/heartdefects/cchd-facts.html

Ewer, A. (2016). Screening for critical congenital heart defects with pulse oximetry: Medical aspects. *American Journal of Perinatology, 33*(11), 1062–1066.

Frank, L. H., Bradshaw, E., Beekman, R., Mahle, W. T., & Martin, G. R. (2013). Critical congenital heart disease screening using pulse oximetry. *Journal of Pediatrics, 162*(3), 445–453.

Hom, L. A., & Martin, G. (2016). Newborn critical congenital heart disease screening using pulse oximetry: Nursing aspects. *American Journal of Perinatology, 33*(11), 1072–1075.

Koppel, R. I., Druschel, C. M., Carter, T., Goldberg, B. E., Mehta, P. N., Talwar, R., & Bierman, F. Z. (2003). Effectiveness of pulse oximetry screening for congenital heart disease in asymptomatic newborns. *Pediatrics, 111*(3), 451–455.

Kumar, P. (2016). Universal pulse oximetry screening for early detection of critical congenital heart disease. *Clinical Medicine Insights: Pediatrics, 10,* 35–41.

Mahle, W. T., Martin, G. R., Beekman, R. H., & Morrow, W. R. (2012). Endorsement of Health and Human Services recommendation for pulse oximetry screening for critical congenital heart disease. *Pediatrics, 129*(1), 190–192.

Mahle, W. T., Newburger, J. W., Matherne, G. P., Smith, F. C., Hoke, T. R., Koppel, R., . . . Grosse, S. D. (2009). Role of pulse oximetry in examining newborns for congenital heart disease: A scientific statement from the AHA and AAP. *Pediatrics, 124*(2), 823–836.

Martin, G. R., & Bradshaw, E. A. (2012). Sensitivity of pulse oximetry for detection of critical congenital heart defects in newborn infants higher than that of antenatal ultrasound with few false positives. *Evidence-Based Medicine, 17*(2), 57–58.

Oster, M., Aucott, S. W., Glidewell, J., Hackell, J., Kochilas, L., Martin, G. R., . . . Kemper, A. R. (2016). Lessons learned from newborn screening for critical congenital heart defects. *Pediatrics, 137*(5), 1–14.

Oster, M., Lee, K., Honein, M., Colarusso, T., Shin, M., & Correa, A. (2013). Temporal trends in survival for infants with critical congenital heart defects. *Pediatrics, 131*(5), e1502–e1508.

Perinatal Quality Collaborative of North Carolina (PQCNC). (n.d.). Critical congenital heart disease. Retrieved from https://www.pqcnc.org/node/13639

Save Babies Through Screening Foundation. (2012). Cora's story: The need for pulse oximetry. Retrieved from http://www.savebabies.org/blog/2012/01/cora%E2%80%99s-story-the-need-for-pulse-oximetry-screening-for-cchd/

Secretary's Advisory Committee on Heritable Disorders in Newborns and Children (SACHDNC). (2012). Implementing point of care newborn screening. Retrieved from http://www.hrsa.gov/advisorycommittees/mchbadvisory/heritabledisorders/recommendations/correspondence/implementpocnewbornscreen.pdf

Thangaratinam, S., Daniels, J., Ewer, A. K., Zamora, J., & Khan, K. S. (2007). Accuracy of pulse oximetry in screening for congenital heart disease in asymptomatic newborns: A systematic review. *Archives of Disease in Childhood: Fetal and Neonatal Edition, 92*(3), F176–F180.

▶ Discussion Points

In an effort to make this example of interprofessional and interagency collaboration an exemplar for understanding persistence, consider the following:

1. Have the stakeholders changed? If so, what is the impact on the overall process of collaboration?
2. Has the focus changed? If so, how should those who are involved in the policy process make changes to reach the desired outcome?
3. Are there other factors that have or are having an impact on the future of the program?

References

Feely, H. B., & Athey, J. L. (1995). *Emergency medical services for children: 10 year report.* Arlington, VA: National Center for Education in Maternal and Child Health.

Institute of Medicine (IOM). (1993). *Emergency medical services for children.* Washington, DC: National Academy Press.

Suggested Readings

DeLeon, P. H., Kjervik, D. K., Kraut, A. G., & VandenBos, G. R. (1985). Psychology and nursing: A natural alliance. *American Psychologist, 40*, 1153-1164.

Gausche-Hill, M., Ely, M., Schmuhl, P., Telford, R., Remick, K. E., Edgerton, E. A., & Olson, L. M. (2015). A national assessment of pediatric readiness of emergency departments. *JAMA Pediatrics, 169*(6), 527-534. Erratum in: *JAMA Pediatrics* (2015), *169*(8), 791.

Preventive Health Amendments of 1984. [P.L. 98-555]. (October 30, 1984). 98 STAT. 2854. (S 2301). 42 USC 201 note.

Schenk, E., & Edgerton, E. A. (2015). A tale of two populations: Addressing pediatric needs in the continuum of emergency care. *Annals of Emergency Medicine, 65*(6), 673-678.

CHAPTER 10

Overview: The Economics and Finance of Health Care

Nancy M. Short

Other people, including the politicians who make economic policy, know even less about economics than economists.

—**Herbert Stein**, *Washington Bedtime Stories* (1986)

KEY TERMS

Adverse selection: A situation in which, as a result of private information, the insured are more likely to suffer a loss than the uninsured. A form of information asymmetry.

Affordable Care Act (ACA): The combination of the Patient Protection and Affordable Care Act of 2010 and the Health Care and Education Affordability Act of 2010. There are nine titles (or sections) within this law; mandatory personal health insurance, as required in this law, is commonly referred to as "Obamacare" and is only one of these titles.

Alternative Payment Models (APMs): A quality payment program for providers administered by the Centers for Medicare and Medicaid Services.

Coinsurance: The share of the costs of a covered healthcare service paid by the consumer, calculated as a percentage (for example, 20%) of the allowed amount for the service. The consumer pays coinsurance plus any deductibles owed. This should not be confused with a health plan that pays for a specific percentage of "essential health benefits."

Comparative effectiveness research (CER): A category of studies to determine the effectiveness of clinical interventions specifically when compared to differing treatments for the same condition or for different subgroups of patients. The newly created Patient-Centered Outcomes Research Institute (PCORI) is charged with identifying priorities and carrying out this type of research.

Essential health benefits: A set of healthcare service categories that, starting in 2014, had to be covered by certain plans. Insurance policies must cover these benefits to be certified and offered in the health insurance marketplace. States expanding their Medicaid programs must provide these benefits to people newly eligible for Medicaid.

Health insurance exchanges (HIXs): Markets set up to facilitate the purchase of health insurance in accordance with the Patient Protection and Affordable Care Act of 2010. Exchanges are either state, federal, or jointly run depending on the state.

Information asymmetry: The condition in which some parties to business transactions have an information advantage over others. There is often information asymmetry between patients and providers regarding therapies and prices.

Means testing: A process undertaken to determine whether a person's income qualifies him or her to participate in a social program. It is often used to determine eligibility for Medicaid coverage of long-term care and to determine eligibility for subsidies for health insurance.

Medicare Access and CHIP Reauthorization Act (MACRA) of 2015: A program that combines parts of three government quality incentive programs into one single program to determine physicians' and advanced practice registered nurses' reimbursement.

Moral hazard: The change in behavior as a result of a perceived reduction in the costs of misfortune (e.g., health insurance changes the costs of becoming ill or injured). A form of information asymmetry.

Opportunity costs: The value of the next best choice that one gives up when making a decision; also called economic costs.

Qualified health insurance plan (QHP): An insurance plan that has been certified by the health insurance marketplace, provides essential health benefits, follows established limits on cost-sharing (e.g., deductibles, copayments, and out-of-pocket maximum amounts), and meets other requirements under the Affordable Care Act. Sometimes referred to as essential minimum coverage.

Quality-adjusted life-years (QALYs): Calculated life expectancy adjusted for the quality of life, where quality of life is measured on a scale from 1 (full health) to 0 (dead). Originally developed as a broader measure of disease burden beyond mortality, QALYs are now used in cost-effectiveness analyses to aid coverage and reimbursement decisions worldwide.

"Repeal, replace, repair, or starve": A slogan referring to a primarily conservative political ideology with regard to the Affordable Care Act. Another possible action to reduce the impact of the ACA would be for Congress not to fund implementation of specific parts of the law—an approach known as "starving" a law.

Risk pool: A multiple-beneficiary risk-sharing arrangement to limit an insurance company's exposure, liability, or risk or some combination of the three. A combination of young, healthy beneficiaries balancing the risk for high expenses for older, sicker beneficiaries is an ideal risk pool.

▶ Introduction

Three important concepts that form the framework for health policy discussions are quality/safety of care, access to care, and cost of care. All health policy discussions boil down to one of these categories or to the synergies among these categories. This chapter focuses on the "cost" category, including some economic theories supporting current health policies and some of the structures created to implement these policies.

Health economics and the finance of health care are often erroneously used as interchangeable terms. How does health finance differ from health economics? In a nutshell, economics is the science that informs the processes of finance. The two disciplines share common ground such as cost–benefit analysis and analysis of risk, but they are not synonymous. Economics is amoral—that is, it is neither a moral science nor an immoral science. The science of health economics can suggest what makes a person, a population, a region, or a nation better off, but philosophy and ethics must be debated elsewhere and are represented by political trade-offs when policy is made. Similarly, the healthcare market as viewed by economists is amoral: When confronted with finite resources, there will be losers and winners. This is a tough concept for nurses to swallow.

Economic theory is based on the principle that all resources are scarce. Politics is the process for determining how scarce resources will be used and apportioned. Policy is the end result of the political process. Health policy is one type of policy determined in the political process and is made largely at the national level but also at state and local levels of government. Health economics is a growing research field within the discipline of economics.

Economic science studies markets such as the labor market for nurses and physicians, the pharmaceutical market, and the insurance market. Together these markets form the universe that is termed the "healthcare market." Within the healthcare market are nonprofit organizations, government organizations, shareholder-owned corporations, and other financial entities. Economics informs policy, and policy determines finance (**FIGURE 10-1**).

To better understand these relationships, think about the supply and demand for oranges. When significant weather events affect the orange crop, prices go up for all products made from oranges. In response to price variation, consumers choose whether they will continue to purchase orange juice or instead purchase a substitute such as apple juice.

In health care, shortages of resources lead to increased demand, discontinuation of manufacturing or loss of a manufacturing site, lack of raw materials at

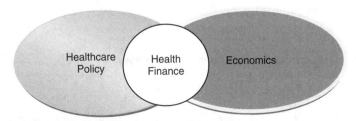

FIGURE 10-1 The intersection of health policy and health finance.

reasonable prices, quality issues in manufacturing, and delays or capacity problems (e.g., labor strikes). In January 2017, nearly 200 drugs were listed as "in shortage" in the United States: Sterile injectables such as saline and atropine sulfate topped the list. Pharmaceutical manufacturers report to the Food and Drug Administration (FDA) when there are shortages, and the FDA posts this information in the form of the Current Drug Shortage Index (https://www.accessdata.fda.gov /scripts/drugshortages/default.cfm). Because pharmaceutical manufacturing is not owned and operated by the U.S. government, the government does not control choices of what and how much to produce. Can consumers choose to go without a medication, or will they simply pay the higher price charged for a medication? Consumers frequently do choose to skip medications, sometimes at great risk. This added risk to health and life makes the healthcare market very different from all other economic markets. There are few ready-to-use substitutes for health care.

▶ Economics: Opportunity Costs

There is no such thing as a free lunch: For every opportunity taken and for every option discarded, there are trade-off costs. When you purchased the 2017 Nissan Juke, you did not purchase the 2016 Kia Soul. You also did not take a vacation, buy a new wardrobe, or pay off your college debt. Not acquiring the Soul, the vacation, the new wardrobe, or eliminating your debt, are the **opportunity costs** of purchasing the Juke.

Opportunity costs may also be described in terms of time spent on an activity (researching the safety of the Juke) and other indirect measures or intangibles. An example of opportunity costs related to health policy is current Medicare policy: 90% of Medicare funds are used for 10% of Medicare beneficiaries. Most Medicare dollars are expended in the final events of a person's life. Because there are finite funds available, legislative policy directing payments for an elderly person's last weeks of life represent an opportunity cost. For example, the funds could also be used for preventive care of 30-year-olds, more school nurses, or health research. These hard choices are the core of perennial political debates at the federal, state, and local levels. The economic consequences of a policy may last for years and may be argued equally eloquently by economists who fall on both sides of an issue.

> The most important contribution economists can make to the operation of the health care system is to be relentless in pointing out that every choice involves a trade-off—that certain difficult questions regarding who gets what, and who must give up what, are inevitable and must be faced even when politicians, the public, and patients would rather avoid them. (Getzen, 2010, p. 429)

▶ Finance: Does More Spending Buy Us Better Health?

Studies continue to show that there is no correlation between increased spending on health care in the United States and reductions in population mortality (Hussey,

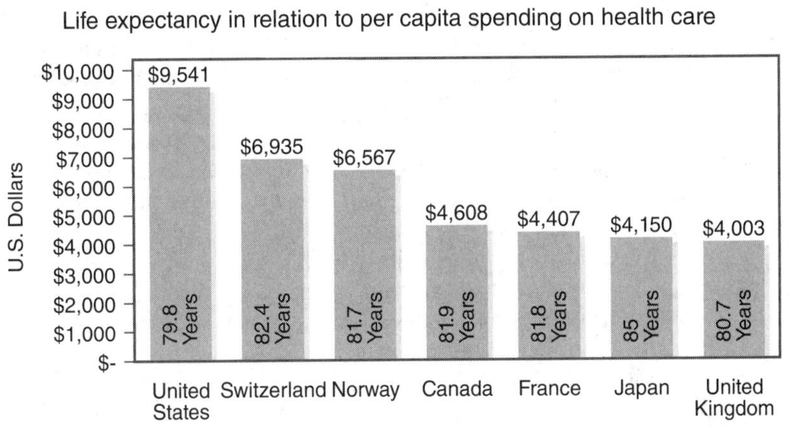

Life expectancy in relation to per capita spending on health care

FIGURE 10-2 **Life expectancy in relation to per capita spending on health care.**

Data from Central Intelligence Agency. (n.d.). The world factbook. Retrieved from https://www.cia.gov/library/publications/the-world-factbook/; Organisation for Economic Co-operation and Development. (2017). OECD Health Statistics 2016. Retrieved from http://www.oecd.org/els/health-systems/health-data.htm

Wertheimer, & Mehrota, 2013). Paradoxically, achieving increased quality may require increased spending, whereas lowering costs may require higher quality or efficiency to avoid rework. In the 1900s, spending on infrastructure that provided clean water and hygiene, vaccination programs, and better access to health care resulted in large improvements in quality of life and life expectancy. As the United States approached $5,000 annual per capita spending on health care, gains in population health and life expectancy slowed. In 2016, U.S. spending reached $9,451 per capita (Organisation for Economic Co-operation and Development, 2017), but the marginal gains to health were almost imperceptible. (**FIGURE 10-2** illustrates U.S. spending compared to other developed countries.) Routinely used indicators of health status—for example, infant mortality, prevalence of chronic diseases, Health Adjusted Life Expectancy, and feeling that one has good health— also do not correlate with per capita spending on health care.

Health care is not a true "normal good" in economic parlance. The market for a normal good or service experiences an increase in demand when income increases. There is a correlation between seeking healthcare goods and services when income rises; however, the necessity for health care even when income is extremely low makes it a special case in economics. In the absence of a national ideology and commitment that health care is a right for all people, a highly regulated market determines the haves and have nots for health care in the United States.

▶ Economics: Health Insurance Market

Health insurance in the United States is a misnomer: What we are actually purchasing is *sickness* insurance. Like other forms of insurance, health insurance is a form of collectivism in which people pool their risks—in this case, the risk of incurring medical expenses. Risk pooling is key to how insurance markets work: Each participant with marginal or poor health and a high risk of accruing high expenses is financially "balanced" by several participants with good health and low risk of high expenses. Barring the participation of individuals who already have disease or injury (preexisting conditions) allows insurers to manage **adverse selection** (explained in a later section). The health insurance mandate in the **Affordable Care Act (ACA)** provided for the enlargement and balance of the **risk pool**. Without the option to refuse to cover preexisting conditions or the increased risk pool created by the ACA's mandate, the business model for the insurance market would collapse: in 2017, many insurers pulled out of the Health Insurance Exchanges because of uncertainty about the continuation of the mandate. To repeal mandated individual health insurance from the ACA and maintain the very popular feature that no one can be denied health insurance because of a preexisting condition, Congress must grapple with how insurers will balance risk pools so as to remain solvent.

As this book went to press, Congress and the Trump administration were engaging in debate over how to **"repeal, replace, repair, or starve"** health-care finance in the United States. In general, liberal thinkers wish to maintain the ACA with possible improvements. Hard-right conservatives have made election campaign promises to repeal and replace the ACA, while more moderate conservatives are more open to repairing what they see as flaws in the law. Changing the manner in which all Americans obtain health insurance is extremely complex; any changes enacted by legislators will take years to implement. The American public is strongly divided about how to finance health care in the country (**FIGURE 10-3**).

The market for health insurance is divided into public and private insurance. The six major government healthcare programs are Medicare, Medicaid, the Children's Health Insurance Program (CHIP), the Department of Defense TriCare and TriCare for Life programs, the Veterans Health Administration program, and the Indian Health Service program. The insurance industry is organized into group and nongroup (or individual) insurance. For example, employer-sponsored health insurance (ESHI) is a form of group insurance. In 2016, more than 15 million Americans purchased individual insurance; by comparison, more than half the U.S. population younger than age 65 had health insurance through their jobs or a family member's job. The National Conference of State Legislatures (2017) reports that the average health insurance premium was $18,142 per family in 2016. The cost of insurance premiums does not include out-of-pocket payments for deductibles, copays, non-covered treatments/medications, or other fees.

One of the primary factors influencing how much you pay for health insurance is the state in which you live. Each state has a department of insurance regulating the industry within its borders. Under the ACA, all 50 states offer either the HealthCare.gov marketplace platform or a state-based marketplace (these marketplaces are also known as health insurance exchanges) designed to help individuals purchase affordable health insurance. The number of participating insurance companies, as well as variable policies and prices, are driven by market forces in each state (Assistant Secretary of Planning and Evaluation, 2016).

Some providers and organizations refuse to accept health insurance; they accept only cash-based financing. This practice, known as direct pay, arguably reduces the cost of health care by eliminating the profits insurers make and eliminating time and resources for practices to work with various insurers; allows patients to choose whomever they want as a provider; reduces gaps in consumer knowledge about prices or costs; and allows providers to lower prices to reflect the savings of having a smaller billing function (**TABLE 10-1**).

Percent who say they would like to see lawmakers do each of the following with the 2010 healthcare law:

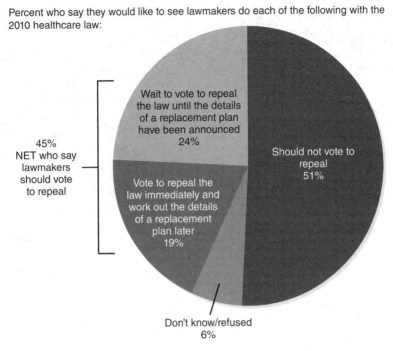

FIGURE 10-3 U.S. public divided on repeal and replacement of the ACA.

Reproduced from Kaiser Family Foundation. (2017c). U.S. public opinion on health care reform, 2017. Retrieved from http://kff.org/slideshow/us-public-opinion-on-health -care-reform-2017/

▶ Finance: Health Insurance Exchanges

Introduced in October 2013, **health insurance exchanges (HIXs)** are intended to create a more organized and competitive market for health insurance by offering a choice of plans, establishing common rules regarding the offering and pricing of insurance, and providing information to help consumers better understand the options available to them. Depending on the state, the HIX serving that state will be implemented by the state government, by the federal government, or jointly by both the state and the federal government. A HIX marketplace is where people (individuals or small businesses) not covered through their employers or by public insurance may shop for health insurance at competitive rates. Private plans, outside of the HIXs, continue to be available; however, private plans are now more likely to be available for purchase only in designated "open enrollment" periods that coincide with those of the HIXs' open enrollment periods.

Insurance plans in the HIX marketplace are primarily separated into four health plan categories—Bronze, Silver, Gold, or Platinum—based on the percentage the plan pays of the average overall cost of providing **essential health benefits** to members. The plan category a person chooses affects the total amount that individual will spend for essential health benefits during the year. The percentages the plans will spend, on average, are 60% (Bronze), 70% (Silver), 80% (Gold), and 90% (Platinum). For example, Bronze plans tend to have the lowest premiums, and they provide an average cost-sharing value of 60%. In other words, a Bronze plan

TABLE 10-1 Free Market (Direct Pay) Compared to Traditional Finance Methods

Insurance	Self-Funded Employer	Medicare and Medicaid	Out-of-Pocket

Traditional: Insurers negotiate discounted rates with the medical providers in their network. Providers charge different amounts to different insurers for the same procedure, but these rates are not publicly available.	**Traditional:** Employers hire a preferred provider organization (PPO), which negotiates discounted rates with medical providers on the employer's behalf. Employers pay claims out of their operating budgets.	**Traditional:** Government determines how much to reimburse medical providers for all procedures on the basis of recommendations from the American Medical Association. Rates are often modest, leading some physicians to refuse to accept or limit such coverage.	**Traditional:** Patients pay medical providers directly. In the past, uninsured patients' bills were based on the artificially inflated prices providers used to begin negotiations with insurers. Some traditional providers are offering cash-only prices that are lower than insurers' negotiated rates.
With direct pay: The idea is that health insurance begins to look more like auto insurance: Insurers estimate the cost of a procedure and send a check to the patient, who compares prices and chooses a provider.	**With direct pay:** Employers partner with medical providers on the basis of their publicly available prices and then pay them directly. Employers pay medical bills out of their operating budget.	**With direct pay:** If most medical providers posted their prices, the government could potentially set reimbursement rates based on the average regional price of a procedure.	**With direct pay:** Patients still pay providers directly, but since price lists are posted publicly, regional providers compete on price, quality, and reputation.

covers an average of 60% of all plan enrollees' covered out-of-pocket costs. This does not mean that 60% of actual costs will be covered for any one given person; it is not the same as **coinsurance**, in which a person pays a specific percentage of the cost of a specific service. These "metal" categories as well as the essential health benefits required by the ACA are the subjects of scrutiny and debate in Congress.

The ACA requires the following essential health benefits to be included in every **qualified health insurance plan (QHP)**:

- Well-baby and well-child care for children younger than age 21
- Oral health and vision services for children
- Preventive services and immunizations
- Ambulatory patient services, including laboratory services
- Chronic disease management
- Mental health and substance abuse coverage at parity with physical ailment coverage
- Hospital/emergency services
- Rehabilitation and habilitative services and devices
- Prescription drug coverage
- Maternity care
- No cost sharing for these services

Additionally, insurers cannot impose annual or lifetime limits on health coverage, and they must offer parents the choice of covering their children up to their 26th birthday through the parent's health insurance coverage. This requirement also applies to those persons who "age out" of the foster care system and were covered by Medicaid.

Federal subsidies are available to help individuals pay for a qualified health plan. There are two kinds of subsidies: advance premium tax credits and cost sharing. Advance premium tax credits help to pay health insurance premiums each month for people with incomes 100–400% of the federal poverty level (FPL). Cost sharing helps pay for all other health costs, such as copayments, deductibles, and coinsurance, for families with incomes 100–250% of the FPL who are enrolling in a Silver-level plan in the marketplace. Both kinds of subsidies are determined based on a sliding scale (means tested). The subsidy is determined during the initial application based on the individual/family's annual projected income. There is no penalty for good-faith estimates that are lower than the actual income at year's end.

The ACA requires citizens and legal immigrants to pay a penalty if they do not have a qualified health plan. The mandate for a qualified health plan can be met if an individual has public health insurance coverage, employer-sponsored health insurance, or an individual health plan purchased from either the HIX marketplace or the private insurance market. The penalties for having no health insurance may be amended by the U.S. Department of Health and Human Services or Congress.

The small business health insurance options program (SHOP) opened to employers with 50 or fewer full-time equivalent (FTE) employees in 2014. (Note: 50 FTEs is not the same as 50 employees.) In 2016, all SHOPs opened to employers with up to 100 FTEs. If a business wants to use SHOP, it must offer coverage to all of its full-time employees (generally those working 30 or more hours per week on average) *and* at least 70% of full-time employees must enroll in the business/SHOP plan (as opposed to being covered by a spouse's insurance or as an individual on the HIX). More information on SHOP can be obtained from the Center for Consumer Information and Insurance Oversight.

Penalties for Not Having a Qualified Health Plan

In 2017, the penalty/responsibility for not having a QHP—that is, the "individual shared responsibility payment"—was $695 per adult and $347 per child younger than 18. The maximum penalty was $2,085 or 2.5% of household taxable income (whichever is greater).

Any penalties are paid when income tax forms are filed with the Internal Revenue Service (IRS) the following year. If a person obtains insurance outside of the marketplace, he or she must report that insurance coverage to the IRS every year when filing the tax return. The insurer and the employer (if applicable) provide the necessary proof of coverage to include in the tax return. There are no liens, levies, or criminal penalties for failing to pay the fee. Penalties beyond 2017 had not been announced when this text was being written.

Exemptions From Penalties

In general, exemptions are income related, hardship related, group-membership related, and health-coverage related:

1. Those who have to pay more than 8% of their income for the lowest-cost premium
2. People who do not pay taxes because their income is too low
3. People with certain religious exemptions
4. Prisoners, while incarcerated
5. Those experiencing a hardship (e.g., victims of domestic violence, persons being evicted from their place of residence)
6. Native Americans and Alaskan Natives
7. People who would have been covered had their state of residence elected to expand Medicaid
8. Mixed-status families (documented and undocumented immigrants within one nuclear family)

FIGURE 10-4 depicts cartoonist Kevin Kallaugher's perspective on President Trump's approach to Obamacare.

▶ Finance: Healthcare Entitlement Programs

Medicare and Medicaid are publicly funded social entitlement programs and are the "third rail" of healthcare politics. Anyone meeting the eligibility requirements for Medicare (Part A) or Medicaid is *entitled* to all the promised benefits, no matter the condition of the government's (state or federal) finances. As an analogy, think of your personal budget: You plan for rent, transportation expenses, utilities, clothing, entertainment, gifts, and the like in your budget, and you balance these amounts against your anticipated income to assure that your income covers your expenses. Expenses for Medicare and Medicaid are projected every year, but unlike your clothing allowance, if the government runs short of revenue (e.g.,

FIGURE 10-4 "Time to Hit the Road"
Courtesy of Kevin KAL Kallaugher, Kaltoons.com

fewer taxes are collected during an economic downturn), there is no legal option to cut back on entitlement programs. Likewise, if expenses for Medicare and Medicaid are higher than projected (e.g., perhaps more seniors are seriously ill), the government cannot choose not to provide payment for the overage in services. If the government fails to meet its obligation, beneficiaries are entitled to sue.

By law, state governments must balance their budgets; the federal government may run deficits up to a ceiling set by Congress. This important concept explains many of the policies at the state and federal levels. In simple terms, Medicare is a federally funded program, and Medicaid is funded by federal and state funds along with some local funds. The full reality is more complex, but these generalities suffice for our discussion. Funding for Medicare comes primarily from general revenues (40%) and payroll taxes (38%), followed by premiums paid by beneficiaries (12%).

In 2015, the Kaiser Family Foundation reported that Medicare provided insurance coverage to 55.5 million people, including those age 65 and older (if they or their spouse made payroll tax contributions for 10 or more years) and younger people with permanent disabilities (after 24 months of receiving Social Security Disability Insurance payments), end-stage renal disease, and amyotrophic lateral sclerosis (Lou Gehrig's disease). Medicare covers most healthcare services but does not cover long-term care services such as nursing home care (Kaiser Family Foundation, 2017b).

- Medicare Part A (hospital insurance program) helps pay for inpatient hospitalizations, skilled nursing home care (up to 100 days), home health (limited post-hospital care), and hospice care. The beneficiary must pay a deductible.
- Medicare Part B (supplementary medical insurance) is voluntary and covers 95% of all Part A beneficiaries. Part B helps pay for physician visits, outpatient hospital services, preventive services, mental health services, durable medical equipment, and home health. Beneficiaries pay a monthly premium plus some copayments.
- Medicare Part C is also called Medicare Advantage. It includes private health plans that receive payments from Medicare to provide Medicare-covered

benefits to enrollees. Plans provide benefits covered under Parts A and B and often Part D.

- Medicare Part D is a voluntary program that helps pay for outpatient prescription drugs and is administered exclusively through private plans. Premiums and cost sharing vary according to the plan purchased. The Affordable Care Act improves coverage by gradually closing the "doughnut hole"—an unusual gap in coverage in which 100% of costs become out-of-pocket expenses. The cost of Part D is increasing at a faster rate than costs for the rest of Medicare.

Prior to the implementation of the Affordable Care Act, Medicare served all eligible beneficiaries without regard to income or medical history. As health reform rolled out, **means testing** was applied to those with very high incomes. In 2017, Medicare beneficiaries with incomes greater than $85,000 for individuals and $170,000 for couples paid premiums ranging from $170.50 to $389.80 per month, depending on the level of income, compared with the standard premium of $121.80. Extra Part D premiums range from $12.70 to $72.90 per month. Beginning in 2018, beneficiaries with incomes greater than $133,500 pay a higher premium subsidy than the current amount due to a provision in the **Medicare Access and CHIP Reauthorization Act (MACRA) of 2015**. Increasing means testing reaches far down into the middle class. The income thresholds for income-related premiums are frozen under current law until 2019, when it is estimated that the number of Medicare beneficiaries subjected to higher premiums will increase from 5% to 10% of Part B enrollees. Some members of Congress and administration officials have proposed increasing means testing until 25% of beneficiaries are subject to higher premiums.

Note: Maryland has a 36-year-old waiver from the federal government to operationalize Medicare in a unique manner. The details are beyond the scope of this chapter; however, some economists believe that Maryland's reimbursement system may become the model for the rest of the nation.

Medicaid was enacted under the Social Security Act in 1965 as a companion to Medicare. It entitles participating states to federal matching funds on an open-ended basis, entitles eligible individuals to a set of specific benefits, is means tested, and allows states to provide broader coverage. In addition to providing health insurance coverage, Medicaid provides assistance to low-income Medicare beneficiaries (dual-eligible), long-term care assistance (nursing home and in-home community-based services), and support for the safety-net system of health care. The largest source of federal funding to the states, Medicaid is the largest health insurance program in the United States.

Medicaid fills large gaps in the U.S. health insurance market, finances the lion's share of long-term care, and provides core support for the health centers and safety-net hospitals that serve the nation's uninsured population and millions of others. Within broad federal guidelines, states design their own Medicaid programs. Medicaid reimburses private providers to provide services to beneficiaries. In 2017, 20% of the U.S. population received health insurance from Medicaid. Disabled and elderly adults make up only 25% of enrollees, but they account for approximately 70% of Medicaid expenditures. Of the 12 million Americans in long-term care, 87% are covered by Medicaid, making Medicaid the major program paying for long-term care (Kaiser Family Foundation, 2017a).

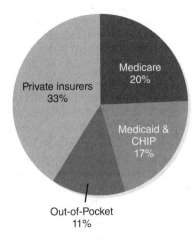

FIGURE 10-5 National health expenditures in the United States by source of payment, 2015.

Data from Centers for Medicare & Medicaid Services. (2016). National health expenditure data. Retrieved from https://www.cms.gov/research-statistics-data-and-systems/statistics-trends-and-reports/nationalhealthexpenddata/nationalhealthaccountshistorical.html

In those 18 states that opted out of the ACA Medicaid expansion plan, Medicaid coverage requires that beneficiaries have low incomes (defined by each state using the federal poverty guidelines) *and* meet one of these categories of need:

- Pregnant or recent postpartum
- Younger than age 18 years
- Older than age 65 years and blind or disabled

These restrictions were in place across all Medicaid programs prior to the implementation of the ACA.

Medically needy persons whose incomes are too high to be eligible for Medicaid may also be covered. (Each state determines eligibility.) In addition, states may define optional eligibility groups. In 2014, the federal poverty level for a family of four was $23,850 in the continental United States and a little higher in Alaska and Hawaii (U.S. Department of Health and Human Services, 2014). As of April 2017, 32 states had expanded Medicaid by eliminating medical need categories and providing coverage to those with incomes at or below 138% of the FPL.

One of the arguments against expanding Medicaid is a fear of increasing the overall health expenditures for the United States (Rosenbaum, Rothenburg, Gunsalus, & Schmucker, 2017). **FIGURE 10-5** indicates the percentage paid by each type of payer in the U.S. healthcare system.

▶ Finance: Payment Models

The long-term goal of the federal government is to move providers (physicians, advanced practice registered nurses [APRNs], hospitals, all other health professionals who are reimbursed by federal programs) from a payment system rewarding volume of care to a model based on the quality of management of the health of populations. The term *population management* can translate into examples such as a ZIP code as defining a population, or a population of patients with diabetes being treated within a specific practice, or the population of patients undergoing hip replacement in a hospital. Since 2016, selected hospitals and providers have acted as "laboratories" to demonstrate the efficacy of various organizational formats and payment models to advance the goal of stabilizing and lowering healthcare costs while maintaining or increasing quality and safety.

Medicare Access and CHIP Reauthorization (MACRA) of 2015 is a complex federal law that ended the prior physician and APRN reimbursement model known as the sustainable growth rate (SGR). Payment for quality of outcomes is at the heart of the changes instituted by MACRA, which took effect in 2017: Providers must choose one program for reimbursement from Medicare. The options under the Quality Payment Program consist of the **Alternative Payment Models (Apms)** and the Merit-Based Incentive Payment System (MIPS). Principles of the Alternative Payment Models are:

1. Changing providers' financial incentives is not sufficient to achieve person-centered care, so it will be essential to empower patients to be partners in healthcare transformation.
2. The goal for payment reform is to shift U.S. healthcare spending significantly toward population-based (and more person-focused) payments.
3. Value-based incentives ideally should reach the providers who deliver care.
4. Payment models that do not take quality into account are not considered APMs in the APM framework and do not count as progress toward payment reform.
5. Value-based incentives should be intense enough to motivate providers to invest in and adopt new approaches to care delivery.
6. APMs are classified according to the dominant form of payment when more than one type of payment is used.
7. Centers of excellence, accountable care organizations, and patient-centered medical homes are examples, rather than categories, in the APM framework because they are delivery systems that can be applied to and supported by a variety of payment models.

Types of payment models include fee-for-service, bundled care, accountable care, shared decision making, and the direct decision support model. Physician and APRN providers must choose whether to participate in APMs or in the MIPS. Both the APM and MIPS programs are beyond the scope of this chapter. **FIGURE 10-6** depicts the overall trajectory of the payment framework models.

▶ Economics: Information Asymmetry

Information asymmetry is the term used by economists to point out that healthcare consumption differs from purchasing other goods and services because of the inability of patients, providers, or payers to possess all the information needed for completely informed decision making. Optimal rational decision making requires "perfect information"—that is, the situation in which consumers are just as knowledgeable as sellers.

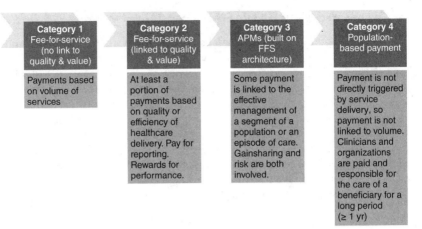

Category 1 Fee-for-service (no link to quality & value)	Category 2 Fee-for-service (linked to quality & value)	Category 3 APMs (built on FFS architecture)	Category 4 Population- based payment
Payments based on volume of services	At least a portion of payments based on quality or efficiency of healthcare delivery. Pay for reporting. Rewards for performance.	Some payment is linked to the effective management of a segment of a population or an episode of care. Gainsharing and risk are both involved.	Payment is not directly triggered by service delivery, so payment is not linked to volume. Clinicians and organizations are paid and responsible for the care of a beneficiary for a long period (≥ 1 yr)

FIGURE 10-6 Centers for Medicare and Medicaid Services' payment framework trajectory.

As an example, imagine you want to buy a car. You gather all the information that you can to eliminate any advantage the car seller may have in terms of the worth of this particular car. Being newly informed, you may choose to go to several dealerships before you find a seller that meets your expectations (or utility).

Now think about the typical healthcare experience. You go to your primary care provider (PCP) for your annual physical examination, and the PCP finds an abnormality and refers you to a specialist. Depending on your level of information, you will blindly trust the specialist or you may "shop around." You may be very hard-pressed to learn about the quality or performance of either your primary care provider or the specialist. If you are referred to a hospital, you are probably unable to learn the nurse-to-patient ratio even though evidence shows that this factor is critical to your well-being. Clearly, information asymmetry is present at many points in this scenario.

Healthcare professionals might argue that they generally know what is "best" for patients. The problem of asymmetric information differs from a simple information problem in that one party possesses knowledge needed to enable rational decision making that the other party lacks. However, the healthcare professional and the insurer have a potential conflict of interest because of the exchange of money. The potential for benefiting monetarily from a decision may affect the decision-making process. In health care, the patient delegates much decision making to the healthcare professional (and sometimes even to the insurer).

Asymmetric information also affects healthcare professionals when patients conceal lifestyle information or state that they are in compliance with a treatment when they are not. In addition, a patient's caregiver may withhold or distort information that would be helpful to the provider. Insurers face information asymmetry as well: Clients (consumers who are the buyers of insurance) know much more about the state of their health and their future plans than an insurer knows.

Two specific types of information asymmetry are adverse selection and **moral hazard**.

Economics: Adverse Selection and Moral Hazard

Economists use the terms *adverse selection* and *moral hazard* to describe the situations insurers face when consumers have greater information about their health than insurers or payers. Adverse selection occurs when a person participates in a health plan based *solely* on the likelihood that he or she will have higher than usual health expenses (e.g., planning to get pregnant). **Moral hazard** occurs when a health plan member uses more health services than that person ordinarily would simply because he or she is insured (e.g., a person with orthodontic coverage gets braces on his teeth for cosmetic purposes only). Insurers and payers may also lack sufficient information regarding the choices and decisions of providers and may be unable to ascertain if a procedure is truly medically necessary.

The patient, who does not pay the bill, demands as much care as possible. In contrast:

> [T]he insurance company maximizes profits by paying for as little as possible; . . . it is very costly for either the patient or the insurance company to prove the "right" course of treatment. In short, information asymmetry makes health care different from the rest of the economy. (Wheelan, 2002, p. 86)

Imagine that you have consciously chosen not to purchase health insurance because you are young and enjoy good health; you decide it is cheaper to pay the annual penalty. Recall that insurers may no longer deny health insurance to those who have preexisting health conditions. Within a few months, you unexpectedly become pregnant and decide that you do not want to pay the full cost of prenatal care, delivery, and postpartum care, so you seek a private insurer such as Blue Cross and Blue Shield (BCBS) to purchase insurance. After the baby is born, and BCBS has paid for the costs of your pregnancy and delivery, you decide that you no longer need insurance and drop your coverage. This is an example of adverse selection.

If millions of people made this kind of choice, it would have dire effects on the insurance market. Insurance markets rely upon having a mix of customers who will not require payouts for healthcare episodes and customers who will. In other words, in the health insurance market, the healthy subsidize the sick. If only the old, the sick, or the disabled purchased health insurance, the market would collapse under the weight of their expenses. The scenario in health insurance is similar to that for other types of insurance, such as fire, life, and automobile—those customers who do not use the benefits subsidize those who do. Mandating the purchase of health insurance is an economic strategy designed to create a sustainable risk pool of beneficiaries.

▶ Finance: Comparative Effectiveness Research and Quality-Adjusted Life-Years

Imagine a system of research in which new discoveries or approaches to reduce or eliminate disease are tested for effectiveness against doing nothing at all. The current gold standard for research in the United States is the randomized control trial (RCT), in which a group of subjects receives a treatment while another group receives no treatment. Effectiveness is decided by whether the disease or condition responded to the new approach, but the new approach is not compared to any other approach.

As a result of the 2009 American Recovery and Reinvestment Act (ARRA) and the 2010 ACA, the federal government made major investments in **comparative effectiveness research (CER)**. CER compares the overall benefits of one therapeutic approach with those of another for the majority of patients. These investments are yielding new information about which treatments work best for which population of patients. But how will this research be used beyond informing provider decisions?

Here is an example of a current dilemma: Solvadi is a new drug developed to treat hepatitis C, a life-threatening disease that often goes unrecognized until it reaches its final stages. Solvadi costs $1,000 per dose, and a full treatment regimen costs $84,000. In March 2014, the high price of this medication led to street protests in San Francisco. Health experts say that treating every person with advanced liver disease (from hepatitis C) in California would cost $6.3 billion if Solvadi was given to all those patients. With a success rate of about 90%, Solvadi is an improvement over older drugs, for which regimens cost only $25,000.

Should public insurance pay for Solvadi? Does a regimen of Solvadi have cost benefits when compared to a liver transplant and lifelong immunotherapy? Is avoiding chronic disease "worth" the cost? How many productive years of life are gained? If California's Medicaid program typically spends $3,500/beneficiary/year, how many new beneficiaries could be covered for the $6.3 billion? Economists and health services researchers tackle these types of questions by conducting CER and using a concept called **quality-adjusted life-years (QALYs)**.

QALY is an economic concept developed in the 1960s to facilitate cost-effectiveness analysis. Economists have attempted to include personal preferences regarding age and health conditions and have created a catalog known as the EQ-5D Index. For instance, if you have colon cancer and you are a 65-year-old white female, your EQ-5D index for QALYs is 0.93. That is, if you live 1 year with colon cancer, it is only worth 93% of a year with full health and no diseases. If you have two conditions at the same time (e.g., colon cancer and neurotic disorder), your EQ-5D index is 0.79. Once economists know how many QALYs a treatment is worth, they can figure out its cost per QALY—the broadest measure of the cost-effectiveness of health care.

In general, a QALY carries an economic value of between $70,000 and $150,000 per quality life-year gained by applying a treatment or approach (Anderson et al., 2014). Will CER be used to determine not only a treatment's effectiveness but also the cost-effectiveness and ultimately payment decisions? CER findings can be translated into practice in a variety of ways, some of which may be more acceptable to the public than others. QALYs have been linked to CER in the United Kingdom by the National Institute for Clinical Excellence and have led to debates about *rationing* care. This "R" word represents a slippery slope for opponents of government funding for CER.

The Patient-Centered Outcomes Research Institute (PCORI) was created under the ACA to coordinate government activity around CER. The ACA does not include cost-effectiveness determinations among the guidelines for PCORI.

PCORI conducts research to provide information about the best available evidence to help patients and their healthcare providers make more informed decisions. PCORI's research is intended to give patients a better understanding of the prevention, treatment, and care options available and the science that supports those options.

▶ Finance: Bending the Healthcare Cost Curve Downward

Historically, physicians and hospitals have been paid for each procedure, test, visit, and consultation; that is, they received more pay for doing "more," whether or not "more" resulted in good patient outcomes. This kind of practice drives up costs for health care. One of the ways the ACA seeks to reduce healthcare costs in the United States is by encouraging providers and hospitals to form networks to provide good-quality care to Medicare beneficiaries while holding costs down. In such a system, providers get paid more if they keep their patients well. One of the challenges for hospitals and providers is that the incentives seek to reduce hospital stays, emergency room visits, and use of expensive specialist and testing services—all the ways that hospitals and physicians make money in the current fee-for-service system.

Unlike in other industries, prices for health care vary dramatically depending on who is paying and on geography. The U.S. system is a bit like shopping in a department store where there are no prices marked on the goods. You check out, and a few weeks later, you receive a bill that reads, "Pay this." Growing movements toward price transparency in health care hope to empower patients to overcome information asymmetry, make wise choices, and foment competition that may lower prices. Physicians and hospitals that rarely competed on cost have been cushioned by third-party payers who pay the bulk of the bills. The advent of the Healthcare Blue Book (https://healthcarebluebook.com/) aims to do what the Kelley Blue Book does for used cars—namely, identify a "fair price" for specific healthcare services in the patient's local area. Some argue that true price transparency will destabilize the healthcare industry. Others think that transparency may confuse consumers (Beck, 2014).

▶ Discussion Points

1. Discuss the role of economists in the healthcare policy process. Read about the work of current health economists (e.g., Joseph Antos, James Capretta, Jeffrey Sachs, and Gail Wilensky) to understand their role.

2. Access the blog created by the journal *Health Affairs* (http://www.health affairs.org/blog/) and use the keyword "economics" to search for the latest articles about healthcare economics.

3. Discuss the gross national product in terms of healthcare expenditures. Which sorts of programs will not receive funding when health care consumes a large percentage of federal expenditures?

4. Define "social capital." How does social capital differ from economic capital? Discuss how you benefit from social capital in your own life. How does social capital determine or affect the health of populations?

5. Research some articles on cost shifting in health care. Identify policies that use this method. Argue the benefits and losses of cost shifting. Also research cross-subsidization in health care. How does this differ from cost shifting?

6. Who finances most long-term care in the United States? Take a poll of your peers prior to researching this question to see what they think is the answer. Are nurses well informed about this economic issue, and does this meet your expectation?

7. How does QALY analysis benefit the young over the old?

8. What does the RAND Corporation do? Review its online series, "Small Ideas for Saving Big Health Care Dollars" (http://www.rand.org/pubs/research_reports/RR390.html). Choose one idea for reducing healthcare spending and discuss three new things you learned, three things that surprised you, and how you can use this information in your own practice.

🔎 CASE STUDY 10-1: *Economic Value of BSN Education for RNs*

Retrieve and read the study *Nurse Staffing and Education and Hospital Mortality in Nine European Countries: A Retrospective Observational Study* by Linda Aiken, PhD (and colleagues), of the Center for Health Outcomes and Policy Research at the University of Pennsylvania School of Nursing. This study shows that increasing a nurse's workload by one patient increases the likelihood of an inpatient dying within 30 days of admission by 7% (odds ratio [OR], 1.068; 95% confidence interval [CI], 1.031–1.106), and every 10% increase in bachelor's degree nurses is associated with a 7% decrease in this likelihood (OR, 0.929; 95% CI, 0.886–0.973). These associations imply that patients in hospitals in which 60% of nurses have bachelor's degrees and where nurses care for an average of 6 patients will have almost 30% lower mortality than patients in hospitals in which only 30% of nurses have bachelor's degrees and nurses care for an average of 8 patients.

Discussion Points

1. State your interpretation of these data. Using these conclusions, discuss the implications for hospital leaders when making staffing decisions.

2. Discover the percentage of BSN-prepared nurses licensed in your state. If possible, discover the percentage of BSN-prepared nurses in a hospital or facility in your area.

3. How easily can an average person find out the RN–patient and BSN RN–patient ratio in hospitals? Why do you think this situation exists? What does it mean to you and your family? Who or which entities can change this situation?

🔎 CASE STUDY 10-2: Economic Impact of States Declining Medicaid Expansion

Recall that Medicaid is a joint federal and state entitlement health insurance program. The ACA of 2010 required all states to eliminate the use of categories to determine eligibility and expand the Medicaid program to all persons younger than age 65 with incomes at or below 138% of the federal poverty level. However, in June 2012, the U.S. Supreme Court ruled that requiring states to expand their Medicaid programs was unconstitutional: Each state could make its own decision on whether to expand the program. By 2016, 32 states and Washington, D.C., had opted to expand their Medicaid programs. Declining expansion means that Medicaid continues as it was prior to the ACA's implementation, with category-based eligibility.

Discussion Points

1. Determine whether your state has expanded its Medicaid program.
2. Explain why a very poor person (income below FPL) living in one of the states that declined Medicaid expansion may be ineligible to participate in the health insurance exchanges.
3. What is the economic effect on the state (and on the hospital or site where you work or are being trained) of having a large population of uninsured people?
4. Why would a state choose not to participate in Medicaid expansion despite the federal promise of paying for the additional beneficiaries?
5. There is no "right" to health care in the U.S. Constitution. Debate the pros and cons of a universal Medicare-for-all healthcare finance program for the United States. Refer to the ANA Code of Ethics to inform your debate.
6. Refer to the following article: Sommers, B. D., Gourevitch, R., Maylone, B., Blendon, R., & Epstein, A. M. (2016, October). Insurance churning rates for low income adults under health reform: Lower than expected but still harmful for many. *Health Affairs, 35*(10), 1816–1824. Answer the following questions: In terms of health insurance, what is "churning"? What effect does churning have on access to care and quality of care? What is the relationship among access to care, quality of care, and cost of care?

References

Anderson, J. L., Heidenreich, P. A., Barnett, P. G., Creager, M. A., Fonarow, G. C., Gibbons, R. J., . . . Shaw, L. J. (2014, March 27). ACC/AHA statement on cost/value methodology in clinical practice guidelines and performance measures: A report of the American College of Cardiology/American Heart Association Task Force on Performance Measures and Task Force on Practice Guidelines. *Circulation.* Retrieved from http://circ.ahajournals.org/lookup /doi/10.1161/CIR.0000000000000042

Assistant Secretary of Planning and Evaluation. (2016, October 24). Research brief: Health plan choice and premiums in the 2017 health insurance marketplace. U.S. Department of Health and Human Services. Retrieved from https://aspe.hhs.gov/system/files /pdf/212721/2017MarketplaceLandscapeBrief.pdf

Beck, Melinda (2014, February 23). How to bring the price of health care into the open. *Wall Street Journal*. Retrieved from http://online.wsj.com/news/articles/SB1000142405270230 365020457937524284208668

Central Intelligence Agency. (n.d.). The world factbook. Retrieved from https://www.cia.gov /library/publications/the-world-factbook/

Centers for Medicare and Medicaid Services. (2017, June). National health expenditure data. Retrieved from https://www.cms.gov/research-statistics-data-and-systems/statistics-trends -and-reports/nationalhealthexpenddata/nationalhealthaccountshistorical.html

Getzen, T. (2010). *Health economics and financing* (4th ed.). Hoboken, NJ: John Wiley & Sons.

Hussey, P. S., Wertheimer, S., & Mehrota, A. (2013). The association between health care quality and cost: A systematic review. *Annals of Internal Medicine, 158*(1), 27–34.

Kaiser Family Foundation. (2017a, January). Status of state action on the Medicaid expansion decision. Retrieved from http://kff.org/health-reform/slide/current-status-of-the-medicaid-expansion -decision/

Kaiser Family Foundation. (2017b, April 16). State health facts: Total number of Medicare beneficiaries. Retrieved from http://kff.org/medicare/state-indicator/total-medicare-ben eficiaries/?currentTimeframe=0&sortModel=%7B%22colId%22:%22Location%22,%22 sort%22:%22asc%22%7D

Kaiser Family Foundation. (2017c). U.S. public opinion on health care reform, 2017. Retrieved from http://kff.org/slideshow/us-public-opinion-on-health-care-reform-2017/

National Conference of State Legislatures. (2017, January 3). Health insurance: Premiums and increases. Retrieved from http://www.ncsl.org/research/health/health-insurance-premiums .aspx

Organisation for Economic Co-operation and Development. (2017). OECD health statistics 2016. Retrieved from http://www.oecd.org/els/health-systems/health-data.htm

Patient Protection and Affordable Care Act of 2010. Pub. L. No. 111–148, § 3022.

Rosenbaum, S., Rothenberg, S., Gunsalus, R., & Schmucker, R. (2017, January 12). Medicaid's future: What might ACA repeal mean? Commonwealth Fund. Retrieved from http://www .commonwealthfund.org/publications/issue-briefs/2017/jan/medicaids-future-aca-repeal

Stein, H. (1986). *Washington bedtime stories: The politics of money and jobs*. New York, NY: Free Press.

U.S. Department of Health and Human Services. (2014, January 22). Annual update of the HHS poverty guidelines. Retrieved from https://Federalregister.gov/a/2014-01303

Wheelan, C. (2002). *Naked economics: Undressing the dismal science*. New York, NY: W. W. Norton.

Online Resources

Alliance for Health Policy (http://www.allhealthpolicy.org): Nonpartisan, well-respected organization providing analytical materials and webcasts by health economists and other health experts.

America's Health Insurance Plan (https://www.ahip.org): The national association for insurance companies providing coverage for healthcare and related services.

California HealthCare Foundation (http://www.chcf.org): This organization's annual chartbook provides a wealth of data and graphics.

Centers for Medicare and Medicaid Services (https://www.cms.gov/NationalHealthExpendData/): National health expenditure data.

Centers for Medicare and Medicaid Services (CMS) Data Navigator (https://www.cms.gov /home/rsds.asp): The Data Navigator introduces healthcare data users to the Medicare and Medicaid program data maintained by CMS. Intended for use by researchers and analysts.

Commonwealth Fund (http://www.commonwealthfund.org): Supports independent research on healthcare issues and makes grants to improve healthcare practice and policy. Not to be confused with the Commonwealth Foundation.

Consumer Expenditure Survey, Bureau of Labor Statistics (https://www.bls.gov/cex/): Details of consumer healthcare expenditures.

Consumer Price Indexes, Bureau of Labor Statistics (https://www.bls.gov/cpi/): Monthly data on changes in the prices paid by urban consumers for a representative basket of goods and services.

Current Population Survey, U.S. Census Bureau (https://www.census.gov): Everything you want to know about the census and the U.S. population.

Dartmouth Atlas of Health Care (http://www.dartmouthatlas.org): Brings together researchers in diverse disciplines—including epidemiology, economics, and statistics—and focuses on the accurate description of how medical resources are distributed and used in the United States.

HealthCare.gov (https://www.healthcare.gov): Federal government website maintained by the U.S. Department of Health and Human Services. The web location for health insurance exchange information.

Kaiser Family Foundation (http://www.kff.org): Nonpartisan, nongovernmental organization in Washington, D.C., providing excellent data, facts, and analysis of healthcare issues and health policy.

Organisation for Economic Co-operation and Development (http://www.oecd.org/): An organization of 35 member countries with the mission to promote policies that will improve the economic and social well-being of people around the world. It works with governments to understand what drives economic, social, and environmental change.

CHAPTER 11

The Impact of Globalization: Nurses Influencing Global Health Policy

Dorothy Lewis Powell and Jeri A. Milstead

KEY TERMS

Commission on Graduates of Foreign Nursing Schools International (CGFNS): An immigration-neutral, nonprofit organization with nongovernmental organization (NGO) consultative status to the United Nations. It evaluates professional and academic credentials for nurses educated outside the United States. It is the only organization named in the U.S. federal statute to administer visa screening of foreign-educated nurses and other professionals in seven healthcare fields (http://www.cgfns.org, 2017).

Global burden of disease: The impact of a health problem as measured by financial cost, mortality, morbidity, or other indicators.

Globalization: "A process of interaction and integration among the people, companies, and governments of different nations driven by international trade and investment and aided by information technology" with "effects on the environment, on culture, on political systems, on economic development and prosperity, and on human physical well-being in societies around the world" (Retrieved from globalization101.org/about-us (p. 1), (visited on 08/29/17)).

International Council of Nurses (ICN): A federation for worldwide advocacy for nursing, with a membership of 130 national nurses associations. Its mission is "to represent nursing worldwide, advancing the profession and influencing health policy" (ICN, 2017, p. 1).

International Monetary Fund: An organization of 189 countries working to foster global monetary cooperation, secure financial stability, facilitate international trade, promote high employment and sustainable economic growth, and reduce poverty around the world.

Migration of human capital: The movement of people, with their stock of knowledge, habits, and social and personality attributes, including creativity, along with the ability to perform labor so as to produce economic value across international borders.

Push–pull factors: Those factors that either forcefully push people into migration or attract them. A push factor is generally some problem that results in people wanting to migrate.

World Bank: A source of financial and technical assistance to developing countries around the world. It is not a bank in the ordinary sense but rather a partnership to reduce poverty and support development.

World Health Organization (WHO): A specialized agency of the United Nations that is concerned with international public health. Its mission is "to combat infectious and noncommunicable diseases and ensure the safety of air, food, water and medicines/vaccines" (WHO, 2017b, p. 1). It was established in 1948; is headquartered in Geneva, Switzerland; and has six regions—African, South-East Asian, European, Eastern Mediterranean, Western Pacific, and Region of the Americas.

▶ Introduction

McLuhan and Fiore (1968) described the world as a global village in which each person is affected by and affects all inhabitants. Franklin Shaffer (2014), president and chief executive officer of the **Commission on Graduates of Foreign Nursing Schools International (CGFNS)**, reminds us that "the world is gradually becoming a borderless society" (p. 3). Shaffer's thoughts compel us to consider health and illness as well as those who address health status, whether direct and indirect care providers or policymakers, in a different way.

Professional nurses have long recognized their potential for influencing health policy around the world. The **International Council of Nurses (ICN)** "rallies nurses to make a major contribution in promoting and shaping effective health policy, given their close interaction with clients and ability to gain an appreciation of the health needs of the population and factors that influence those needs" (Benton, 2012, p. 1). Benton, who was chief executive officer at ICN in 2012, noted that "nurses associations can serve as key vehicles for influencing policy, both nationally and globally" (p. 2). He also observed that "initial improvements in the profession can be traced to the organization's commitment of individuals working under the auspices of nursing associations" but with recognition that "policy development has traditionally been nursing's area of slowest advancement" (Benton, 2012, p. 2). Multiple groups and nurse leaders note that "nurses must do more than care for patients and conduct research. . . . They need to also be actively involved in shaping health policy" (Abood, 2007, p. 2).

Globalization has the potential to link nations around the world. It affects all sectors of society, including health care. However, there are uneven benefits and other effects within and across global regions and sectors of society, particularly within and across developing countries. Former President Barack Obama, in an interview with *The New York Times* the week before he left office, took note of the "clash of cultures brought about by globalization and technology and migration" (Kakutani, 2017). Nursing and other healthcare professions and institutions are profoundly affected by the globalization process, including its disparate effects on developed and developing countries (Seloilwe, 2005).

In this chapter, we conduct a general analysis of globalization and its positive and negative effects on critical issues regarding nursing and access to quality health care in developed and developing countries. We also discuss nursing's involvement in healthcare policy formulation and politics from a global perspective, differentiating between developing and developed countries. Finally, we examine the various factors affecting the out-migration of nurses from less developed countries and the consequent impact on health care in those countries.

The roles and responsibilities of nurses in developed and developing countries have much in common. Neither nurses in developed countries nor their counterparts in developing countries are as involved in policy formulation and politics as they could be—and probably should be (Benton, 2012).

▶ Globalization and Its Impact on Nursing and Health Care

Globalization is "a process of interaction and integration among the people, companies, and governments of different nations driven by international trade and investment and aided by information technology . . . with effects on the environment, on culture, on political systems, on economic development and prosperity, and on human physical well-being in societies around the world" (Levin Institute, 2016). Globalization is a controversial phenomenon, particularly with regard to its impact on poor and developing countries. On the one hand, globalization benefits multinational corporations and industrialized nations and extends to poor and developing countries an opportunity to improve their economies and raise their standards of living through foreign collaboration. On the other hand, globalization can cripple developing countries by harming local businesses and services and eroding the culture and traditions of local populations (McCubbrey, 2016).

There is a worldwide shortage of healthcare workers, with the greatest shortage being nurses (Khaliq, Broyles, & Mwachofi, 2009; Senior, 2010). This imbalance is critical to understanding the effects of public policy on the global migration of nurses. Developing countries experience severe shortages of nurses triggered, in part, by "international funding agency requirements aimed at promoting growth, increasing employment, stabilizing prices and currencies, evolving better balances of payment equilibrium, and encouraging balanced budgets in targeted countries" (WHO, 2006a).

The impact of loan policies, such as those of the International Structural Adjustment Programs of the **World Bank** and the **International Monetary Fund** (begun in the mid-1980s), resulted in reductions in the number of health workers employed within various sectors of government, particularly health and education sectors, even as recruitment was restricted or frozen (WHO, 2006a). The competing expectations of meeting international loan payments on time and balancing the public budget have the effect of reducing public expenditures on critical public services, including adequate nursing care. These reductions in expenditures frequently take the form of hiring freezes, severely limiting the number of new nurses allowed to enter the workforce, failing to replace practicing nurses lost due to HIV/AIDS, reducing benefits and salaries, adhering strictly to retirement guidelines, suspending any financial promotions, increasing the nurse-to-population and nurse-to-patient ratios to unsafe levels, and limiting career and professional development opportunities (Shah, 2013).

One might question why nurses affected by restrictive workplace conditions and the inability to effectively care for their patients fail to advocate for better working conditions and accessible patient care. In the past, national nursing associations have often tried to broker favorable conditions of service for nurses and midwives but were barred in their efforts to act as a labor union; they were allowed to have some input only into regulating professional and educational issues within the Nursing Council, a quasi-governmental agency charged with statutory requirements to regulate nursing and midwifery (WHO, 2006a).

Regulatory bodies and associations are concerned with scope of nursing practice, providing guidance on practice and education for nurses and midwives; examining ethics, conduct, and competency of professional nurses; and maintaining a register of qualified nurses (WHO, 2006a). While nursing associations may also seek to have some influence on human resources policies within a country's Ministry of Health, little has been achieved on a worldwide scale. The exception is in South Africa, where there is an autonomous and independent nursing council that receives no government funding (WHO, 2006a); it is similar to nursing councils in developed countries. Such autonomy makes it possible for nurses to have greater authority over advocacy and influence on nursing practice and work conditions. By contrast, all other nursing councils in Sub-Saharan Africa and other developing countries have a statutory link with the Ministry of Health, the official agency for health.

The chief nursing officer (CNO), who is the highest-ranking nursing official in the country, is considered a key stakeholder in driving nursing and midwifery workforce strategies in collaboration with **World Health Organization (WHO)** policy and management functions (WHO, 2015). Ideally, according to the WHO (2015) document on *Roles and Responsibilities of Government Chief Nursing and Midwifery Officers*, the person in this role provides "leadership and influence, policy advice, planning and developing health systems and services, and promotes WHO programs for health status improvement" (p. 11). Countries differ in their abilities and level of execution of the CNO role. WHO provides training materials and conferences to facilitate CNO competencies.

Recommendations and Actions for Sustainable Development Goals

In 2016, the ICN expressed its strong support for the recommendations of the United Nations' High-Level Commission on Health Employment and Economic Growth (HEEG) at a ministerial meeting held in Geneva, Switzerland (WHO, 2017a). In the report entitled *Working for Health and Growth: Investing in the Health Workforce*, the Commission on HEEG identified 10 recommendations and five immediate actions to transform the health workforce for the achievement of the United Nations' Sustainable Development Goals. These recommendations will require major interventions and action by national governments, led by their ministries of health, education, employment, and finance, as well as the international community. The recommendations are expected to stimulate the creation of health and social jobs to promote economic growth (High Level Commission, 2014).

The United Nations' SDGs listed in **FIGURE 11-1** offer an opportunity for nurses to demonstrate how their actions make a difference and how they help shape decision-making processes and healthcare policies. Nurses' ability to effect change is just as important as their technical ability to deliver safe and effective care. Policy development is a practical tool for change, and participation in policymaking is a logical extension and expression of the nursing profession's care and compassion.

The 2006 World Health Report demonstrates an inverse relationship among the burden of disease, the global proportion of healthcare workers, and expenditures on health by WHO regions (WHO, 2006b, p. 9) (**FIGURE 11-2**). There is a direct relationship among the distribution of high burden of disease, low quantity and quality of health workers, and suboptimal level of dedicated resources. As shown in Figure 11-2, approximately 24% of the **global burden of disease** is found in the African region, which has only 2% of the global health workforce and the least financial support of all six WHO regions. By contrast, the populations

FIGURE 11-1 United Nations' sustainable development goals.

Reproduced from United Nations. (n.d.). Sustainable development goals: 17 goals to transform our world. Retrieved from http://www.un.org/sustainabledevelopment/news/communications-material/

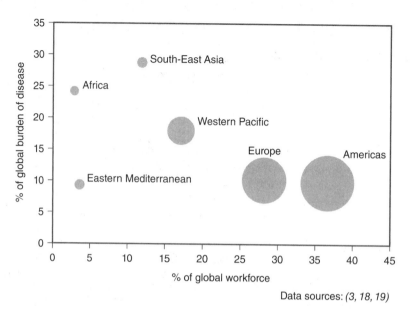

Data sources: *(3, 18, 19)*

FIGURE 11-2 Distribution of health workers by WHO region, level of health expenditure, and burden of disease.

Reproduced from WHO. (2006). Health workers: A global profile. In *Working together for health: The World Health Report 2006* (pp. 1–17). Retrieved from http://www.who .int/whr/2006/06_chap1_en.pdf. Used with permission of the World Health Organization.

of United States and Europe have about 10% of the global burden of disease, with the United States employing 38% of the global healthcare workforce, while Europe employs another 27%. Health expenditures for these two countries rank as number one for the United States and number two for Europe, according to WHO (2006b, p. 9).

Logic suggests that the quality of health outcomes is negatively impacted by the continuously dwindling number of health workers and minimal financial resources to support adequate healthcare facilities accessible to the population served. Other factors that negatively affected health outcomes include failure to provide adequate pay and incentives for healthcare staff, failure to maintain a sufficient number of staff to ensure proper care and medicines are administered, and inadequate access to realistic health promotion and disease prevention. Given the opposite parameters, the result would likely be more accessible care, more staff with better staff-to-patient ratios, and availability of greater numbers of healthcare dollars, regardless of notable imperfections in the system.

McCubbrey (2016, p. 1) documented the following potential negative impacts of globalization on developing countries:

- "Free trade" exacerbates income inequality between industrialized countries and developing countries.
- Commerce is increasingly dominated by transnational corporations, which may seek to maximize profits without regard for the developmental needs of individual countries.

- Protectionist policies of industrialized countries preclude many products from developing countries from being exported.
- Volume/volatility of capital flow increases risks of currency and banking crises.
- Foreign investment in developing countries leads to a "race to the bottom" in which targeted countries hover close to dangerously lower environmental standards.
- Cultural uniqueness is lost in favor of homogenization and a universal culture that draws heavily on the American culture.

These negative impacts of globalization are more likely to be present in developing regions of the worlds, such as Sub-Saharan Africa and Latin America, whereas positive impacts of globalization are more likely to be evident in Eastern Asia, where countries such as China, Japan, Korea, Taiwan, Malaysia, Indonesia, and Singapore are among the greatest beneficiaries of globalization. Globalization has driven economic growth in the latter countries through robust exports, large flows of foreign investments, and rising social indicators, as well as by tapping into large world markets, technology, human capital, and cheaper import markets (McCubbrey, 2016). Successful economies, such as Eastern Asia, are quite different from those countries included in the lower economic tier of developing countries.

Migration of Human Capital

Another characteristic of globalization is **migration of human capital**—that is, relocation of people from a nation considered their home country to a destination country in an effort to improve their working conditions, salary, and opportunities. Both developed and developing countries experience challenges associated with migration and the geographic shortage of nurses. The Organization for Economic Cooperation and Development (OECD) is "a group of 34 member countries that discuss and develop economic and social policy . . . and are democratic countries that support free market economies" (OECD, 2015). OECD has reported data comparing migration from the top 25 sources of healthcare workers for 2000/2001 to similar migration for 2010/2011 (International Migration Outlook, 2017). The most recent comprehensive nurse migration data are reported in *International Migration Outlook 2017* (OECD 2017).

The provider density ratio is a means of comparatively gauging, by country, the number of professional nurse and midwife providers for every 1,000 population (WHO, 2006b). A larger ratio—that is, a larger number of providers per population—likely signals higher levels of job satisfaction and higher quality and accuracy of care than a smaller ratio (Kingma, 2007). According to WHO, 1.7 million healthcare workers migrated in 2009 (Batalova, 2014). The WHO data track aide-level healthcare workers (including nursing, psychiatric, and home health aides) and registered nurses from foreign countries. The nonprofessional or lay worker group accounted for the largest group of healthcare migrants—463,000 individuals—representing 27% of healthcare worker migrants. Professional registered nurses and midwives were the second largest group immigrating to the United States in 2009, representing 23% of all health worker migrants. Among the aide-level workforce, 41% of these migrants came from Asia, 17% from Latin America, 17% from the Caribbean, 10% from Africa, and 15% from North America, Europe, and Oceania.

Factors Affecting Out-Migration

Globalization and the severe and worsening imbalance of nurses/midwives to population density, combined with the inability of nurses to care for the varied health needs of specific populations (particularly in low-income and developing countries), has contributed to the extensive migration of nurses out of their home countries. When they emigrate, they often leave behind a skeletal workforce whose wages, benefits, nurse-patient ratios, quality of life, and workplace satisfaction are unsatisfactory and unsafe (Kingma, 2007).

Migrants are people who make choices about when to leave and where to go, even though these choices are sometimes extremely constrained. In the healthcare context, the term *migrant* does not refer to refugees, displaced persons, or others forced or compelled to leave their homes (UNESCO, 2017). Today, overall migration patterns reflect world economic trends (Levin Institute, 2016) in relation to the "swell in international capital investments and manufacturing businesses seeking cheap land and cheap labor" (p. 7). Associated with migration are **push–pull factors**, which serve as major contributors to the emigration of nurses from developing and low-income countries where working conditions and rewards are increasingly unsatisfactory.

Push factors are those factors that "drive people away from their home countries," whereas *pull factors* are those factors that "attract workers to where they end up" (Levin Institute, 2016, p. 14). Key push factors for migration include poverty-level incomes, low wages (particularly in rural areas), low standards of living, and lack of employment opportunities in poorer countries. Additional push factors contributing to healthcare workers' emigration include a constantly dwindling workforce, patient care concerns, little anticipation of gaining any new nurses, a resurgence of communicable diseases, poor healthcare human resources management systems, inefficiencies in the public health sector, and limited career and professional opportunities. Nurses in "push" countries often experience feelings of powerlessness that contribute to their migration from low-income countries to higher-income countries. In the latter countries, an ongoing shortage of nurses simultaneously creates a "pull" phenomenon, fueling vigorous international recruitment campaigns.

Push and pull factors associated with the worldwide shortage of nurses present a critical challenge for countries seeking to control the movement of populations. For a long period of time, most nations seemed to be satisfied with the status quo regarding the movement of people across national boundaries. The Levin Institute (2016) describes the chief pull factors for healthcare workers in developed countries as higher standards of living and higher wages, a constant demand for nurses, and political and religious freedom. These factors typically afford immigrants higher wages in the new country for the same work done at home and offer them the opportunity to send money to their families back home. According to the World Bank, these kinds of remittances totaled $529 billion worldwide in 2012. There is growing recognition that "the developed world fills its vacancies by enticing nurses from other countries, while developing countries are unable to compete with better pay, better professional development, and the lure of excitement offered elsewhere" (Senior, 2010, p. 1).

The Caribbean Community Market (CARICOM, 2017) is a multinational, English-speaking organization composed of 20 countries from the Bahamas to South America. CARICOM's main purposes are to promote economic integration and cooperation among its members, to ensure that the benefits of integration are equitably shared, and to coordinate foreign policy. The Regional Nursing Body (RNB) of CARICOM links nursing in the member states together through the chief nursing officers of the countries, who provide advisory services to the ministers of health of CARICOM. The RNB advises the organization on matters related to improvements of nursing and its contributions to health care in the region; identifies needs for basic, post-basic, and continuing education for nurses; monitors nursing and healthcare trends in the region; updates nursing legislation; and engages in programs of quality assurance in nursing.

The RNB is an important regional force in advancing education, practice, research, and the policy agenda relative to nursing and midwifery (UIA, 2017). The mandated relationship between the RNB and CARICOM gives nursing the capacity to guide its own professional development and self-regulation. The University of the West Indies at Mona is expected to share nurse graduates with other CARICOM member states and in competition with more distant international locations.

Jamaica loses many generalist nurses and specialist nurses to developed countries and neighboring islands each year. Jamaica, along with regional and international partners, initiated a Managed Migration Program for the Caribbean region with the goal of meeting its own need for nurses and midwives while simultaneously accommodating the inevitable pull by neighboring islands and developed countries—specifically, Canada, the United Kingdom, and the United States (Salmon, Yan, & Hewitt, 2007).

Filipino nursing schools have been educating professional nurses for export (inclusive of English language competence) since 1965. Even while recognizing the importance of this out-migration, the schools continue to train nurses in the national Tagalog language and prepare them to work in Filipino hospitals and patient care settings—particularly in rural areas, where patients tend to follow more traditional ways of life and speak more traditional languages.

▶ The Importance of Understanding the Cultural Context

Nurses cannot work successfully in any healthcare situation if they do not grasp the importance of having a basic understanding of the culture of the patient and the healthcare system. Philosophy about health, disease, customs, and traditions influences whether a person believes he or she has a health problem and, if so, how the problem should be acknowledged and treated. For example, Fadiman (1997) wrote a classic book about her work with the Hmong people. The Hmong, who live in mountainous regions of Southeast Asia, believe that a person with epilepsy has a special gift. According to their belief system, during seizures, the patient should be revered, not treated as if having a disease. When people from this region emigrate to another country and seek health care from a system that considers status epilepticus to be a medical emergency, major challenges arise in terms of communication between the patient/family and the provider.

Researchers must be cognizant of cultural norms when planning to study a disease, population, or issue. For example, "'saving face' can imperil the research process" (Chen et al., 2013, p. 149) if researchers are not aware that on-site staff fear that participants might disclose something that might embarrass the study. Researchers also should realize that some cultures value individual effort less than collective effort; this can affect how the study results are written and disseminated.

Opportunities for conducting global research may be limited by one's own mindset. In 2014, *Journal of Nursing Scholarship* began a series of commentaries on the global state of nursing (Gennaro, 2014). The editorial board emphasized that all nurses must think globally while acting locally. This author challenges nurses to think globally and act globally to address health issues common to many countries.

The American Academy of Nursing (AAN), a prestigious group of nurse leaders, is organized through expert panels. The Expert Panel on Global Nursing and Health created a task force to examine cultural competence on a global level. The members of the task force had experience as nurses and researchers in many cultures and worked diligently to create a document without ethnocentric biases. In this effort, the group worked with members of the Transcultural Nursing Society. The final version of the guidelines they developed, which was published in *Journal of Transcultural Nursing* (Douglas et al., 2014), was adopted by the ICN. As this chapter was being written, the Expert Panel on Emerging Infectious Diseases was preparing a document (policy brief, white paper, or article for publication) that addresses the policy implications when "local" diseases have the potential to become global issues.

Nurses are often the first providers to see clearly when and how the health-care system is, or is not, effectively meeting patient needs (Abood, 2007) and supporting their own needs in the work environment. Nurses not only see the impact of healthcare policies on individual patients but also understand the need for more comprehensive changes in policies that address many health-related issues (Benton, 2009; Shariff, 2014). During troubling times, with serious global healthcare issues, nurses have first-line insights into the level of adequacy of providers, services, resources, and environmental support to fight communicable and noncommunicable diseases; public health practices to prevent the spread of contagion; (in)adequate access to care; availability of medications; and availability of life-sustaining resources such as food and water, conditions of living, and social practices that support good health.

Addressing nursing's insights and ability to inform these issues, Princess Muna Al-Hussein of Jordan, speaking during a 2014 Nursing Leadership in Global Health Symposium at Vanderbilt University (WHO, 2014b), noted that "global health is facing unprecedented challenges, and nurses worldwide are potentially at the heart of meeting them. Nurses worldwide represent a force of abilities that can shape and advance health care" (Rivers, 2014, pp. 1, 2). Princess Muna spoke in favor of programs "that support Sustainable Development Goals with emphasis on alleviating poverty, promoting the health of mothers and infants, and strengthening the health workforce" (WHO, 2014b, p. 1). The holder of several honorary posts in nursing, she has taken a special interest in nursing and midwifery to enhance quality, equity, and efficiency of care (WHO, 2014b).

During the sixth Global Forum for Government and Chief Nursing and Midwifery Officers (CNOs and CMOs), she called for continued support for CNOs and CMOs, educational institutions, WHO Collaborating Centers for nursing and midwives, and professional associations to support universal healthcare coverage (WHO, 2014a, 2016).

▶ Nurse Involvement in Policy Decisions

To what extent have nurses been involved in influencing governmental policies that affect health, the delivery of care, and nursing practice? Research conducted by Asp et al. (2014), for example, identified a lack of knowledge of neonatal danger signals among women in rural Uganda. This research opens up opportunities for nurse interventions for neonates who otherwise might die. Asp and colleagues also identified a link between media exposure and birth preparedness among women in southwestern Uganda.

Nursing Education to Improve Involvement in Policymaking

There is a strong relationship among nursing education, post-secondary education, leadership, and participation in advocacy and policymaking. Professional nursing education in the United States, as an example of a developed country, includes a focus on health policy and advocacy, with students in baccalaureate, master's, and doctoral programs being targeted for policy education. Academic outcome competencies and curriculum guidelines include advocating for "patients, families, communities, the nursing profession and changes in the health care system . . . [and] . . . advocacy for vulnerable populations and promoting social justice" (American Association of Colleges of Nursing [AACN], 2008, p. 20). Building on the advocacy foundation of baccalaureate nursing education, the AACN's (2011) *Essentials of Masters' Education in Nursing* prepares nurses to "use their political efficacy and competence to improve the health outcomes of populations and improve the quality of the healthcare delivery system" (p. 20). At the doctoral level, "political activism and a commitment to policy development are essential elements of professional nursing practice" (AACN, 2006).

Nursing education in developing countries has a primary focus on clinical practice and generally lacks a curricular focus on advocacy. The involvement of health professionals, especially nurses, in policymaking and the development of health programs requires skills that have not been part of the spectrum of competences for even senior-level nurses in developing countries, with the exception of limited instruction on strategic policy development. The entry-level government-sanctioned nursing programs in most developing countries maintain a primary focus on clinical practice, and the standard state-certified curriculum does not emphasize either advocacy or strategic policy development.

Historically, on a worldwide scale, nurses with entry-level education generally did not advocate or seek to influence their practice or health policies. Nursing, considered to be a female profession, was also limited by the culturally perceived subordinate role of women, especially in developing countries. Physicians were considered leaders of the healthcare team and were largely male, which in turn meant they had a greater potential than women to elevate their roles and authority. Despite these stereotypical gender and role conflicts, a greater sense of collegiality, collaboration, and teamwork has emerged in many regions of the world, primarily in developed countries. Many developing countries, meanwhile, continue to operate within the context of a male-dominated society.

Facilitators of and Barriers to Advocacy and Policymaking

Despite worldwide efforts to recognize and promote nursing involvement in policymaking, the profession of nursing continues to underperform in terms of its potential to influence policy within the legislative and policymaking arena. A study by Shariff (2014) offers insight into how identified factors influence the extent of advocacy practiced by nurses in developing countries, particularly in Sub-Saharan Africa.

Shariff (2014) examined a subset of data from East African nations on factors that act as facilitators of and barriers to nurse leaders' participation in health policy development. A Delphi survey methodology was applied, with the research including expert panelists (national nurse leaders), three iterative rounds, statistical analysis, and consensus building. Consensus results identified four facilitative factors:

- Being involved (having experience and exposure, being accorded opportunity, being present at all stages of policy development, seeking opportunity to be involved, and being an active participant)
- Being knowledgeable and skilled (developing health policy, benefiting from role models, possessing university education, and having curriculum content related to health policy)
- Being supported (benefiting from role models, supportive mentorship, and networks for support and for sharing experiences)
- Being perceived in a positive manner (considered a valuable partner in policy development, appointed to policymaking positions, and engaging with policymakers and the media)

▶ Conclusion

Nurses have the opportunity to influence all aspects and sectors of society. When this opportunity is viewed from the vantage point of residents of developed countries versus developing countries, strategies for impact may vary due to tradition, local policy, and culture. Nurses have the potential to bring to policy discussions or committees in the workplace their observed objective perspectives on the contribution of some policies (institutional, local, or national) regarding the health or illness of patients, families, and communities while maintaining a subject's anonymity. They can provide objective input based on the knowledge, values, and skills of their profession, augmented by their specialized and personal experiences and exposure.

Ethical and legal responsibilities require nurses to act on behalf of their patients, to safeguard their rights and well-being, and to promote egalitarian human rights. Some nurses feel called upon to address social and policy issues, including advocating, like Florence Nightingale, for egalitarian human rights. Many nurses working in health care are motivated to assume some kind of advocacy role so as to influence changes in policies, laws, or regulations that govern the larger healthcare system (Abood, 2007). Advocacy adds a welcome dimension to the professional practice of nursing, which offers involved nurses an opportunity to have some control over patient care and outcomes (p. 1).

▶ Discussion Points

1. List at least three health problems at your local level that have implications at the global level. Which data did you need (and from which sources) to determine the global nature of the problem?
2. If you have not been involved in health issues in a country or culture different from your own, which steps would you take to find a good fit for your talents (e.g., your specialty, experience, personal demographics)?
3. Discuss some challenges and successes encountered by the nurse heroes noted in the following international vignettes. Compare these experiences with some of your own. Which advice would you give to colleagues or nurses early in their careers to prepare them for the challenges and successes they will encounter?

☌ *CASE STUDY 11-1:* The Resurgence of Polio

Imagine you work in a rural clinic in Bolivia. You have completed an examination of a 10-year-old child who presented with a high fever (104°F) that has lasted for 2 days, pain and stiffness in all joints, and an inability to stand or walk. You suspect polio and recognize that the disease has had a resurgence in incidence in this country. Ask yourself the following questions.

International Setting/Level of Analysis

1. Am I practicing in a country that offers the polio vaccine to everyone?
2. Which governmental level offers the vaccine?
3. How do I find out about the government structure and function?
4. If I am not familiar with the type of government (e.g., parliamentary, monarchy, democracy, dictatorship), what resources are available to educate me?
5. Which level of government is most likely to hear my concerns?
6. Are there governmental (i.e., public) policies that encourage or discourage vaccination for polio?

(continues)

⌕ *CASE STUDY 11-1:* The Resurgence of Polio
(continued)

Policy Process

1. Which component(s) of the policy process does this health problem most likely "fit"?
2. If this is a matter that should be put on the government agenda, what methods could I use when approaching officials?
3. How can I phrase the problem so that officials will pay attention?
4. Who would be important to enlist in expressing my concerns?
5. If this matter needs a government response, what are the formal and informal means of communicating with officials?
6. Is there a person with prestige or influence who will help carry my message to the government?
7. Which policy tools can I use to design a government response to the problem? Is a law or regulation already in place that addresses this problem? If so, where was the breakdown in implementation?
8. Were the legal objectives clear when written? Were the program objectives changed during implementation?
9. Was the program or law ever evaluated? By whom? For what purpose?
10. Were any recommendations made? If so, were the recommendations followed?

Sociocultural System

Policies that are studied without regard to the human systems in which they function have little relevance. One must start by identifying the context—that is, the values of those who are affected by and affect the policy.

1. In the rural area in which you are practicing, is vaccination an accepted method of disease prevention? If not, what are the arguments against it?
2. If the procedure is accepted, was this child vaccinated? If not, why not?
3. Who was responsible for vaccinating the child?
4. Does polio hold a special meaning in this culture?
5. Is there a clear system of patriarchy or matriarchy? Does family hold a special meaning? Is the family a nuclear unit or an extended unit?
6. Is the patient/family part of a minority group that is treated differently from the majority? Is that person/family adherent in other areas of health care?
7. Are there religious or personal philosophical reasons why vaccination was not administered?
8. Are there myths about polio that keep some people from accepting vaccination? Do you believe these myths? If not, how can you help others dispel the myths?
9. Are there foods, clothing, sanitation practices, or language differences (vernacular phrases, intonations, regional or tribal accents) that could be barriers to vaccination? Is there geography or history that has contributed to the problem under study?

Economic and Political Systems

1. If there is a government mandate to vaccinate, was funding made available?
2. Was there enough vaccine available for the population?
3. Did other governmental priorities supersede vaccination programs?

4. Is vaccine still available? Would pharmaceutical companies be asked to produce more vaccine for a small population? If so, what is the cost, and who will pay for it?
5. Which interest groups could be rallied to support a current government program? A new program?
6. Which private resources could be tapped to assist with solving the problem?
7. Could resources such as the legal system, media, or interest groups be enlisted to address the problem?

The Health System
1. Is there a governmental health system available to help with the vaccination question?
2. At which level (national, regional/district, local/tribal) would this system exist? If not, how are children protected against common diseases?

EXHIBIT 11-1 Personal Stories of International Nurse Policy Leaders

The Caribbean Community
Hermi Hyacinth Hewitt, OD, PhD, MPH, RN, RM, FAAN

Dr. Hermi Hewitt, with advanced degrees from Tulane University and the University of Iowa, is an iconic leader in Jamaica and throughout the English-speaking Caribbean Community (CARICOM) and beyond. Established in July 1973, CARICOM is a progressive development from the former Caribbean Free Trade Association (CARIFTA). The 15 member states of the CARICOM trade block have gone beyond being a mere free-trade area to encompass programs for sustained economic development within the region as well as unified trade, economic, and foreign policies with states outside the region.

For nearly 40 years, Dr. Hewitt has excelled as an educator, leader, and advocate, becoming one of the strongest and most powerful policymakers for nursing in the Caribbean. She was instrumental in the development and pursuit of advancements in nursing in Jamaica and throughout the region. Most notable were the following accomplishments:

- Transformation of the hospital certificate RN training program into an entry-level BSC program at the University of the West Indies–Mona
- Initiation of access to BSC nursing education for practicing nurses throughout the Caribbean region through technology
- Designation of UWI-Mona as a PAHO/WHO Collaborating Center for nursing and midwifery
- Cultivation of global partnerships to strengthen academics, research, and publications among nurses in the region
- Implementation of a master's-level clinical nurse specialist role in geriatrics to enhance care to elderly persons along the wellness–illness continuum

(continues)

EXHIBIT 11-1 Personal Stories of International Nurse Policy Leaders   *(continued)*

- Facilitation of a mandate by the Regional Nursing Body (RNB) to require practicing RNs without a professional practice degree to upgrade to a bachelor's level
- Collaboration with various area governments to institute managed migration of nurses to maintain an adequate nursing workforce for the region

Dr. Hewitt has described various governmental, professional, and institutional entities with which advocacy and collaboration were required for progress in nursing (personal communication, February 2, 2017). Major negotiators included CARICOM (through the RNB), the hospital board chairman and chief executive officer, the university faculty of medical sciences, the chief nurse at the Ministry of Health, the Nursing Council of Jamaica, the National Nursing Organization, and several funding sources.

Policy advocacy activities, according to Dr. Hewitt, are usually confronted with multiple challenges to efforts to facilitate change. Within the context of her own setting, Dr. Hewitt notes the lack of adequate qualified nursing faculty to implement a new baccalaureate program at UWI, a major challenge associated with migration, and the resistance to change among hospital nursing faculty, along with reassignments of hospital nursing faculty to other hospital duties. Cultural challenges were also significant, especially in transforming the culture from a hospital educational culture to a university culture of teaching, research, and community involvement. The inadequacy of physical facilities, along with major budgetary needs and other competing priorities at the university, were often overwhelming obstacles, taking considerable time for resolution. Long-term changes can span more than one administration, and lack of continuity in leadership and vision can compromise momentum and direction. Despite the challenges faced by Dr. Hewitt and her colleagues, they successfully opened a new 17,014-square-feet nursing building at UWI-Mona in January 2009. Trying to attract and maintain the type and number of faculty and resources needed is a constant struggle, requiring ongoing projections, evidence, and networks of support. Nursing leadership, like that demonstrated by Dr. Hewitt, is advocacy at its best.

The Making of a Nurse Leader, Policymaker, and Politician in the CARICOM

Audrey Gittens, RN, BScN, MScN, DNP

Audrey Gittens entered this world to be a leader and to bring about positive change wherever she would be planted. On reflection, she sees her pathway toward becoming a nurse leader in the Caribbean as divinely inspired. As a young woman in 1994, she was confronted with the difficult decision of whether to accept a public service post or to enter the nursing profession. Constantly seeking truth, she sought out various nurses to explore the reality of what nursing truly is. She was greatly influenced by a nurse–midwife who left an indelible mark on her, including the realization that there is no other profession as rewarding as nursing.

The importance of a mentor and coach became evident when Dr. Gittens was a second-year nursing student. Her own words reflect this guidance best:

I approached the then principal of the school, Aberdeen Browne, and informed her that I would like to be the chief nursing officer [of the country within the Ministry of Health]. She laughed, commended me on my ambition, but told me that her [own] desire is to be the holder of the post before I do. She, however, asked me to concentrate on becoming a nurse and then get back to her at the end of my training. I did.

According to Dr. Gittens, Ms. Browne "provided guidance, applauded when I performed well, and challenged me whenever she was not pleased with any aspect of my performance. I gained strength from her encouragement as she boldly told me that I was a natural leader. I fed off this encouragement and presented myself for several leadership roles" (personal communication, February 15, 2017).

Dr. Gittens ably prepared herself academically for practice and leadership in nursing as well as public service. She holds certificates in nursing, midwifery, and administration. She earned a BSc and an MSc from the University of the West Indies at Mona, Jamaica, in 1997 and 2004, respectively. In 2013, she completed her doctor of nursing practice (DNP) degree at Duke University School of Nursing. Dr. Gittens's love of nursing, educational preparation, leadership qualities, vast network of relationships and associations at all levels of community and government, and commitment and sheer tenacity to make a difference have facilitated a dynamic career.

As a relatively young nurse, Dr. Gittens became the president of the National Nurses Association (NNA) of St. Vincent-Grenadines (SVG) and served this professional organization as public relations officer, secretary, and committee member. (SVG is a member of CARICOM.) Her political aspirations surfaced, leading her to agitate and champion the nursing workforce to join a national disobedience movement to protest against the government of SVG in 2000, rallying for better working conditions for nurses. It was the success of this act of advocacy that confirmed for her that she could make a difference for nurses and health care in general. As a staff nurse and the president of NNA, Dr. Gittens negotiated an increase in salary for nurses, a night-duty differential, and closed the pay gap between nurses and other health professionals with comparable responsibilities. Other leadership and policy roles she achieved include:

- Appointed and served as chief nursing officer for SVG for 7 years.
- Chairman of the Regional Nursing Body of CARICOM for 7 years.
- Negotiated a relationship with the Caribbean Examination Council for the management of the CARICOM Regional Examination for Nurse Registration.
- Provided leadership on the review of policies and procedures for evaluation and approval for CARICOM-wide nursing education programs.
- Contributed to drafting new competencies for midwives and nursing assistants.
- Coordinated a policy-level meeting with top government officials in Guyana to encourage a Guyanese nursing affiliation with the RNB of CARICOM. After several rounds of high-level negotiations, Guyana joined the RNB. It has since benefited from a regional nursing curriculum, a professionally managed licensure service, enhanced instructional and evaluation processes, and internationally recognized standards for entry into professional practice for Guyana's nurses.
- Initiated and helped negotiate a contract with a professional management service for managing the Regional Examination for Nurse Registration (RENR).
- Contributed to new competencies for midwives and nursing assistants.

(continues)

EXHIBIT 11-1 Personal Stories of International Nurse Policy Leaders   *(continued)*

- Appointed in 2006 as the first chair of the community college board of governors in SVG. Dr. Gittens's responsibilities included the merger of a technical college, a nursing school, a teacher's college, and an A-1 (advanced level) post-secondary institution into a highly functional community college with far-reaching and notable impact on SVG and the CARICOM region. She resigned as board chair in 2013 after 7 years of service.
- Was elected in a national election as vice president of the women's arm of the governing Unity Labour Party and later as deputy chair of the Unity Labour Party (one of four parties in Jamaica).

Dr. Gittens credits her accomplishments and her commitment to continuous lifelong learning (formally and informally); peer relationships and mentors; engagement with individuals, groups, and communities; a sense of comfort with advocacy, policymaking, and politics; and personal commitment to risk taking and the belief that she can make a difference.

See http://today.caricom.org/ for more information about this part of the world.

Early Nurse Advocacy for Health Policies in Botswana

Serara Selelo-Kupe, RN, BSc, MA, ME, EdD

This vignette reflects the context of pre-independence (from British rule) nursing in Bechuanaland Protectorate, southern Africa (which became the Republic of Botswana in 1966), and the policy role and strategies of Dr. Serara Selelo-Kupe beginning during the latter part of the 1960s that advanced registered nurse education in the country. Dr. Selelo-Kupe chronicled the history of professional nursing in this region of Africa in her 1993 book, *An Uneasy Walk to Quality: The Evolution of Black Nursing Education in the Republic of Botswana, 1922–1980*. The book served as the source for this vignette, along with this author's collegial relationship with Dr. Selelo-Kupe dating back to the early 1980s. I last visited with her in her home in Gaborone in March 2014.

Several significant trends and events occurred during the latter part of the 1960s in Botswana:

- A practice of sending girls with A-level secondary school diplomas and the necessary qualifications abroad to study nursing and post-graduate nursing
- The inauguration of a national nurses association (the Nurses Association of Botswana), which was to play a significant role in the education and socialization of professional nurses in the next decade
- The appointment of a new chief nursing officer, Dr. Selelo-Kupe, in mid-1999 in the Ministry of Health and Wellness (MOH)

The Nursing Council, which advises the MOH, regulates the practice of nursing in Botswana and oversees nurse training and education. Dr. Selelo-Kupe, a native of Botswana, received her basic nursing preparation from McCord Zulu Hospital in South Africa, a BS in nursing education from the University of Ottawa in Canada, and master of arts, master of education, and doctorate in education degrees from Columbia University in New York City. She was exceedingly well prepared, with a U.S. orientation to nursing education and practice, a strong determination and commitment to quality, and highly respected professional nursing status. Though small in stature, she was powerful, fearless, and convincing with her pen, her voice, and her strategic thinking—qualities that ultimately led to her becoming a recognized worldwide advocate for nursing.

When Dr. Selelo-Kupe began her work for the MOH, there were five nursing students enrolled in the four-year diploma program and two tutors or teachers. Soon after assuming her position as CNO in 1999, she inspected the one authorized national hospital training school for nurses in the mining town of Lobatse, 70 kilometers from the current capital of Gaborone. She was very troubled and concerned by her findings:

"I was sadly disappointed by the training conditions, including student accommodation, classroom, facilities, and all that is necessary for the education of nurses. I was left in no doubt why there is such a high attrition rate of candidates with better educational qualification. I honestly feel that the hospital has not got suitable facilities for the training of nurses, nor is it adequately staffed for the purpose." (Selelo-Kupe, 1993, p. 145)

Based on this straightforward, objective evidence, Dr. Selelo-Kupe recommended to the director of medical services that the school at Lobatse be moved to Princess Marina Hospital in Gaborone as soon as possible. She offered succinct, concrete reasons why this solution would address the observed deficits: (1) More doctors practiced in Gaborone with multiple areas of specialization, which would improve teaching; (2) her own proximity to the Gaborone Hospital meant she could help the tutors in developing the program and supervise the program's implementation more closely; (3) the improved condition of the Princess Marina Nurses Home (i.e., the dormitory for nurses) would boost morale of students; and (4) the availability of the hospital laboratory in Gaborone would aid in teaching natural sciences.

The school moved one month later, and the student housing accommodations were deemed excellent. The classrooms were limited, but a teaching facility was quickly erected consisting of a large classroom, a nursing arts laboratory, and an office for the two tutors. Student and faculty morale were high. By December 1969, there was a new policy regarding the education of nurses and "a new program aimed at relating the training of nurses to their responsibilities within the new health care system" (Selelo-Kupe, 1993, p. 146).

Dr. Selelo-Kupe's influence continued to be manifested in the growth and development of nursing in Botswana, throughout Africa, and around the world. She has served on the World Health Organization's Committee on Nursing, consulted with USAID/Howard University, served on the board of directors for the ICN, and was instrumental in the development of the first degree program in nursing for black nurses in all of Africa south of the equator. Today, the home for the School of Nursing is within the University of Botswana in Gaborone.

References

Abood, S. (2007, January 31). Influencing health care in the legislative arena. *Online Journal of Issues in Nursing.* Retrieved from http://www.nursingworld.org/MainMenuCategories /ANAMarketplace/ANAPeriodicals/OJIN/TableofContents/Volume122007/No1Jan07 /tpc32_216091.html

American Association of Colleges of Nursing (AACN). (2006). *Essentials of doctoral education for advanced nursing practice.* Washington, DC: Author.

American Association of Colleges of Nursing (AACN). (2008). *Essentials of baccalaureate education*. Washington, DC: Author.

American Association of Colleges of Nursing (AACN). (2011). *Essentials of master's education in nursing*. Washington, DC: Author.

Asp, G., Odberg Pettersson, K., Sandberg, J., Kabakyenga, J., & Agardh, A. (2014). Association between mass media exposure and birth preparedness among women in southwestern Uganda: A community-based survey. *Global Health Action, 7*, 22904.

Batalova, J. (2014). Immigration and the health workforce in the mid-2000's in the United States. In A. Siyam, *Migration of health workers: WHO code of practice and the global economic crisis* (pp. 1–220). Geneva, Switzerland: World Health Organization.

Benton, D. (2009 May 13). Economics, health, and nursing. *International Nursing Review 56*(2), 158.

Benton, D. (2012, January). Advocating globally to shape policy and strengthen nursing's influence. *Online Journal of Issues in Nursing, 17*(1). doi:10.3912/ojin.Vol1an057N001Man05

CARICOM: Caribbean Community. (2017). CARICOM: Who we are. Retrieved from https://caricom.org/about-caricom/who-we-are

Chen, W. T., Shiu, C. S., Simoni, J. M., Chuang, P., Zhao, H., Bao, M., & Lu, H. (2013). Challenges of cross-cultural research: Lessons from a USA-Asia collaboration. *Nursing Outlook, 9*(13), 145–152.

Douglas, M. K., Rosenkoetter, M., Pacquiao, D. F., Callister, L. C., Hattar-Pollara, M., Lauderdale, J., . . . Purnell, L. (2014). Guidelines for implementing culturally competent nursing care. *Journal of Transcultural Nursing, 25*(2), 109–121.

Fadiman, A. (1997). *The spirit catches you and you fall down*. Sharon, MA: Big Hearted Books.

Gennaro, S. (2014).Commentaries on the global state of nursing. *Journal of Nursing Scholarship, 46*(3), 144.

International Council of Nurses (ICN). (2017). Our mission, strategic intent, core values and priorities. Retrieved from http://www.icn.ch/who-we-are/our-mission-strategic-intent-core-values-and-priorities/

International Migration Outlook. (2015). Retrieved from oecd.org/migration/international migration-outlook/1999124/124x.htm

International Migration Outlook. (2017). OECD Publishing, Paris. Retrieved from https://dx .doi.org/10.1787/migration_outlook-2017-en.

Kakutani, M. (2017, January 6). Obama's secret to surviving the White House years: Books. *The New York Times*. Retrieved from NYTimes.com/2017/01/16/books/obamas-secret-to -surviving-the-white-house-years-book.html?rref=Collective%2Fbyline%2Fmichiko -kakutani&action=click&contentCollection=undefined&region=stream&module-stream -unit&version=latest&contentPlacement-10&pgtype=collection

Khaliq, A. A., Broyles, R., & Mwachofi, A. (2009). Global nurse migration: Its impact on developing countries and prospects for the future. *Nursing Leadership, 10*(3). Retrieved from ncbi.nlm.nih.gov/pubmed/19289910

Kingma, M. (2007, June). Nurses on the move: A global overview. *Health Services Research*. https://www.ncbi.nlm.nih.gov/pmc/articles/PMC1955376/

McCubbrey, D. (2016, September 20). Negative and positive effects of globalization for developing country businesses. Retrieved from https://www.boundless.com/users/235420 /textbooks/business-fundamentals/international-business-for-the-entrepreneur-14 /globalization-opportunities-and-threats-to-developing-country-business-55 /negative-and-positive-effects-of-globalization-for-developing-country-business-253-15556/

McLuhan, M., & Fiore, Q. (1968). *War and peace in the global village*. New York, NY: McGraw-Hill.

Organization for Economic Cooperation and Development. (2015). History. Retrieved from http://www.oecd.org/about/history/

Rivers, K. (2014, March 6). Nurses hold key to meeting global health challenges. *Vanderbilt University Medical Center Reporter, 1-2*. Nashville, TN: University Web Communication. Retrieved from http://news.vanderbilt.edu/2014/03/nurses-hold-key-to-meeting-global-health-challenges /global-nurse-conf-jr111/

Salmon, M., Yan, J., & Hewitt, H. A. (2007, June). Managed migration: The Caribbean approach to addressing nursing services capacity. *Health Services Research, 42*(3 Pt 2): 1354–1372. doi:10.1111/j.1475-6773.2007.00708.x

Seloilwe, E. S. (2005). Globalization and nursing. *Journal of Advanced Nursing, 50*(6), 571.

Selelo-Kupe, S. (1993). *An uneasy walk to quality: The evolution of black nursing education in the Republic of Botswana, 1922–1980.* Botswana, Southern Africa: W. K. Kellogg Foundation.

Senior, K. (2010, May 12). Wanted: 2.4 million nurses, and that's just in India. *Bulletin of the World Health Organization, 88*(5). Retrieved from ncbi.nlm.nih.gov/pubmed/20461210

Shaffer, F. A. (2014). Ensuring a global workforce: A challenge and opportunity. Guest Editorial. *Nursing Outlook, 62,* 1–4.

Shah, A. (2013, March 24). Structural adjustment: A major cause of poverty. *Global Issues: Social, Political, Economic and Environmental Issues That Affect Us All.* globalissues.org/article/3/structural-adjustment-a-major-cause-of-poverty.

Shariff, N. (2014). Factors that act as facilitators and barriers to nurse leaders' participation in health policy development. *BMC Nursing, 13,* 20.

Union of International Associations. (2017). *Regional Nursing Body, CARICOM Community (RNB).* Retrieved from www.uia.org/s/or/en/1100056832

United Nations. (n.d.). Sustainable development goals: 17 goals to transform our world. Retrieved from http://www.un.org/sustainabledevelopment/news/communications-material/

United Nations Education, Scientific, and Cultural Organization (UNESCO). (2017). *Learning to live together migrant and migration.* Retrieved from unesco.org/new/en/social-and-human-sciences/themes/international-migration/glossary/migrant

World Health Organization (WHO). (2006a). *Health workers: A global profile.* Geneva, Switzerland: Author.

World Health Organization (WHO). (2006b). *Working together for health: World health report.* Geneva, Switzerland: Author.

World Health Organization (WHO). (2014a, May 20). *Keynote speaker: HRH Princess Muna Al-Hussein of Jordan.* Sixth Global Forum for Government Chief Nursing and Midwifery Officers, Geneva, Switzerland.

World Health Organization (WHO). (2014b, May 20). 6th Global Forum for Government Chief Nursing and Midwifery Officers. Retrieved from http://www.who.int/hrh/news/2016/global-forum_govchiefnursing2016/en/

World Health Organization (WHO). (2015). Roles and responsibilities of government chief nursing and midwifery officers. Retrieved from who.int/hrh/nursing-midwifery/15178-gcnmo.pdf?ua=1

World Health Organization (WHO). (2016). Government Chief Nursing and Midwifery Officers discuss strategies on the future of nursing and midwifery workforce. Retrieved from http://www.who.int/hrh/news/2016/discuss_strategies/en

World Health Organization (WHO). (2017a). High level commission on health and economic growth. Retrieved from http://who.int/hrh/com-heeg/en/

World Health Organization (WHO). (2017b). Mission statement. Retrieved from who.int/bulletin/mission_statement.en

CHAPTER 12

An Insider's Guide to Engaging in Policy Activities

Nancy M. Short and Jeri A. Milstead

▶ Strategies to Recognize Political Bias in Information Sources

Political language . . . is designed to make lies sound truthful and murder respectable and to give an appearance of solidity to pure wind.

—**George Orwell**, *Politics in the English Language*

Bias is the presence of a preference that interferes with or inhibits impartial judgment. Bias is exhibited by unfair actions and policies stemming from prejudiced thinking. In essence, bias may be thought of as "having an agenda." Most of us, and most of the organizations we inhabit, have an agenda; therefore, few sources are bias free. Just because a source is biased, however, it does not mean that you cannot obtain important information from the source. You must identify ideological or political bias when using sources to influence or craft health policy.

You need to know your primary source: What are the interests? Which language is being used (inflammatory, educational, persuasive)? Whom does the source represent? How might the information presented be relevant to you? Toward which purpose is this source geared? When was the source last updated with current information? Where does the source get its funding? If the source is an organization, who serves on the board of directors—that is, who is setting the agenda?

Often you must do some homework to discover if a source is biased: It is *not* sufficient to note that the source declares itself to be nonpartisan. Do you think that the American Nurses Association (ANA) is biased? Would you freely, without hesitation or annotation of materials, use content from the ANA? The ANA is a trade association/special-interest group for professional nurses and educators. It is biased in favor of the welfare of its members and all nurses. If you search for endorsements of political candidates by ANA, you will learn that ANA predominantly supports Democrats. This is not earth-shattering news and should not prevent you from using ANA materials; however, it should inform you about how and when to use these references.

There are thousands of special-interest groups and organizations in the United States. In the following subsections, we take a look at two influential organizations located in Washington, D.C.

Heritage Foundation

Heritage Foundation (http://www.heritage.org/) is widely considered one of the world's most influential public policy research institutes. A right-wing think tank, Heritage Foundation enjoyed particular prominence during the Reagan administration. The word "conservative" is prominent in several places on the website, including the mission statement of the organization.

Who is setting the agenda? Senior executives of equity firms, lawyers, authors, journalists, and a college professor comprise the board of directors.

What are Heritage Foundation's interests? The website has an extensive list of topics and accompanying position statements that are too numerous to list here. You can expect sources with a conservative political ideology to advocate for a range of regulations on all businesses (market forces allowed to guide commerce), strong defense and military, limited government social programs (conservatives believe individuals are responsible for their own welfare), support for the rights of the unborn, and opportunities to own and carry firearms. In contrast, such sources tend to frown on "political correctness."

When was the site updated? Position and opinion statements are very current and are in step with the news cycle within the past 48 hours.

Where does Heritage Foundation get its funding? Initial funding was provided by Joseph Coors, of the Coors beer empire, and Richard Mellon Scaife, heir to the Mellon industrial and banking fortune. Heritage Foundation is a 501(c)3 nonprofit organization. Its annual report states that "we rely on the financial contributions of the general public: individuals, foundations and corporations. We accept no government funds and perform no contract work." Heritage Foundation receives funding from organizations with connections to the Koch Brothers, the Lambe Foundation, Donors Trust and Donors Capital Fund, and the conservative Bradley Foundation. In 2016, it had revenues in excess of $100 million.

Families USA

Families USA (http://familiesusa.org/) calls itself "The Voice for Healthcare Consumers." Families USA is an influential left-wing lobbying organization, although it frequently refers to itself as a nonpartisan media operation. Descriptive words and phrases that predominate on this organization's website include *social activism, community organizing, justice, equity,* and *protect the disadvantaged*—typical of a liberal or progressive ideology. Nevertheless, the word "liberal" is never used on this site.

Who is setting the agenda? Ron Pollack, founder of Families USA, has been most important in setting its agenda. He stepped down from his position as director/chief executive officer in March 2017. He is a well-known firebrand in Washington, D.C., who has successfully argued to the Supreme Court (he is a lawyer) for secure food aid for low-income Americans as well as for federal litigation that resulted in the creation of the Women, Infants, and Children (WIC) program for malnourished mothers and infants. The board of directors for Families USA includes a Catholic nun with a history of activism for social justice, leaders from humanitarian foundations, a physician who has worked for a Democratic senator and governor, a librarian who is a champion for Medicaid, a faculty member of Harvard Medical School, the director of a large labor union, and academics with backgrounds indicating liberal philosophies.

What are Families USA's interests? The main interest is to secure affordable, quality health care for all people in the United States. The organization promotes a patient- and community-centered health system.

When was the site updated? A blog provides analysis of current policy debates on healthcare finance; entries are no more than 3 days old. Other resources are much older—available slide shows are 11 months old.

Where does Families USA get its funding? ProPublica reports that Families USA's 2014 990 tax return showed revenues of $7 million. Donors include the Kellogg Foundation, Gordon and Betty Moore Foundation, and others. As you can see, learning about Ron Pollock, finding the 990s, and discovering which causes the Kellogg Foundation and other donors usually support takes some digging.

Summing it up, you should never assume that any reference or source is unbiased. Do not take content as factual until you have determined what the agenda and motivations of the authors or publishers may be. This kind of critical thinking requires you to be a skeptical, sophisticated user of data and information. This is not to say that you cannot use references from organizations such as Heritage Foundation or Families USA; however, seeking balance in your understanding is important. Balance your knowledge by reading and exploring a variety of points of view. As a starting point, **TABLE 12-1** describes the five major political parties (and their general ideology) in the United States.

▶ Creating a Fact Sheet

You must be prepared when you visit a congressional or state legislative office. Novices to the policy and politics world often visit their representative with others as an activity related to a conference or convention. At conferences, you may be handed materials to take with you to a legislative meet-and-greet.

TABLE 12-1 Political Parties in the United States and Their Ideological Perspectives

Democratic	Republican	Libertarian	Green Party	Constitution
■ Raise incomes and restore economic security for the middle class	■ Preserve the U.S. Constitution	■ Civil liberties	■ Environmentalism	■ Restore honesty, integrity, and accountability to government
■ Create good-paying jobs	■ Require a balanced budget for federal government	■ Non-interventionism	■ Nonviolence, anti-war positions	■ Federal government should only be involved in government roles as outlined in the U.S. Constitution; the best government is local government.
■ Fight for economic freedom and against inequality	■ Repeal and replace the Affordable Care Act	■ Laissez-faire capitalism	■ Decentralization of wealth and power to promote social justice	■ Restore "true capitalist" principles to U.S. economic policies
■ End systemic racism	■ Maintain a strong military	■ Abolition of the welfare state	■ Participatory grassroots democracy	
■ Guarantee civil rights (especially for vulnerable groups)	■ Make America energy independent	■ Minimum government	■ Feminism and gender equity	
■ Protect voting rights	■ Secure U.S. borders	■ Role of government is to protect the rights of every individual, including the right to life, liberty, and property	■ Respect for diversity: promote LGBT rights	
■ Secure environmental justice	■ Promote hard work to end poverty		■ Community-based economics	
■ Ensure the health and safety of all Americans	■ Promote family		■ Personal and global responsibility	
	■ Promote religious liberty		■ Future focus and sustainability	
			■ Ecological wisdom	

© Neil Toenner/Shutterstock. © heticlor/Shutterstock. Courtesy of Libertarian Party. Courtesy of Green Party. Courtesy of Constitution Party

These materials are intended to be left with the member or staff to serve as a reminder or give a nudge to action after you leave the office. This kind of fact sheet (also known as a "leave-behind") is a reasonable way to get introduced to the process but is not a highly effective way to share a message. The most effective meeting is one-to-one (e.g., face-to-face) with the member or health staff (legislative aide).

You should prepare a fact sheet that is customized to your message. Criteria for a fact sheet are as follows:

- Keep the document to one page; you may use both the front and the back.
- Use attractive, easily readable font (of at least 12), and eliminate all typos and spelling errors.
- Title your issue at the top of the page. Use plain English—no medical terms.
- State your "ask," succinctly at the top of the page directly under the title.
- Do not use citations or references. This is not an academic document.
- Bullets, lists, tables, and text boxes must be clearly readable (never use a tiny map or graph).
- List organizations in support of your position (state-level organizations for state issues).
- Know who opposes your "ask," and be ready to address this opposition verbally.
- Your full contact information (name, credentials, phone, email) must be readable. Unless you have permission to represent your place of work, do not give the impressions that you are speaking on your employer's behalf.

For more information about how to construct a fact sheet and see samples, visit http://www.cthealthpolicy.org/toolbox/tools/fact_sheets.htm.

▶ Contacting Your Legislators

It is crucial that healthcare professionals know how to contact their legislators, agency heads, government staff, and other policymakers. We recommend calling or emailing to avoid security testing and delays imposed on standard mail and packages. Do not send an attachment—no one will open it because it may contain a virus or malware.

A. In general:
    1. Know the correct title and spelling of the Member's (or staff's) name and correct address. If in doubt, call the office and ask (staff are eager to provide this information). If there are credentials, get them right!
    2. Direct your message to the right level: federal issues to U.S. senators and representatives in Washington, D.C.; state messages to state senators and representatives at the state capital.
    3. Be polite. Choose language that is not confrontational or angry.
    4. Avoid healthcare jargon, such as "I'm an APRN working in SICU with GSW patients."
    5. If you use Twitter or other social media, be very careful about what you say—your messages may be read by many others and potentially misinterpreted.

Example of a Fact Sheet for Folic Acid Supplementation for the Prevention of Neural Tube Defects

Asking That You:

- ✓ **Expand the Women, Infants, and Children (WIC) program** to allow the purchase of **over-the-counter folic acid supplements**
- ✓ **Increase funding for the WIC program** to allow the program to cover these supplements for **pregnant women already enrolled in WIC**

Fast Facts About Neural Tube Defects

➤ The neural tube is present in early fetal development and develops into the infant brain and spinal cord

➤ Neural tube defects (NTDs) result when the fetal neural tube doesn't close properly, resulting in spinal cord or brain defects

➤ NTDs are among the most common congenital defects in the United States
- ■ 3,000 pregnancies are affected by NTDs in the United States every year
- ■ 840 infants die of NTDs in the United States every year

➤ Types of NTDs:
- ■ Spina bifida is the most common NTD involving the spinal cord
  - ○ Infants with spina bifida have disabilities that range widely in severity
  - ○ Disabilities related to spina bifida are permanent and lifelong, resulting in significant economic impacts

Lifetime Costs for an Infant With Spina Bifida

Medical costs	$513,500
Special education and developmental services	$63,500
Estimated lost parental economic output	$214,900
Total anticipated lifetime costs	**$791,900**

- ■ Anencephaly is the most common NTD related to the brain and results in the death of nearly all afflicted infants

CONTACT: I. M. Involved, BS, BSN, RN, CCRN
Iminvolved@gmail.com   512-555-1100

Facts About NTDs and Folic Acid

➤ Folate is required for proper DNA synthesis and function

➤ Folic acid supplementation is associated with a decreased risk for NTDs

➤ Folic acid supplementation provides maximum benefit for NTD prevention when started 1 month before conception and continued through the first 2–3 months of pregnancy

➤ The U.S. Preventative Services Task Force (USPSTF) has determined that the net benefit of supplementation is substantial and the risks are minimal

➤ USPSTF recommends that all women who are pregnant or may become pregnant take a daily supplement containing 0.4 to 0.8 mg of folic acid

Projected Costs of Proposed WIC Expansion

North Carolina WIC Participation Totals (2012 data)

Total number of WIC participants in N.C.	284,995
Total number of pregnant women participating in WIC in N.C.	27,052

North Carolina WIC Expansion Anticipated Costs (2014 dollars)

Annual current food costs for WIC program in N.C.	$127,920,051.00
Folic acid supplement cost, per pregnant WIC participant	$1.94
Estimated annual cost of proposed WIC expansion in N.C.	$52,480.88

Summary

➤ Addition of folic acid supplement coverage would expand WIC program food costs by **less than 0.04%**

➤ Folic acid supplementation has the potential to prevent **2–3 cases of spina bifida** per year among infants born to WIC program participants in N.C.

➤ Potential taxpayer cost savings could exceed **$1.1 million annually**

Supporting Organizations

Centers for Disease Control and Prevention
Flour Fortification Initiative
U.S. Preventative Services Task Force
International Clearinghouse for Birth Defects Surveillance

World Health Organization
American College of Obstetrics and Gynecology
U.S. Food and Drug Administration
International Federation for Spina Bifida and Hydrocephalus

      6. Do your homework. What is the position of the Member on similar issues? Know whether the member has sponsored or opposed similar legislation.

B. Via email: Keep your message to three paragraphs.

First paragraph:

      1. Use a salutation: Dear Senator or Dear Representative (or Mr., Ms., Mrs., Dr.).

      2. State who you are (e.g., name, constituent, APRN/MD/DO).

      3. Declare your support/opposition to a specific issue; state a bill number if possible. Legislative Aides (LAs) keep track of "support" and "do not support" messages.

Second paragraph:

      1. Rationale: one or two reasons to support your position; be brief (limit to one regular page).

      2. Use ordinary language—no medical terminology, three- or more-syllable words, vague words, or vernacular/local lingo.

      3. Identify any major opposition and include your response to it; include a talking point that the Member may use later.

      4. Include a personal story if you have one—it can be very persuasive evidence. Do not use names or circumstances that are considered privileged or private.

Third paragraph:

      1. Make your "ask." Be specific: vote for/against a bill or amendment; hold a hearing; call a press conference (*not* just "support" or "oppose").

      2. Do *not* thank the representative or senator in advance—save this for after he or she has acted.

      3. Offer to be the contact for this issue.

      4. Close with "Sincerely," plus your name/credentials, address, and preferred phone number.

C. If you call the Member/staff's office:

      1. You probably will not talk with the Member. Ask for the Health LA, and write down the name of the person to whom you speak.

      2. Do not expect to talk with the staffer more than 5 minutes, so use notes and talk in a conversational tone—do not read your message, as it will be obvious that you do not know your own words.

D. If you fax a message, be sure you have the right fax number; otherwise, it may get lost and may not be read by relevant staff. Again, be brief, be focused, and use ordinary language.

E. What *not* to include:

      1. *All* reasons you support or oppose the policy—pick one or two reasons. You should write only one-page emails or letters.

      2. Threats: "If you don't vote for this bill, I will not vote for you."

      3. "Thank you"—save it until you know the Member's action, then be sure to write a thank-you note.

F. Follow up:

      1. Within 2 weeks, email or phone the Member's office: Received email? Any questions? Any action on the issue? Anything I can do?

▶ What to Expect When You Visit Your Policymaker

1. Make an appointment—don't just show up.
2. You may visit in pairs, but if there are many of you, make sure the staff know in advance so that they can arrange a place large enough to accommodate all of you.
3. Dress professionally. Do not show up in jeans or clothing with offensive logos.
4. Don't expect to see the policymaker in person; you probably will talk with a staff member. Staff are very important. Depending on the prestige and length of time in the position, a policymaker may have a small or large staff; each staffer will have one or more specific areas to cover, such as health, agriculture, economic development, or transportation. Staff are responsible for filtering information that is presented to the policymaker.
5. Research the person you are visiting. If it is a legislator, go to the relevant website—you probably will find information about his or her education, family, interests, and community service, as well as current service on committees. There may be a picture.
6. Know the district or constituency that the policymaker represents. This will give you clues about the person's interests and background. Note any leadership positions the person has held. It is best to visit your own representative, but if you have a particular area of interest, you can choose a person who is the chair or an officer of a relevant committee.
7. Expect your visit to last no more than 5 to 10 minutes—so be focused with your message.
8. Shake hands and look the people you meet in the eye. Speak clearly and with authority.
9. Do not spend much time in "pleasantries"—get to the point of your visit.
10. State why you are there—the specific issue/bill number, your position ("for" or "against"), and why.
11. Be prepared to defend your position. Use evidence-based research (translated into ordinary language), best practice, and other supports.
12. Focus on only one issue per visit. You may be tempted to interject several issues, but you have a very limited amount of time, so do not undercut yourself.
13. Have one or two 1-page documents that support your issue ready for the staff after you leave. For example, you may have "talking points" that summarize your issue. If you are representing an organization, make sure its logo appears on the documents.
14. Leave your business card so that the staff can contact you.
15. Hand-write a thank-you note within two weeks after your visit.

▶ Preparing to Testify

You may be asked to testify at a hearing about an issue in which you are involved. A hearing is an official meeting of a committee or group of policymakers (i.e., legislators) in which they "hear" arguments for and against an issue. You must follow protocols about who and when and how long you testify.

1. Know where the hearing room is located. Be there before the hearing begins.
2. You may be required to sign in as a witness. You will be called in the order in which you sign in.
3. Know the name of the committee chair and who will be attending the hearing.
4. Provide copies of your testimony to each member of the committee. Distribute these copies to their staffs.
5. Have with you a one- to two-page testimony document in a font large enough to read without glasses. If your issue demands a longer response, provide copies to the committee staff.
6. Dress as a professional (e.g., no jeans or hoodies). You are representing your organization or issue. Look credible.

Tips on Testifying

1. Always address the chair first, then any particular members. For example, if a member asks a question, you respond by saying, "Mr. Chairman, Representative (or Senator) XXX, . . . Do this *every time* you speak. You may want to practice with a colleague.
2. Do not read your testimony. You have provided written copies to each member of the committee, so now is your time to have a "conversation" with them.
3. Make a single point. Now is *not* the time to bring up all the issues relevant to your case.
4. Provide a personal story that emphasizes your point; state it quickly.
5. You have only a very short time to testify (3–5 minutes),* but you may be able to extend this window if there are questions from committee members. To make best use of the opportunity, have your rationale in your head so you do not hem and haw and waste time.
6. Speak clearly and loudly. Stand up straight. Dress conservatively and appropriately. Act as a professional. Do not slouch. Do not say "Uh . . ." during your precious speaking time.
7. Do *not* use medical terminology or other confusing language. For example, do not use abbreviations or acronyms (e.g., CABG, IV, MI).

---

* There may be a three-light bulb system used for keeping time. As one U.S. senator said, "Talk when the light is green, talk fast when the light is yellow, and talk damned-fast when the light is red!"

8. If you refer to research or evidence, summarize it.
9. Speak positively and with conviction. Use "power" words (e.g., *expertise, overwhelming evidence, significance*).
10. Do *not* equivocate; that is, do not say "kinda," "sorta," "maybe," or "like."
11. Do *not* threaten anyone or become violent. You are there as a guest.
12. Always close the loop—that is, bring your remarks back to how this issue will affect the constituents of the policymakers and your patients. Otherwise, you are likely to be seen as self-serving.
13. Be prepared to answer any questions from those who oppose part or all of the bill. Again, have a response in your head that you can pull out for a 30-second reply.
14. If you cannot think of a response to a question, go back to your original position and restate your argument. Remember: Just because you are asked a question does not mean you have to answer it. If you get nervous and the question stumps you, keep to your point.
15. If you are asked a question that you cannot answer immediately, tell the questioner that you will get back to him or her with a solid answer promptly.
16. Thank the chair and committee for hearing your testimony. Tell them you are available for comments or questions.

Providing Testimony for a Regulatory Hearing

Jacqueline Loversidge

When providing comments in writing or as written/oral testimony at a hearing, it is important to follow these guidelines:

- Be transparent about your identity, background, and representation status; that is, be clear about whether comments/testimony represent an organization's position or your own.
- Be specific regarding whether the position you are representing is in support of or in opposition to the regulation. Give examples using brief scenarios or experiences when possible.
- Assure there is a body of credible evidence to back up your position. Explain major points using common language; avoid nursing/medical jargon.
- Know the agency's position and respond to those concerns.
- Know the opposition's position and respond to those concerns.
- Convey a willingness to negotiate or compromise toward mutually acceptable resolutions.
- Demonstrate concern for the public good rather than self-interest.
- Be brief and succinct. Limit your remarks to one or two pages. Regulatory agencies may limit the number of minutes for oral testimony; 5 minutes is average.

Regulatory agencies charged with public protection are more likely to address concerns that deal with how the public may be harmed or benefited rather than concerns that give the impression of turf protection and professional jealousy.

Demonstrate support for your position by asking colleagues who represent a variety of organizations, professions, and interests to submit comments; inter-professional solidarity projects a powerful message. When a significant number and variety of professionals and organizations form a coalition around a single issue, their collaboration demonstrates an elevated degree of concern and a high level of commitment toward finding a solution. In this way, the volume and breadth of interest expressed in a proposed regulation can serve as the deciding factor in assisting an agency to assess support or nonsupport for the proposed regulation.

▶ Participating in Public Comment Periods (Influencing Rule Making)

The U.S. federal government requires all agencies to post proposed rules to the *Federal Register* (https://www.federalregister.gov/) and provide for public commentary to be collected for a specific time interval. All comments must be summarized and the summary made public prior to a rule being adopted. Professional nurses are extremely well positioned to provide public comments on proposed rules and regulations affecting healthcare delivery, patient care, working conditions for nurses, and many other aspects of the healthcare universe that are subject to regulation.

An excellent site for participation is located at https://www.regulations.gov/. On this site, you may search for regulations by keyword, by date, by agency of origin, and by category.

Tips for Submitting Effective Comments

A comment can express simple support or dissent for a regulatory action. However, a constructive, information-rich comment that clearly communicates and supports its claims is more likely to have a positive impact on regulatory decision making.

The following tips are meant to help the public submit comments that have an impact and help agency policymakers improve federal regulations:

- Read and understand the regulatory document on which you are commenting.
- Be concise, but support your claims.
- Base your justification on sound reasoning, scientific evidence, and/or how you will be impacted.
- Address trade-offs and opposing views in your comment.
- There is no minimum or maximum length for an effective comment.
- The comment process is not a vote: One well-supported comment is often more influential than a thousand form letters.
- Attempt to fully understand each issue. If you have questions or do not understand a part of the regulatory document, you may ask for help from the agency contact listed in the document.

- If a rule raises many issues, do not feel obligated to comment on every one. Instead, select those issues that concern and affect you the most and/or you understand the best.
- If you disagree with a proposed action, suggest an alternative (including not regulating the issue at all), and include an explanation and/or analysis of how the alternative might meet the same objective or be more effective.
- Identify your credentials and experience that may distinguish your comments from others. If you are commenting in an area in which you have relevant personal or professional experience (e.g., registered nurse, APRN, scientist, attorney, hospital executive), say so.
- You may provide personal experience in your comment, as may be appropriate. The stories every nurse has to share can be powerful.
- Include examples of how the proposed rule would impact you negatively or positively.
- Keep a copy of your comment in a separate file. This practice helps ensure that you will not lose your comment if you have a problem submitting it using the web form.

Form Letters

Organizations often encourage their members to submit form letters designed to address issues common to their membership. Many in the public mistakenly believe that a submitted form letter constitutes a "vote" regarding the issues concerning them. Although public support or opposition may help guide important public policies, agencies make determinations for a proposed action based on sound reasoning and scientific evidence rather than on a majority of votes.

Visit https://www.regulations.gov/docs/Tips_For_Submitting_Effective_Comments.pdf for more information on submitting effective comments.

▶ How to Write an Op-Ed

A brief history: *Op-ed* is an abbreviation for "opposite the editorial page" (although it is often mistaken for "opinion-editorial"). This sort of newspaper article expresses the informed opinions of a named writer (often an expert) who is usually unaffiliated with the newspaper's editorial board. An op-ed differs from an editorial, which is usually unsigned and written by the newspaper's editorial board members. An op-ed is also distinct from a "letter to the editor," in which a reader responds to a previously written article.

The first modern op-ed page was created in 1921 by Herbert Swope of *The New York Evening World*; he realized that the page opposite the editorials was "a catchall for book reviews, society boilerplate, and obituaries." Swope explained:

> It occurred to me that nothing is more interesting than opinion when opinion is interesting, so I devised a method of cleaning off the page opposite the editorial, which became the most important in America . . . and thereon I decided to print opinions, ignoring facts.

Beginning in the 1930s, radio began to threaten the primacy of print journalism, a process that later moved even more quickly with the rise of television. To combat this trend, major newspapers such as *The New York Times* and *The Washington Post* began including more openly subjective and opinionated journalism, adding more columns, and growing their op-ed pages. Today, digital blogs and social media threaten print media as the preferred method for obtaining information and forming opinions.

Op-eds are an excellent way for individuals, organizations, businesses, and institutions to articulate a unique position on a particular issue. Think of an op-ed as persuasive writing in its most compelling form. *It is not simply educational—it must offer a solution to an issue that has a political solution.* Unlike a letter to the editor, an op-ed combines an influential opinion with facts, figures, and examples to deliver a thoughtful viewpoint to the thought leaders who often read a newspaper's opinion pages. These articles are also the "bread and butter" of online media outlets, such as *Huffington Post, Daily Caller,* and *The Health Care Blog.* Critical to the success of an op-ed is to write about a topic that is timely and on the public's radar. Prior to attempting to write an op-ed, you should read op-eds in the newspaper, journal, or digital source to which you plan to submit your own article.

Newspapers have policies on how to submit articles to their opinion page, and most limit the length to 500-750 words. The length limit is also a "suggested" length: Editors have a certain amount of space to fill, so an article that is too short or too long is unacceptable. Digital editors usually require a head shot of the author and a very short biographical sketch, so include this material as an attachment. The email to the editor, with the op-ed attached, should be written as a brief note (in a letter format) pitching your writing. Use an email address that you use frequently, and tag the email to give you a receipt notice.

"Striking while the iron is hot" is essential for op-eds. For this reason, writing an op-ed ahead of an event, holding it until you see the right time, and submitting it as an event unfolds may be your best assurance of getting it published. For example, if the Nobel Prize is awarded for research into the physics of brain injury, it is timely to submit your op-ed on why the legislature needs to pass a law regarding tackle football in pee-wee leagues. Your op-ed about violence against nurses in emergency departments is timely if the legislature is debating workplace violence. Right after the president orders a bombing run on a chemical factory in Syria is not the time to try to get your op-ed on legislative funding for diabetes education published; your article will not find space on the op-ed page.

As a professional nurse, you have expertise that nonclinicians (most people) do not have. You have experiences that you can draw on to illustrate problems in the healthcare system and the need for government intervention.

Good sources for more help can be found at the Duke University and Health System's News Office (https://styleguide.duke.edu/toolkits/writing-media/how-to-write-an-op-ed-article/), Harvard's Kennedy School of Government communications program (http://shorensteincenter.org/wp-content/uploads/2012/07/HO_NEW_HOW-TO-WRITE-AN-OPED-OR-COLUMN.pdf), and The Op-Ed Project (http://www.theopedproject.org).

Four Steps Toward Writing an Op-Ed

Step 1: Identify your topic	■ Select an area that you know a lot about, feel passionate about, and have a policy solution for or in which the public would benefit from reading your persuasive opinion. ■ Timeliness: Is your topic current? Does it have broad appeal to those who will read the blog, newspaper, or journal?

Step 2: Begin crafting the first draft	■ Establish your credibility by stating your credentials and declaring your expertise. Do not forget that you are also a mother/father, daughter/son, sibling, and so on; this role may also add credence to your opinions.
	■ Use a "grabber". The first paragraph must grab the reader's attention within 10 seconds.
	■ Use active voice.
	■ Use a cost–quality–access framework.
	■ Explain the scope of the problem:
	  • How it affects the public or a population or community. Use data and statistics if available.
	  • Use a poignant, heart-wrenching personal story, if applicable.
	  • Identify stakeholders who disagree with you; describe why they disagree and inoculate their argument(s).
	  • Identify ethical dilemmas as appropriate.
	  • Identify any health or healthcare disparity issues.
	■ Specify policy-based solutions:
	  • Include evidence or science on why this policy solution is helpful.
	  • Be *highly specific* and accurate in describing which sphere of government is involved and which action needs to be taken.
	  • Offer policy solutions that nongovernment sectors (industry) can adapt to solve the problem.
	■ Make a call to action: Describe one or more actions that readers can take *today* to solve this problem. Direct your writing to excite the readers by explaining and clearly linking the policy problems to practical solutions. Make the readers feel compelled to actively support the policy solution.
	■ Predict what may happen if the problem is not fixed.

Step 3	■ Let your first draft rest. After you have walked away from the writing for a few hours, reread it and edit it for clarity and succinctness. ■ Eliminate medical jargon. Perhaps have a nonclinician friend read it for understanding. ■ Clarity: Ask yourself, "Is it clear what I'm asking the reader to do?"
Step 4	■ Follow all instructions: Do not go over the word limit established for the targeted publication. ■ Permission: Do not mention your employer unless you have permission to do so. If you work where there is a communications or public relations department, check in with it (or read the website) to assure yourself of any rules pertaining to work-related stories. Do not violate Health Insurance Portability and Accountability Act (HIPAA) rules. Even with these restrictions, most nurse stories for a large market can be written and scrubbed of wording that may be a violation of institutional policies. If you meet resistance from your employer but believe your story should be shared, contact the editor of the publication and seek help in writing the piece in such a way that will be acceptable to all parties.

▶ For Serious Thought

1. World's best op-ed: http://www.chicagotribune.com/news/nationworld /politics/ct-talk-huppke-obit-facts-20120419-story.html
2. Omar Ahmad talks about political change with pen and paper at TED 2010: http://www.ted.com/talks/omar_ahmad_political_change_with _pen_and_paper.html
3. The Op-Ed Project: http://www.theopedproject.org
4. *The New York Times*: http://www.nytimes.com/pages/opinion/index.html
5. *Chicago Tribune*: http://www.chicagotribune.com/news/opinion /editorials/
6. *Raleigh News & Observer*: http://www.newsobserver.com/opinion/
7. *The Chronicle* (Duke University's daily newspaper): http://www .dukechronicle.com/section/opinion/
8. National Nurses United: http://www.nationalnursesunited.org/site /entry/101-voice-respect\
9. Listen to a clip of journalist Suzanne Gordon speaking to school nurses about the media's image of nurses and nursing: http://suzannecgordon .com/lectures-workshops/
10. Read five to eight examples of congressional testimony on ANA's site: http://www.rnaction.org/site/PageServer?pagename=%2Fnstat_congressional _testimony#ACA
11. Reaching for Health Equity: http://www.cdc.gov/minorityhealth/strategies 2016/
12. "Your health depends on where you live" Ted Talk by Bill Davenhall: https://www.ted.com/talks/bill_davenhall_your_health_depends_on_where _you_live?language=en
13. Families USA on health equity: http://familiesusa.org/issues/health -equity
14. Health Resources and Services Administration's Office of Health Equity: http://www.hrsa.gov/about/organization/bureaus/ohe/
15. Campaign for Equity of Care: http://www.equityofcare.org/

▶ Recommended Nonpartisan Twitter Feeds

@Politifact
Rand Congressional @RAND_OCR
Fact Check @factcheckdotorg
Kaiser Family Foundation Health News @KHNews
Alliance for Health Policy @AllHealthPolicy
@CSPAN
Commonwealth Fund (not Foundation) @Commonwealthfnd

▶ Recommended E-Subscriptions

■ Kaiser Health News updates: Subscribe to this daily email at http://khn .org/email-signup/. Once you enter your email address, you will be given a choice to select the subscriptions you want. Select "First Edition" and KHN Morning Briefing. You also may want to subscribe to Breaking News Alert.

- Congressional Bill Tracker: http://dyn.realclearpolitics.com/congressional_bill_tracker/.
- Subscribe to bills that *your* elected officials introduce at https://www.govtrack.us/congress/bills/subjects/house_of_representatives/5947?congress=113. Type in the names of your representatives as "sponsors" or "co-sponsors."
- Subscribe to *Health Affairs Health Policy Brief* at http://www.healthaffairs.org/1260_opt_in.php. Check the box for Health Policy Brief.
- Congressional Quarterly (CQ) Roll Call: Sign up for a free trial to track state and federal policy updates at http://cqrollcall.com.
- Subscribe to the American Nurses Association's *Daily SmartBrief* at http://www.smartbrief.com/ana/index.jsp?campaign=story.
- Subscribe to the American Association of Nurse Practitioners' *Daily SmartBrief* at https://www.smartbrief.com/signupSystem/subscribe.action?pageSequence=1&briefName=aanp&campaign=in_brief_signup_link&utm_source=brief.
- Subscribe to the *New England Journal of Medicine*'s Health Policy and Reform blog at https://cdf.nejm.org/register/reg_multistep.aspx?ea=health-policy-and- reform&promo=ONFQSU23&cpc=FMAAALLV0612C. Select "health policy & reform."

▶ Influential Organizations Affecting Health Policy

- Library of Congress for text/summaries of legislation: http://thomas.loc.gov
- U.S. House of Representatives: http://www.house.gov
  - Committee on Ways and Means: http://waysandmeans.house.gov
  - Committee of Energy and Commerce (oversees Medicare and Medicaid): http://energycommerce.house.gov
  - Committee on Appropriations: http://appropriations.house.gov
- U.S. Senate: http://www.senate.gov
  - Health, Education, Labor and Pensions Committee (HELP): http://help.senate.gov
  - Finance Committee: http://finance.senate.gov
- White House: https://www.whitehouse.gov
- *Federal Register*: https://www.federalregister.gov/
- U.S. Department of Health and Human Services: https://www.hhs.gov
- Bureau of Health Workforce: https://bhw.hrsa.gov/
- Centers for Medicare and Medicaid Services: https://www.cms.gov/
- Medicare Payment Advisory Commission: http://www.medpac.gov/
- American Nurses Association: http://www.nursingworld.org
- National Quality Forum: http://www.qualityforum.org/
- Baldrige National Quality Program: http://baldrigefoundation.org/
- Institute for Healthcare Improvement: http://www.ihi.org/ihi
- National Association for Healthcare Quality: http://www.nahq.org/
- National Academy of Medicine (quality series): https://nam.edu

- National Committee for Quality Assurance: http://www.ncqa.org/
- American Academy of Applied Science: https://www.eurekalert.org
- Kaiser Family Foundation: http://www.kff.org
- Commonwealth Fund: http://www.commonwealthfund.org/
- Center for Studying Health System Change: http://www.hschange.com/
- Urban Institute: http://www.urban.org/health/index.cfm
- American Enterprise Institute: http://www.aei.org/
- Heritage Foundation: http://www.heritage.org/
- Cato Institute: http://www.cato.org/
- Physicians for a National Health Program: http://www.pnhp.org/

▶ How to Become a Change Agent in Policy: Betty Sturgeon—One Exemplary Nurse's Story

A personal and professional story of one nurse in Nebraska serves as a resource for many current nurse practitioners (NPs), student NPs, and patients. Betty Sturgeon made a difference in Nebraska by (1) demonstrating nurse practitioner political activism; (2) implementing interprofessional team education and practice four decades before the concept was fostered as it is now; (3) serving as a pioneer NP in Nebraska; and (4) facilitating the practice of NP care in a university's student health center so that hundreds of college students would learn about this type of health provider and this type of care.

Ms. Sturgeon, age 93, died in 2017 (Obituary, *Omaha World Herald*, January 12, 2017). She lived her professional life daily as a NP who made a difference for several populations in this state. She taught in a university NP program and also taught a physical assessment course for students in the School of Pharmacy. Her facilitation of NPs working in this university's student health center would change the knowledge base of hundreds of students regarding health provider possibilities. Finally, as one of the first few NPs four decades ago in Nebraska, Ms. Sturgeon literally "set the scene" for what NPs could later do in 2015 at the state legislative level. The professional behaviors that she exemplified daily resulted in advocacy behaviors in two academic departments in a university and in its student health center. Her service as one of the first NPs in Nebraska laid the groundwork for all who have practiced since then. In addition to the specific legislative policy advocacy articulated in this chapter, she personified the kinds of lived advocacy one does daily to effect change.

Index

O

P